Helvécia

Dom Smaz

Lars Müller Publishers

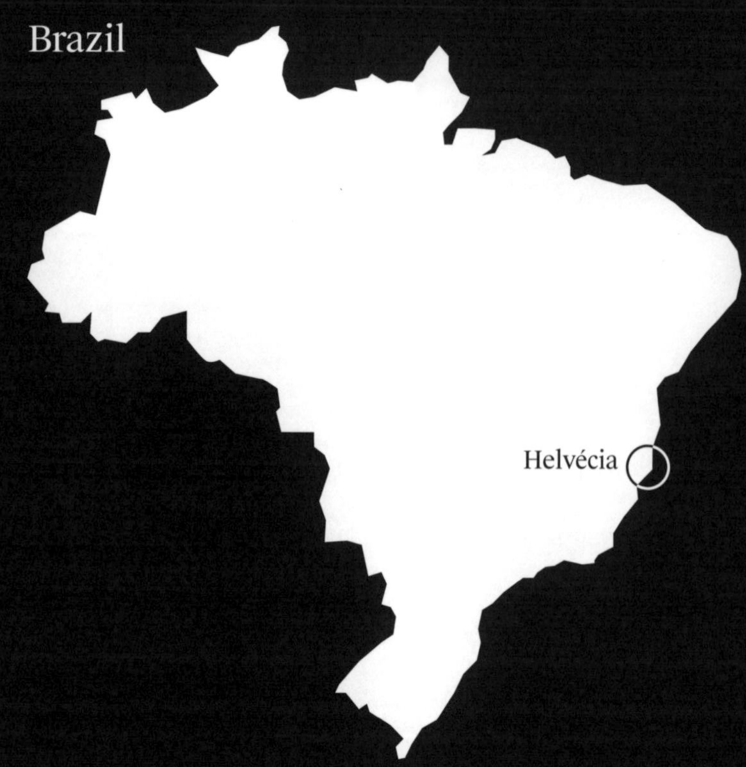
Brazil
Helvécia

Christian Doninelli

Interviews:

Conducted by Milena Machado Neves

Milena Machado Neves and Christian Doninelli

Milena Machado Neves and Christian Doninelli

Flávio dos Santos Gomes

Izabel Barros, Rohit Jain, Shalini Randeria

For Léon

Foreword

My mother is Brazilian. She came to Switzerland and met my father, a native of the Canton of Vaud. Then I arrived, born in 1983 in Lausanne, which is where I grew up. Ever since I was little, I have regularly visited Brazil. When I was a teen and right in the middle of trying to find myself and forge an identity, I took up photography. At some point, I wanted to tackle Brazil, its history and culture. For me, that had to be through photography. So I began making longer and longer visits during which, to understand the place, I took pictures of Brazilian men and women from a point of view that focused on their extreme social contrasts. These are due to a colonial society that has not yet been fully digested.

In the spring of 2014, I was staying in Rio de Janeiro for several months when I met Milena, who is from northeastern Brazil, specifically Teixeira de Freitas, in the south of the State of Bahia. In late 2014, we decided to take a road trip to the place where she grew up. We crossed regions like the State of Espírito Santo, with its valleys of green pasture that strangely reminded me of the Swiss canton of Fribourg, when, after nearly eight hundred kilometers and around fifty minutes from our destination, I read a sign along the road announcing "Helvécia." Puzzled, I asked Milena what she knew about the place and she explained that it is a *quilombo*, a former refuge for enslaved people who had escaped bondage or had been recently freed. I then learned from Milena that the place-name comes from the Latin, Helvetia, the allegorical female figure personifying the Swiss Confederation.

I began researching the place and discovered that Helvécia was a former colony where Swiss and German immigrants once grew coffee. Time passed. Around a year later, the urge to delve into this story started to gnaw away at me. I suggested to Milena that she delve into the story with me. In late 2015, we went there and set off on our discovery of the village and its 2,500 inhabitants. Milena would deal with the research and I with capturing this story in images.

Dom Smaz

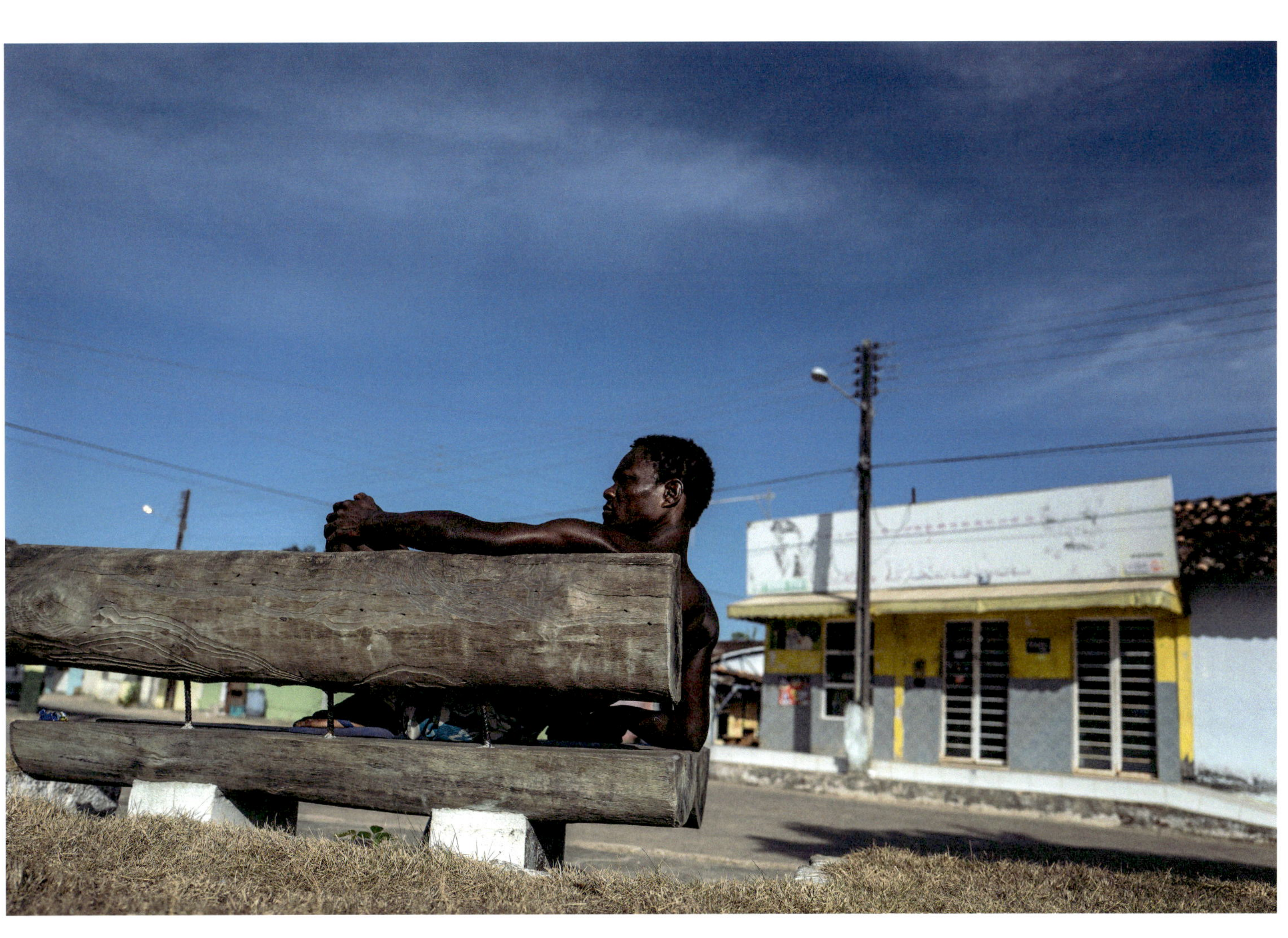

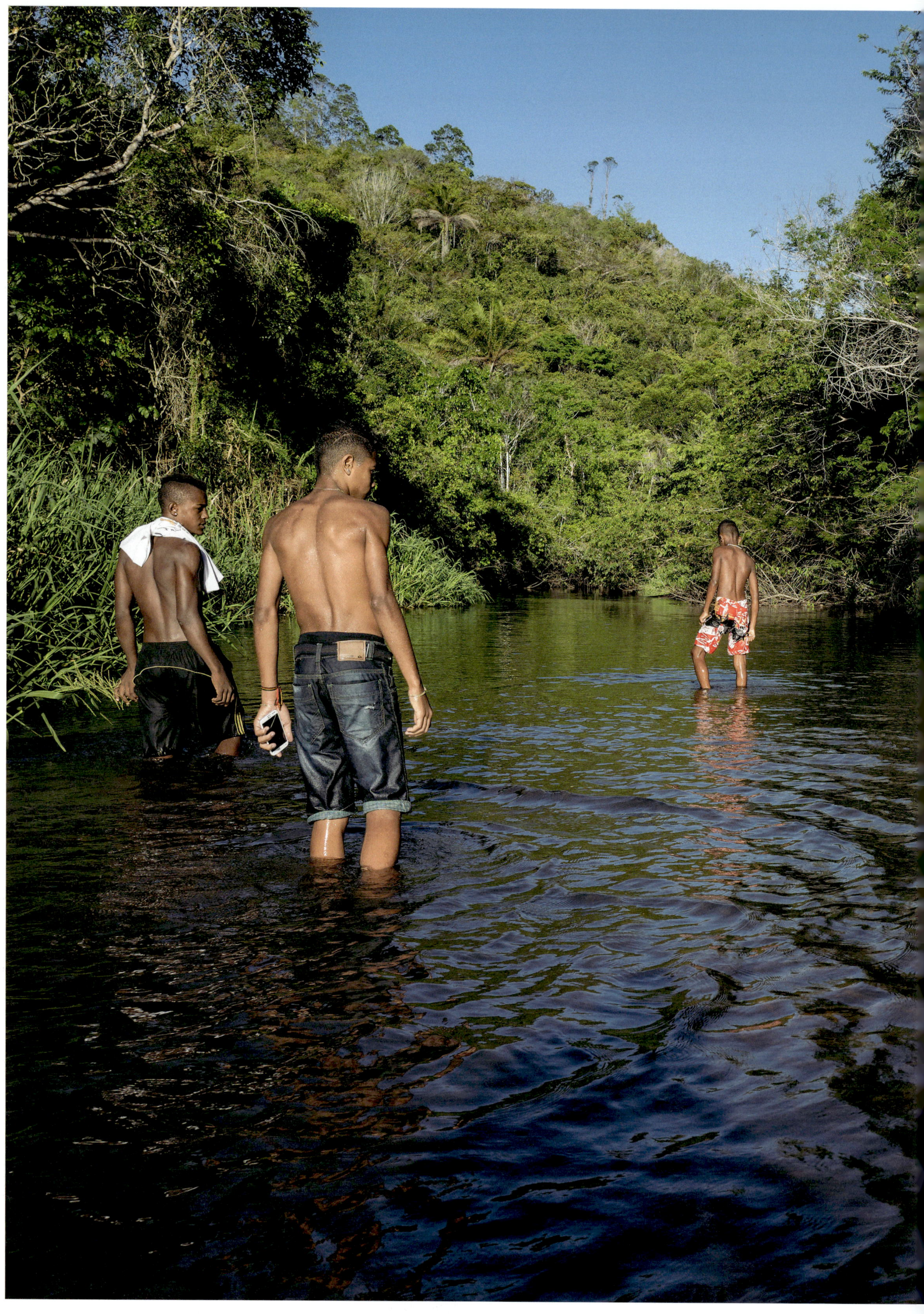

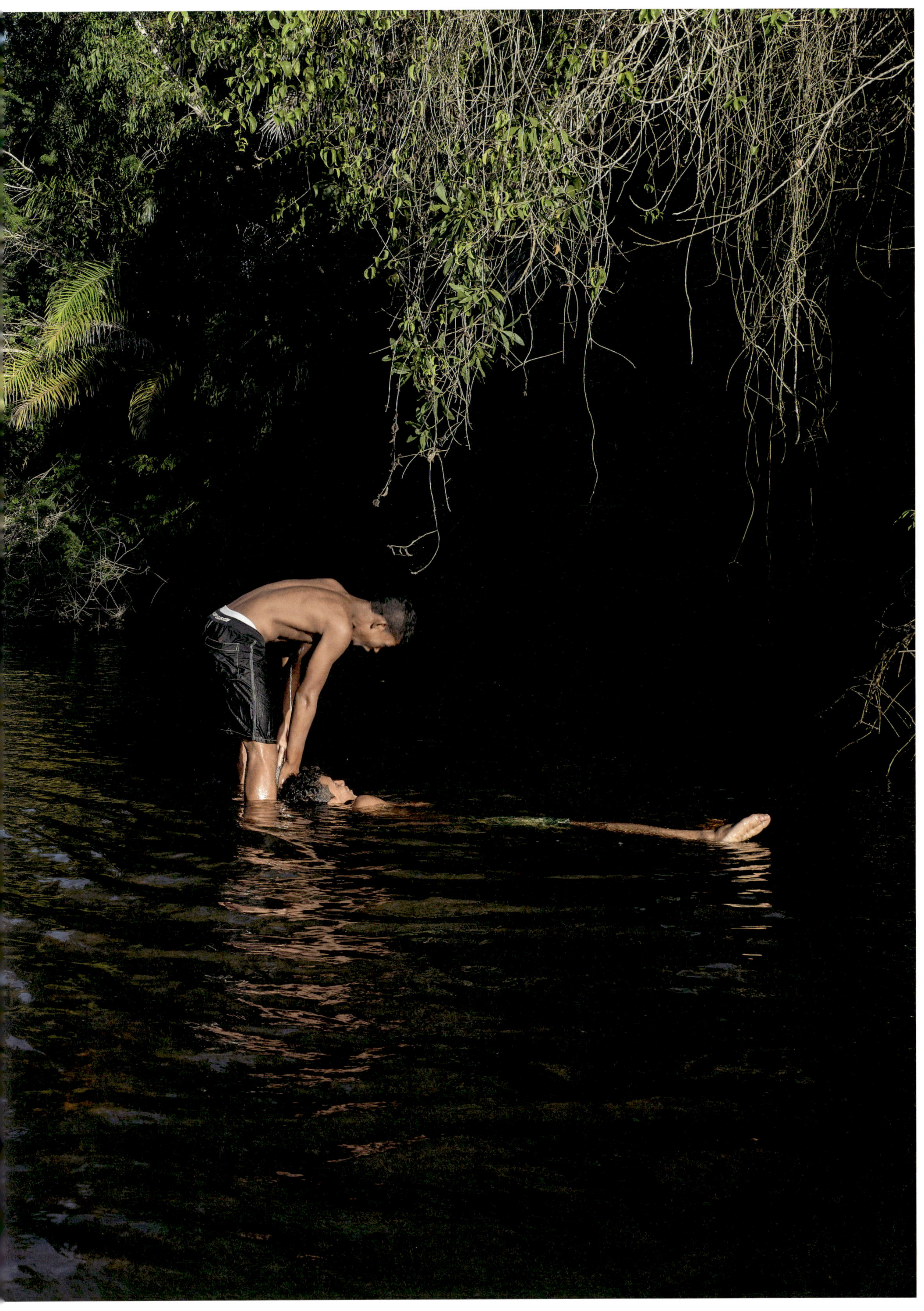

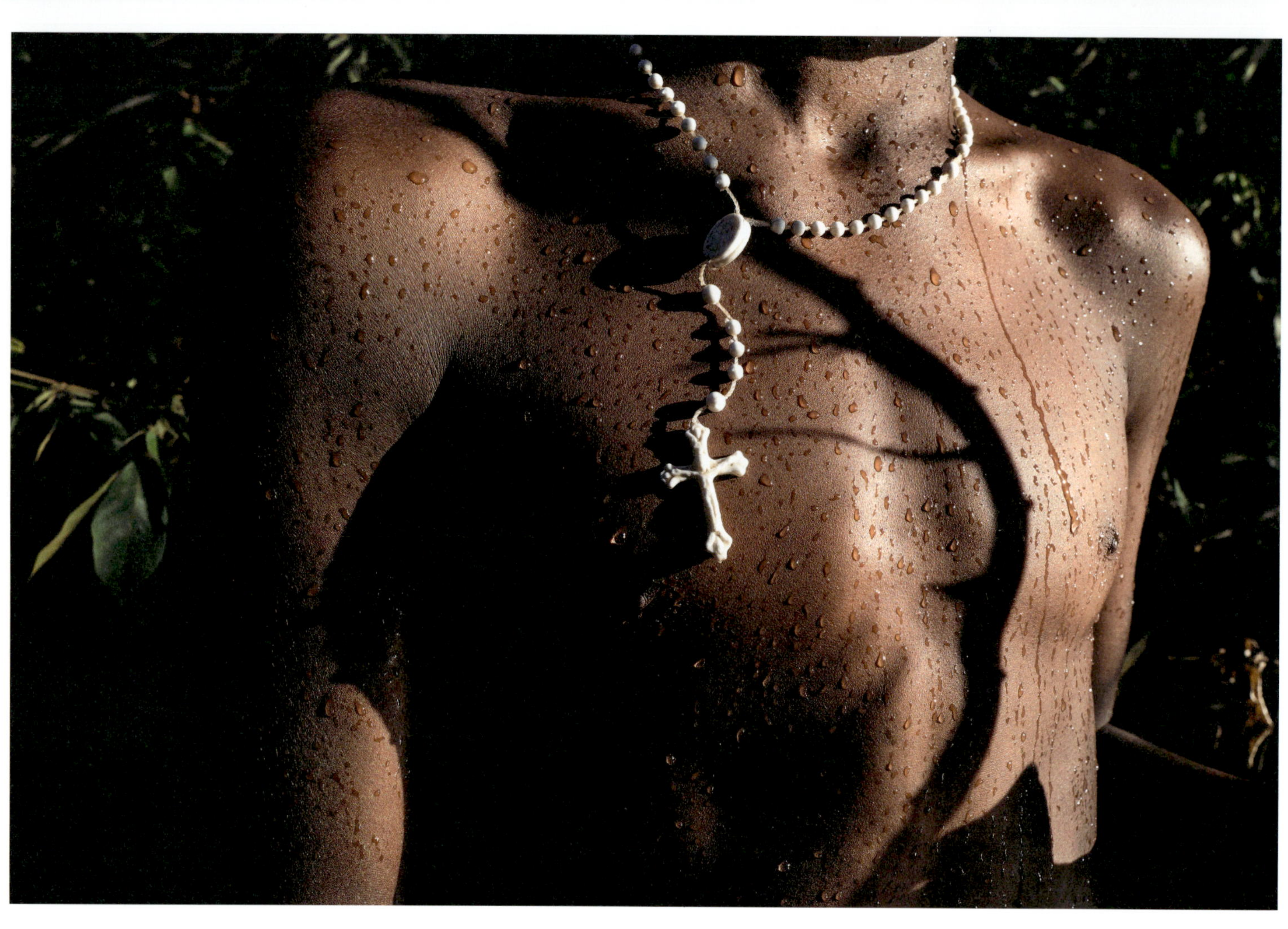

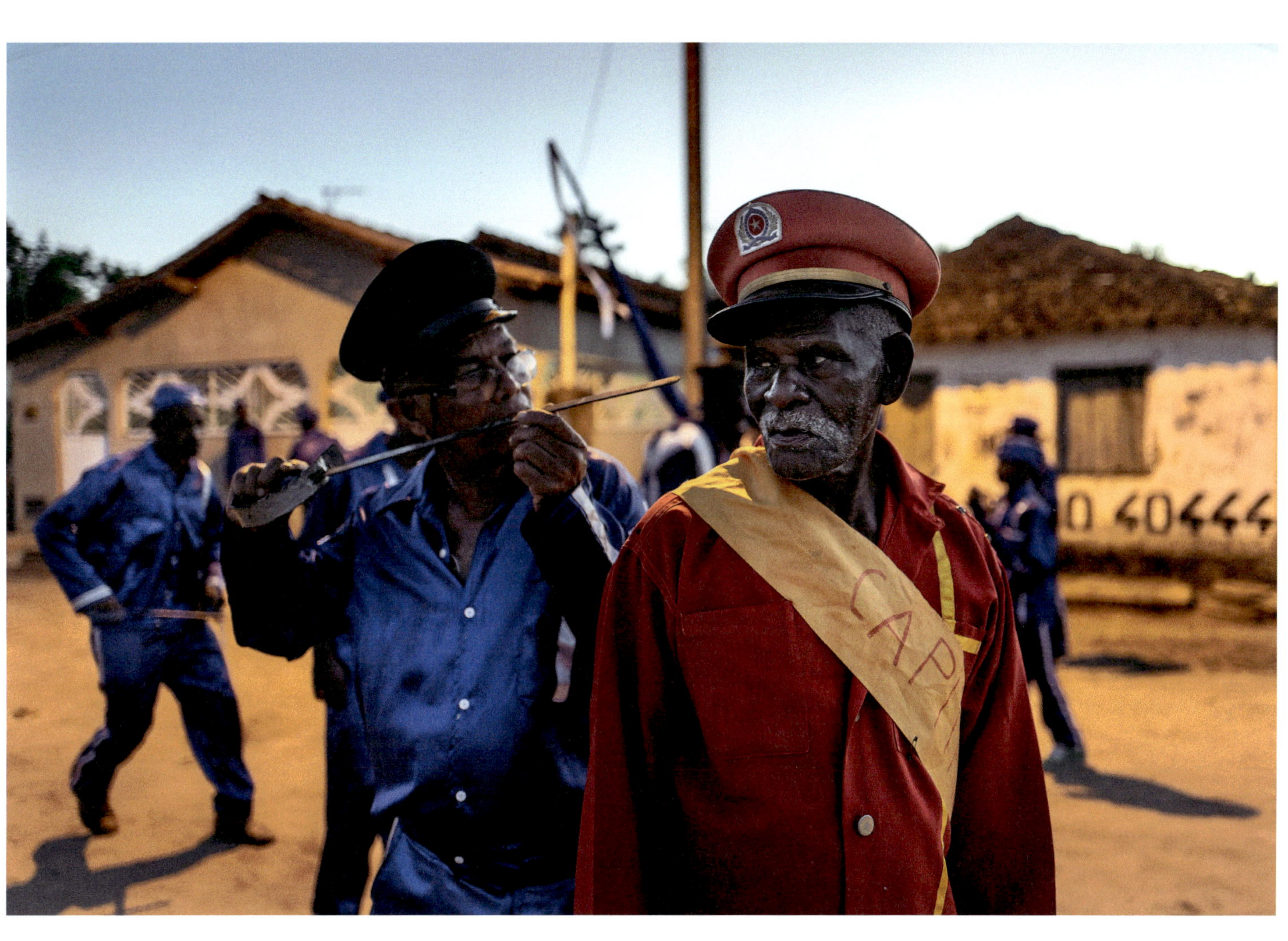

0 40444
CAP

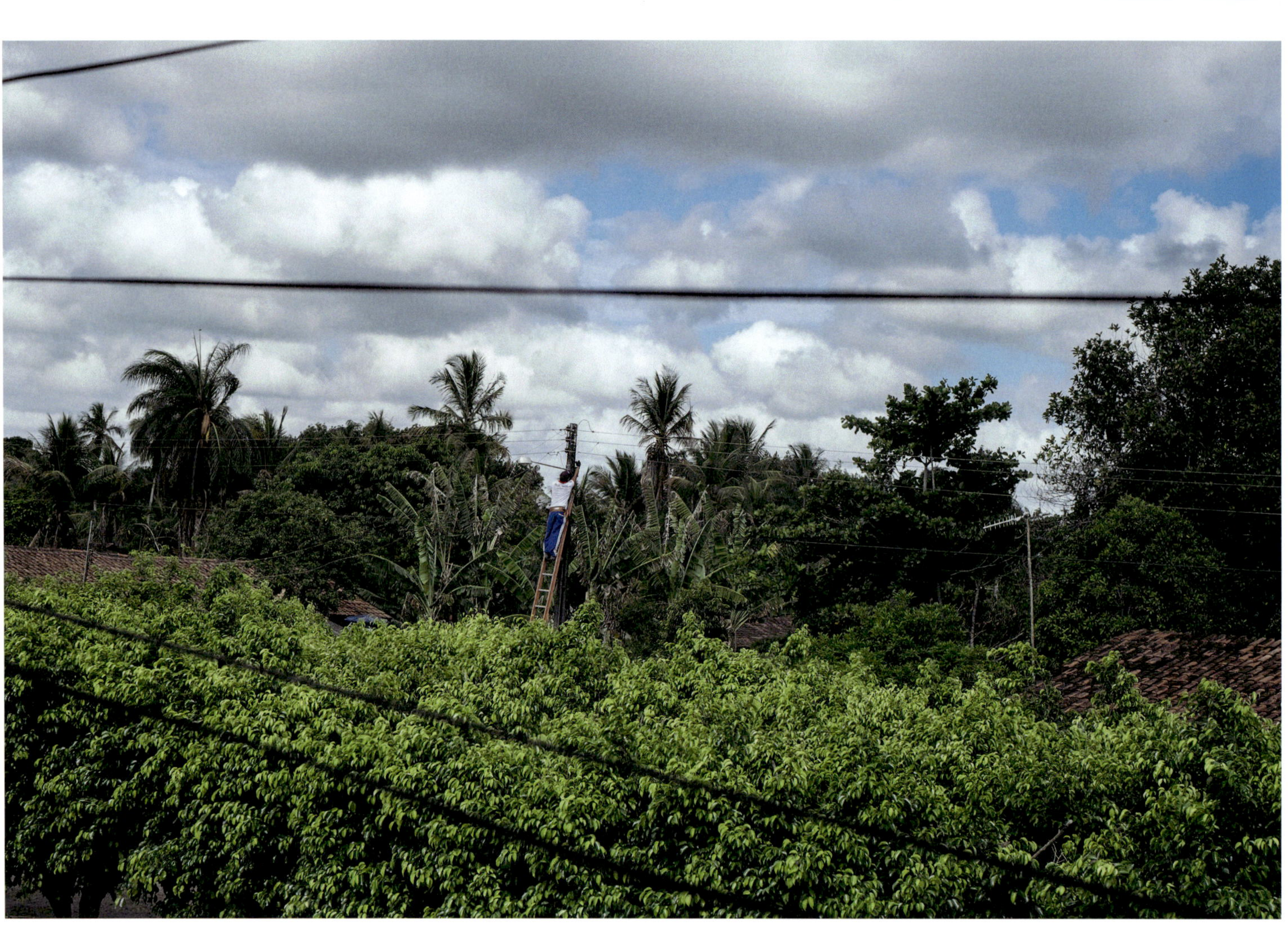

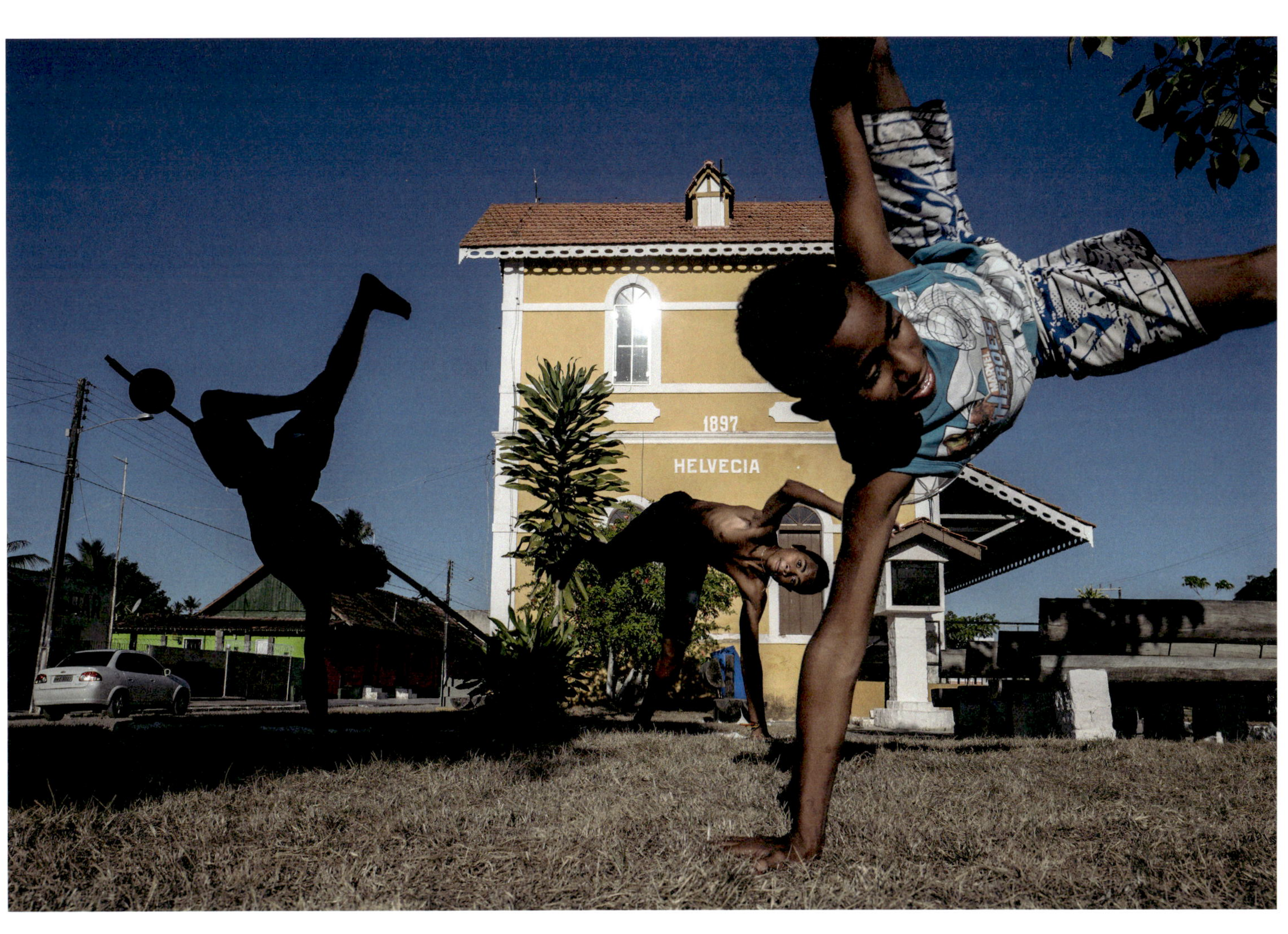

1897
HELVECIA

Christian Doninelli

The Brazilian sun has yet to reach its zenith and the heat is already suffocating. At the center of the village, three teens show supple grace executing various moves in *capoeira*, a martial art that has its roots in Africa. In the background, on the yellow ocher façade of the disused train station a name stands out, an unexpected name in such a place, to say the least, HELVÉCIA, which is followed by a date, 1897, the year the building went up. Taken aback, the passing visitor cannot help but wonder by what whim of history did an isolated locale like this, lost in a sea of eucalyptus, manage to inherit such a place name. As this outsider strolls down the streets of the town, the mystery only deepens for those streets are tread by a mostly Black population, and the Black inhabitants are far more numerous than in the other hamlets, villages, and towns in the South of the State of Bahia. A realization dawns very quickly, the most African of Brazilian villages bears a Swiss name.

On site the mystery proves difficult to unravel. Stopped and asked at random, several passersby confess they know next to nothing about the origins of their community. "In the old days, there was a big landowner whose wife was called Helvécia," a young waitress leaning on the bar volunteers. "Out of love, he gave her name to his lands." A client sitting at the table opposite now speaks up, "Nooo! Helvécia's the name of a town in Switzerland." They begin, visitor and locals, to arrive at the truth without quite managing to get there.

Meanwhile, the three young capoeiristas have taken off. To escape the heat, they have gone for a dip in Rio Peruípe without suspecting that on its banks, less than two hundred years ago, their African ancestors trudged ashore in leg irons.

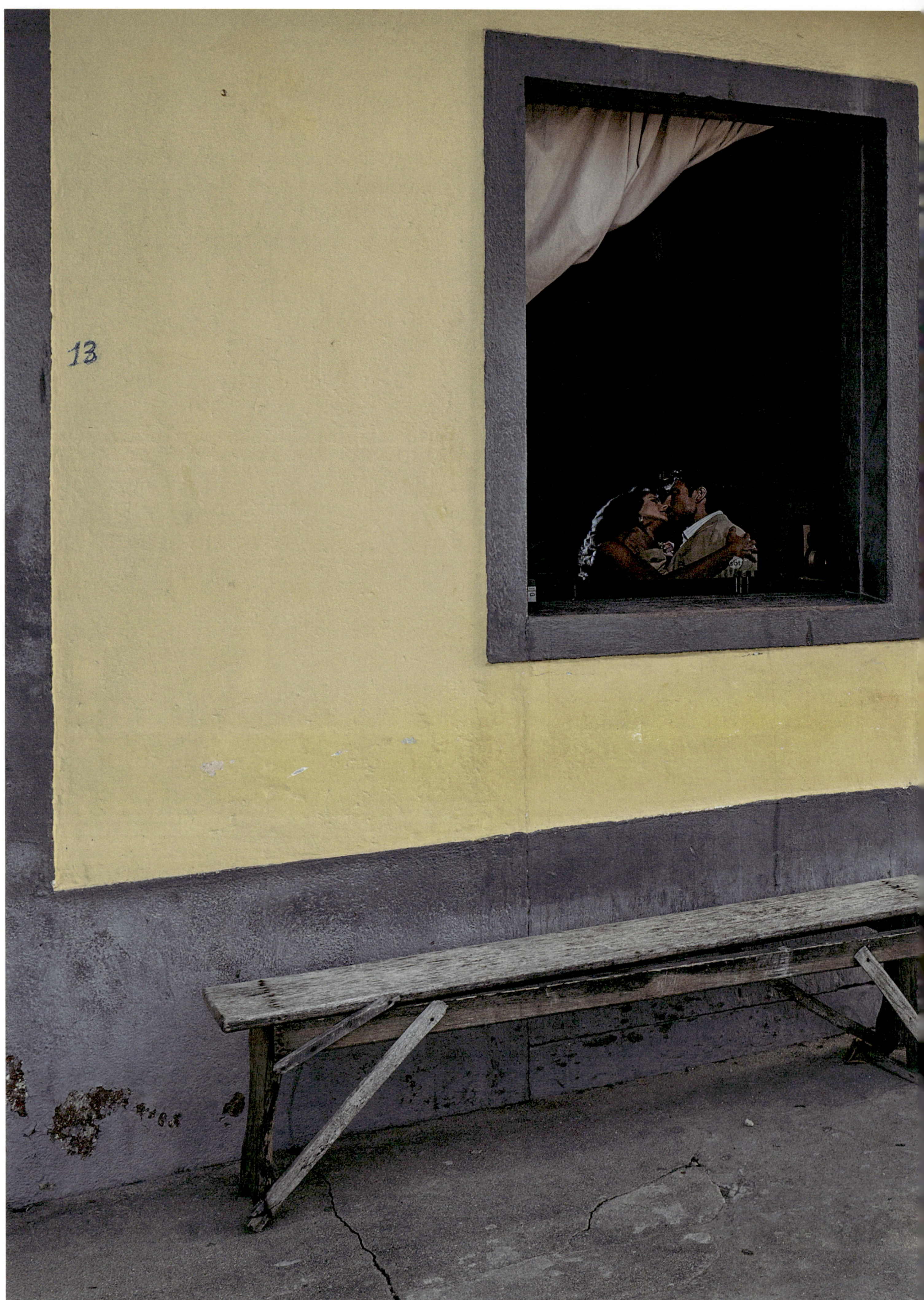

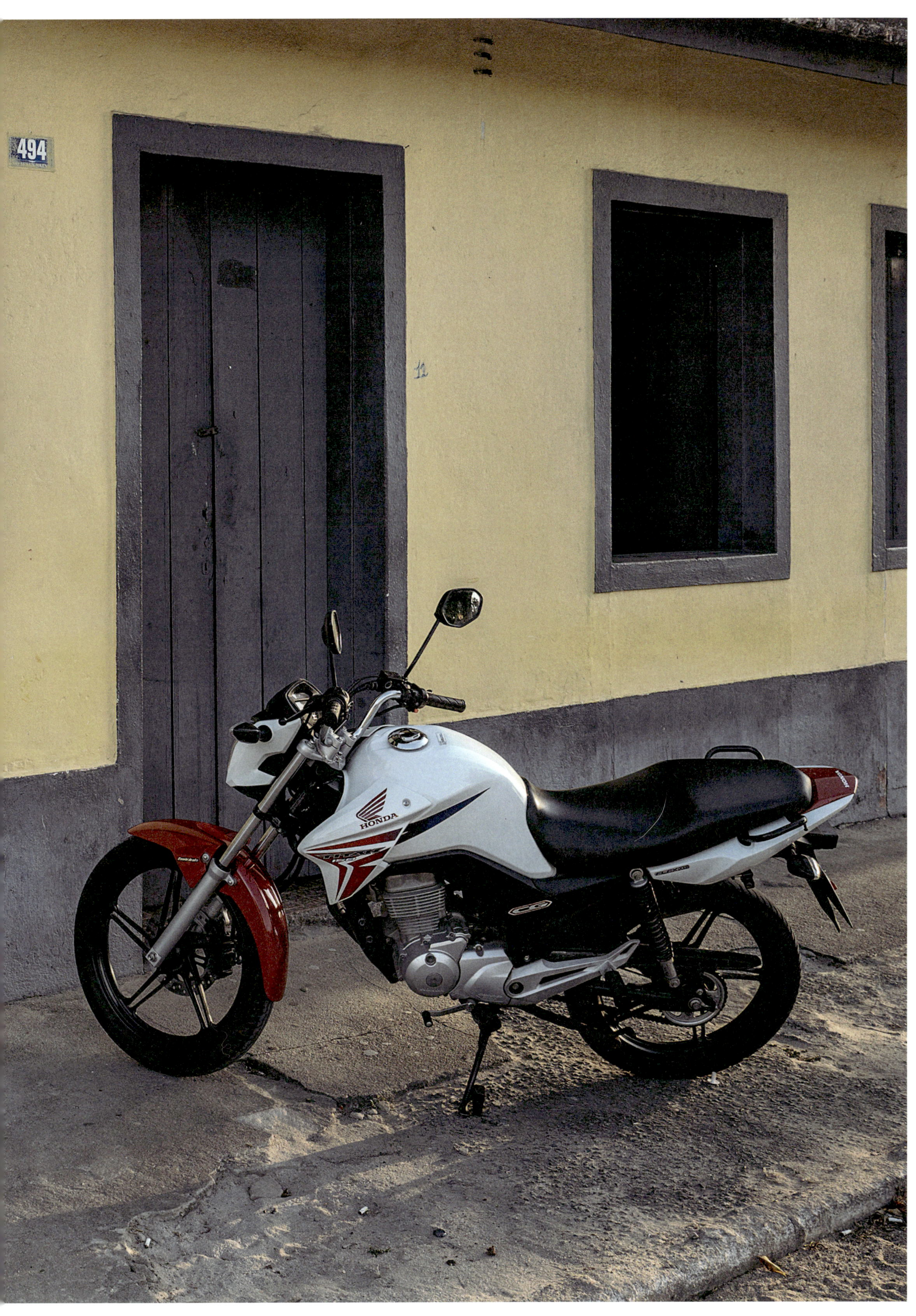
494

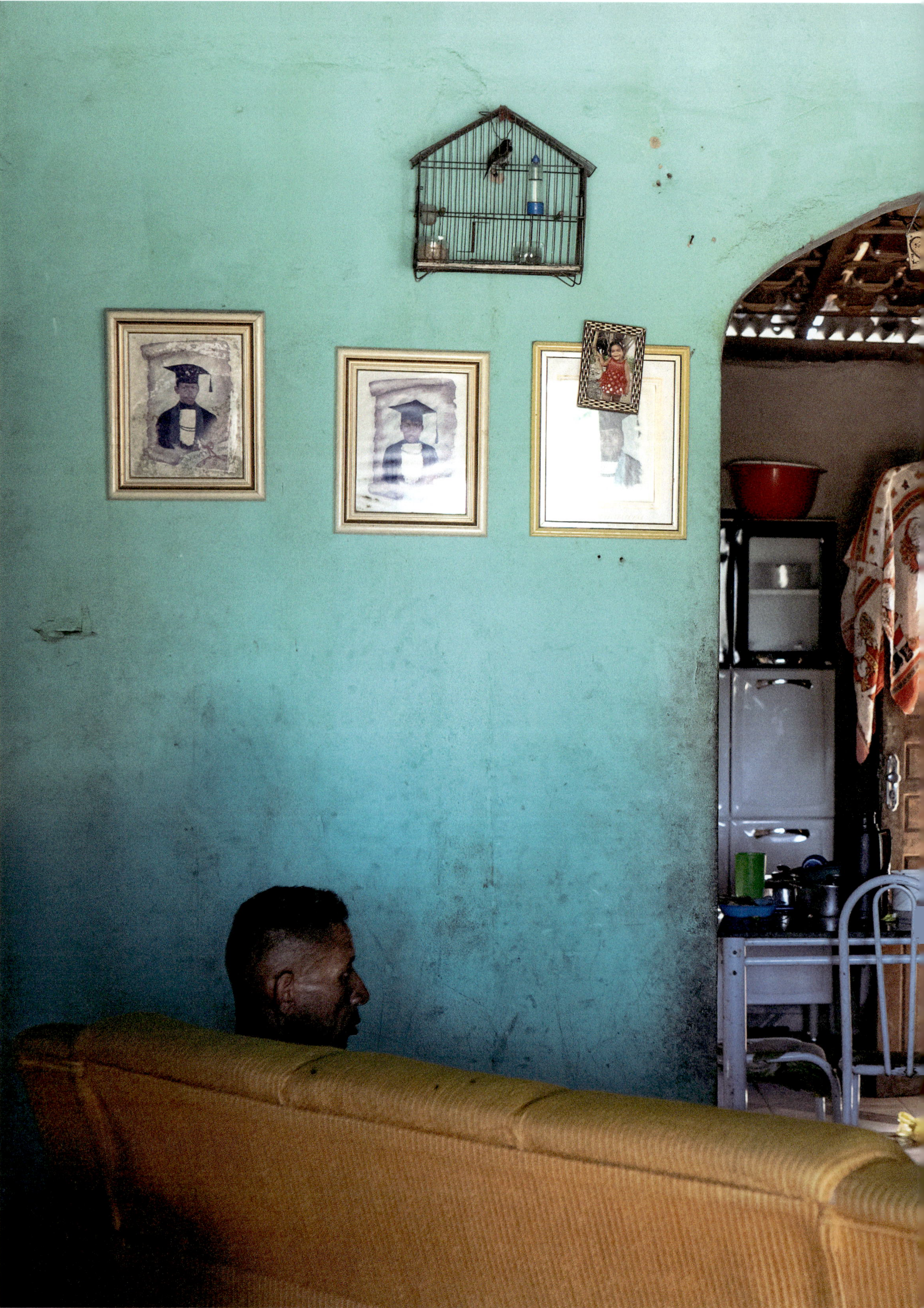

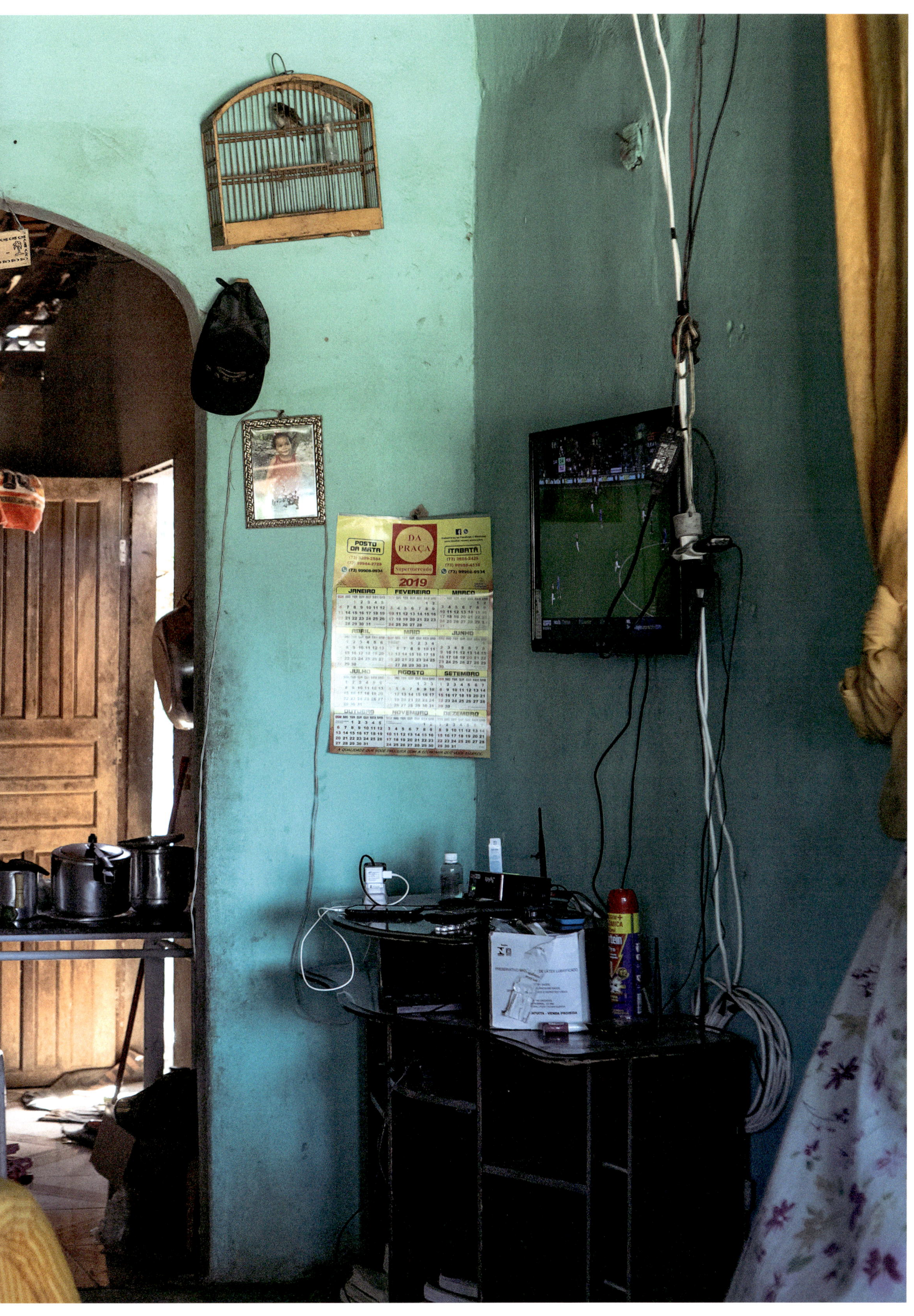

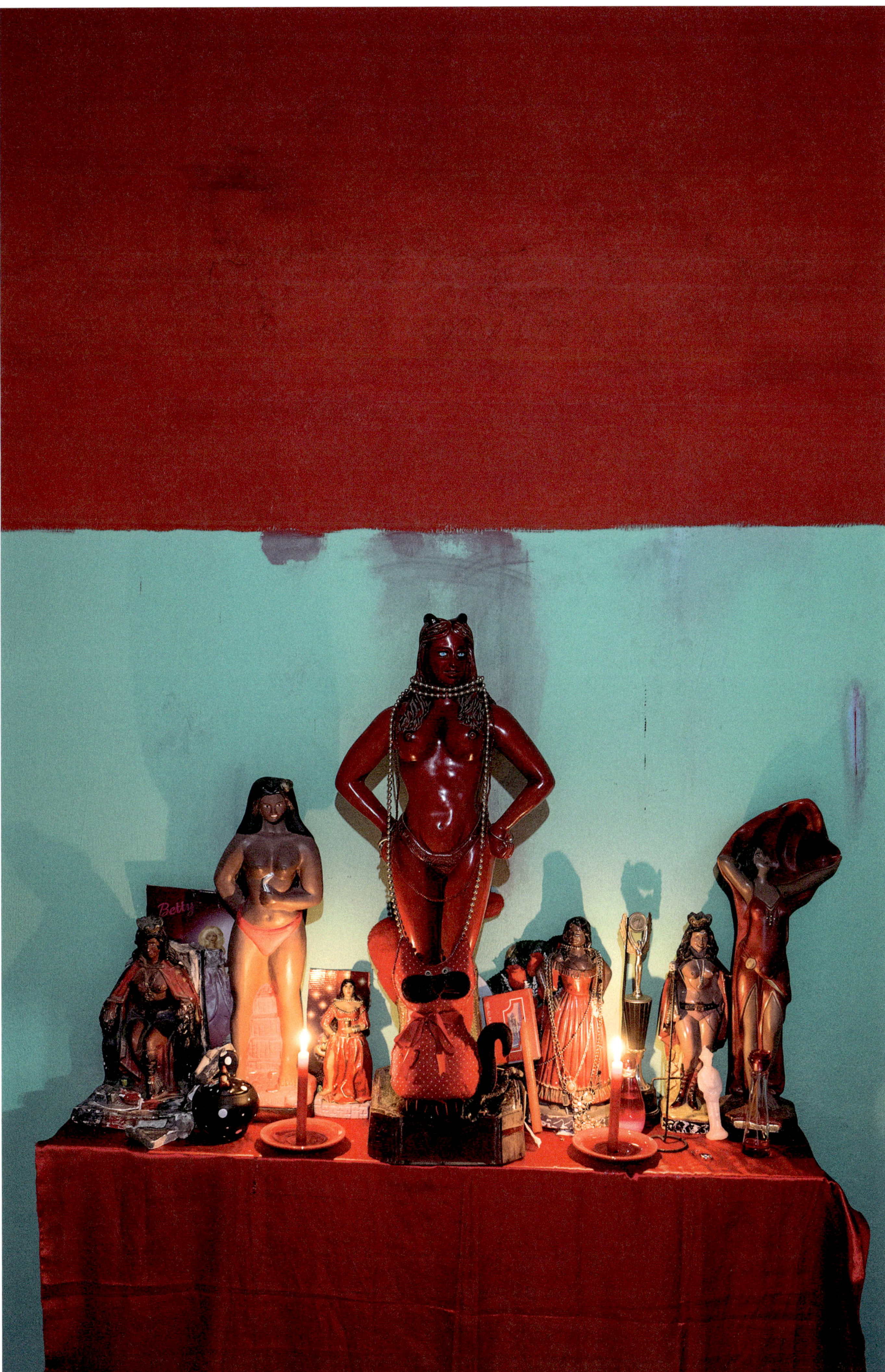

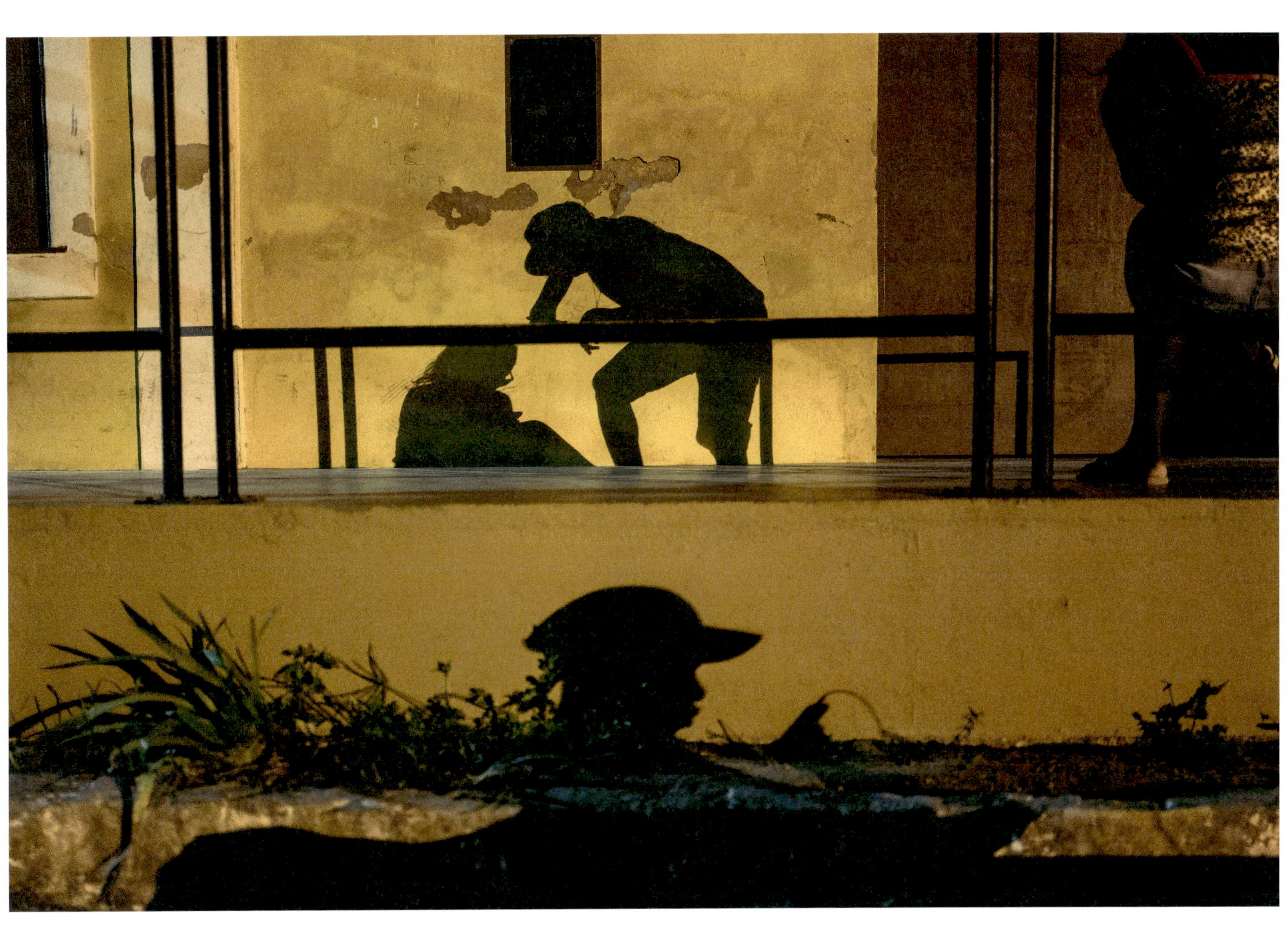

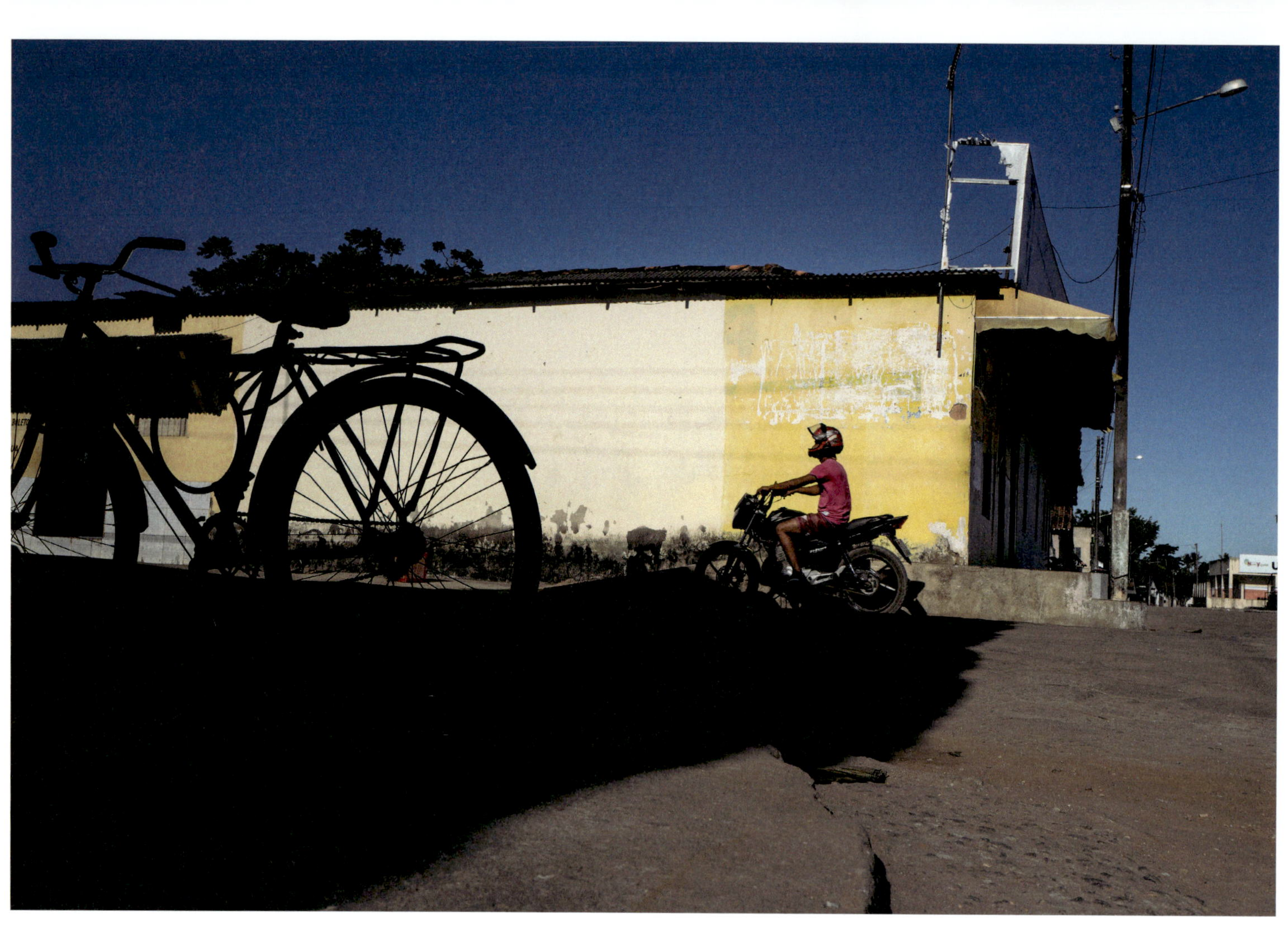

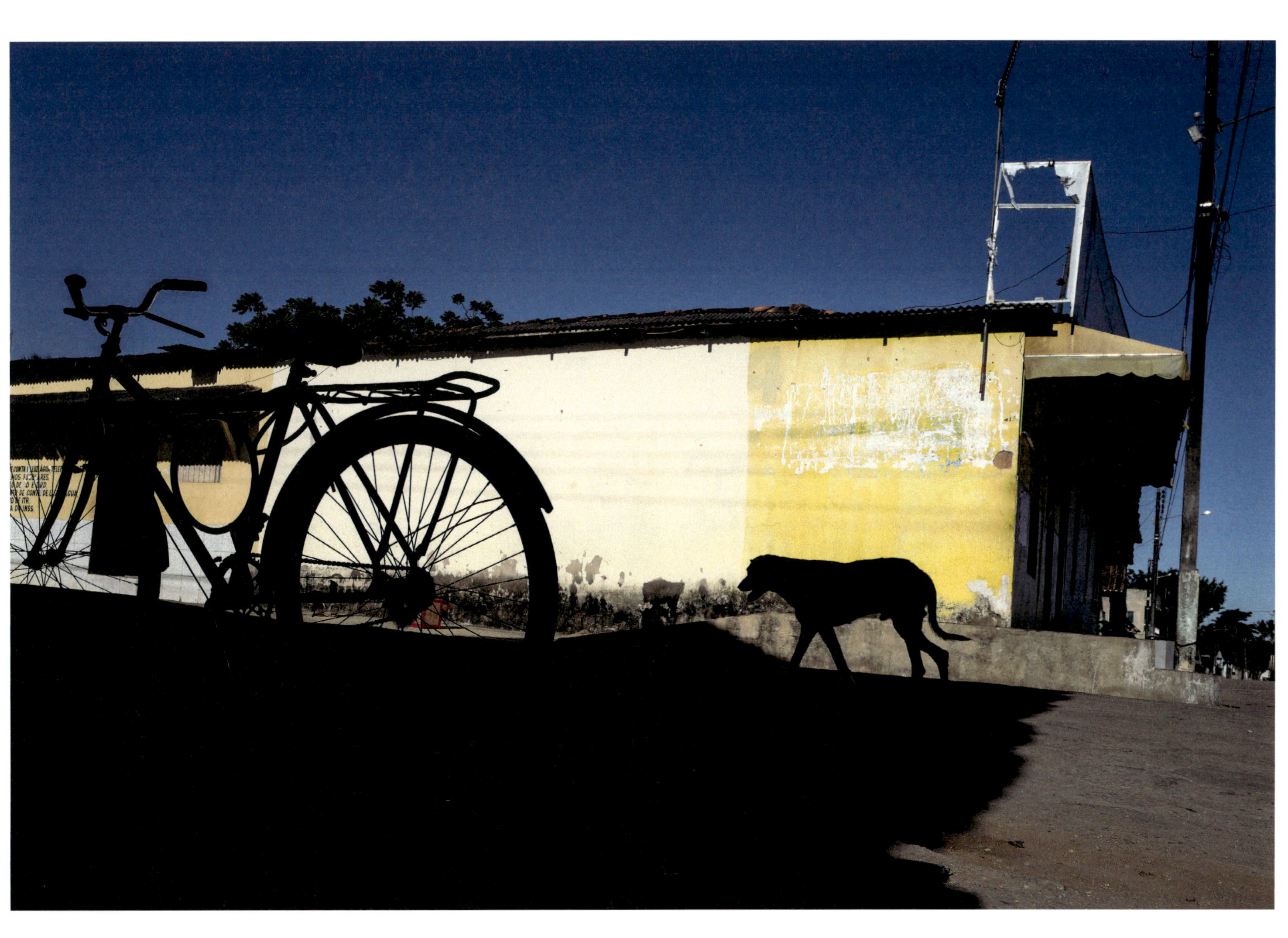

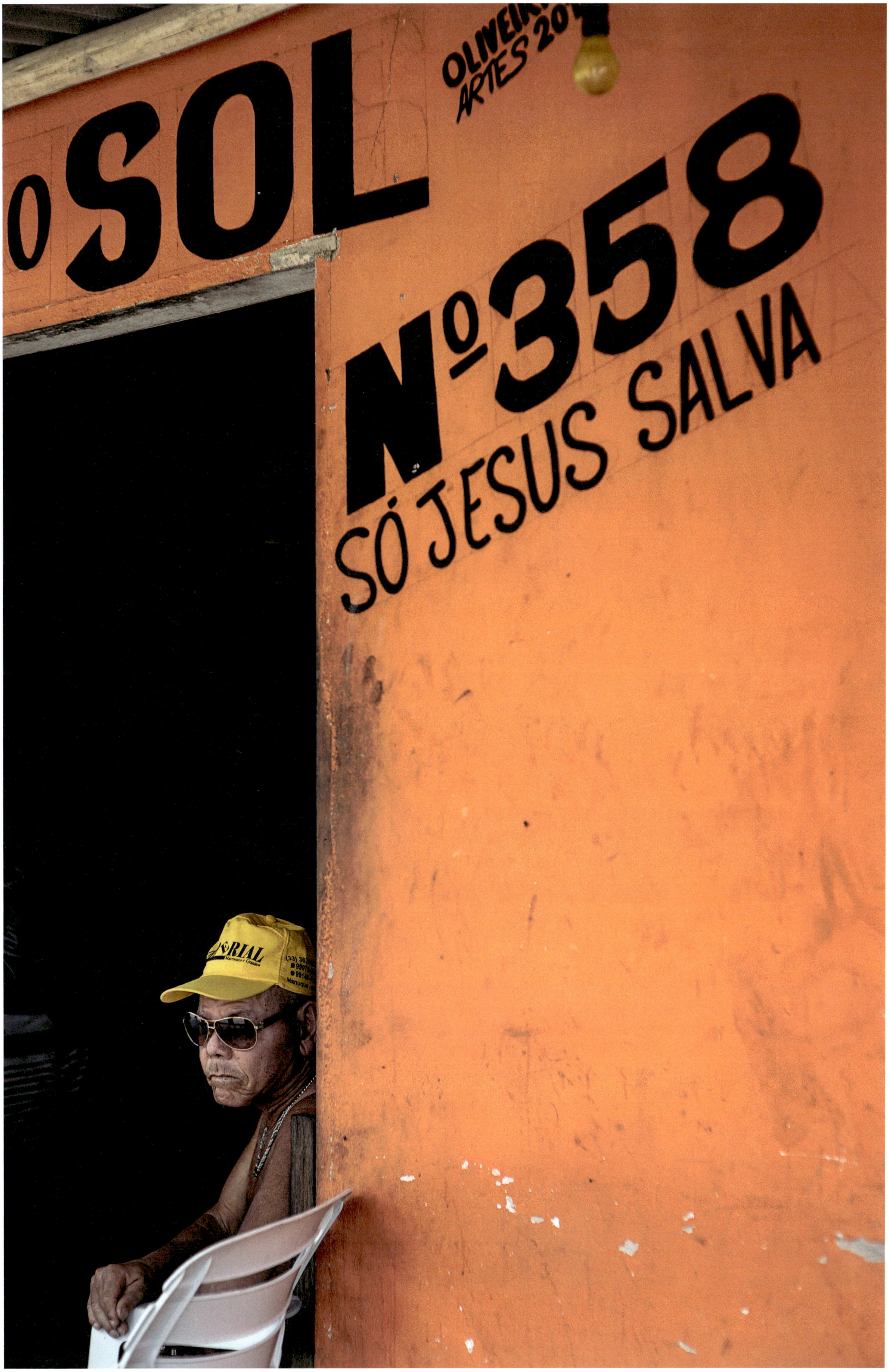

o SOL

OLIVEIR
ARTES 20

Nº 358
SÓ JESUS SALVA

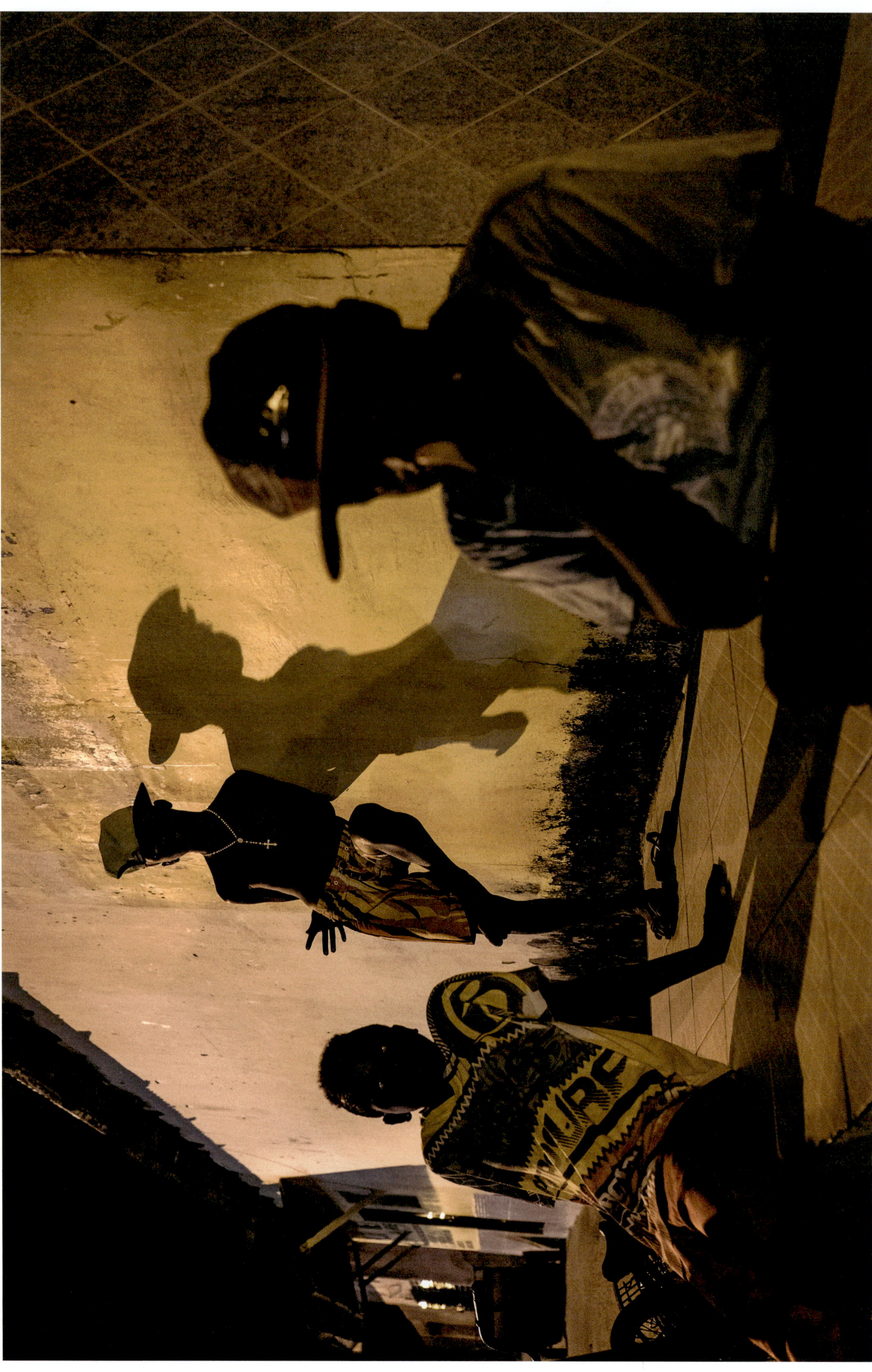

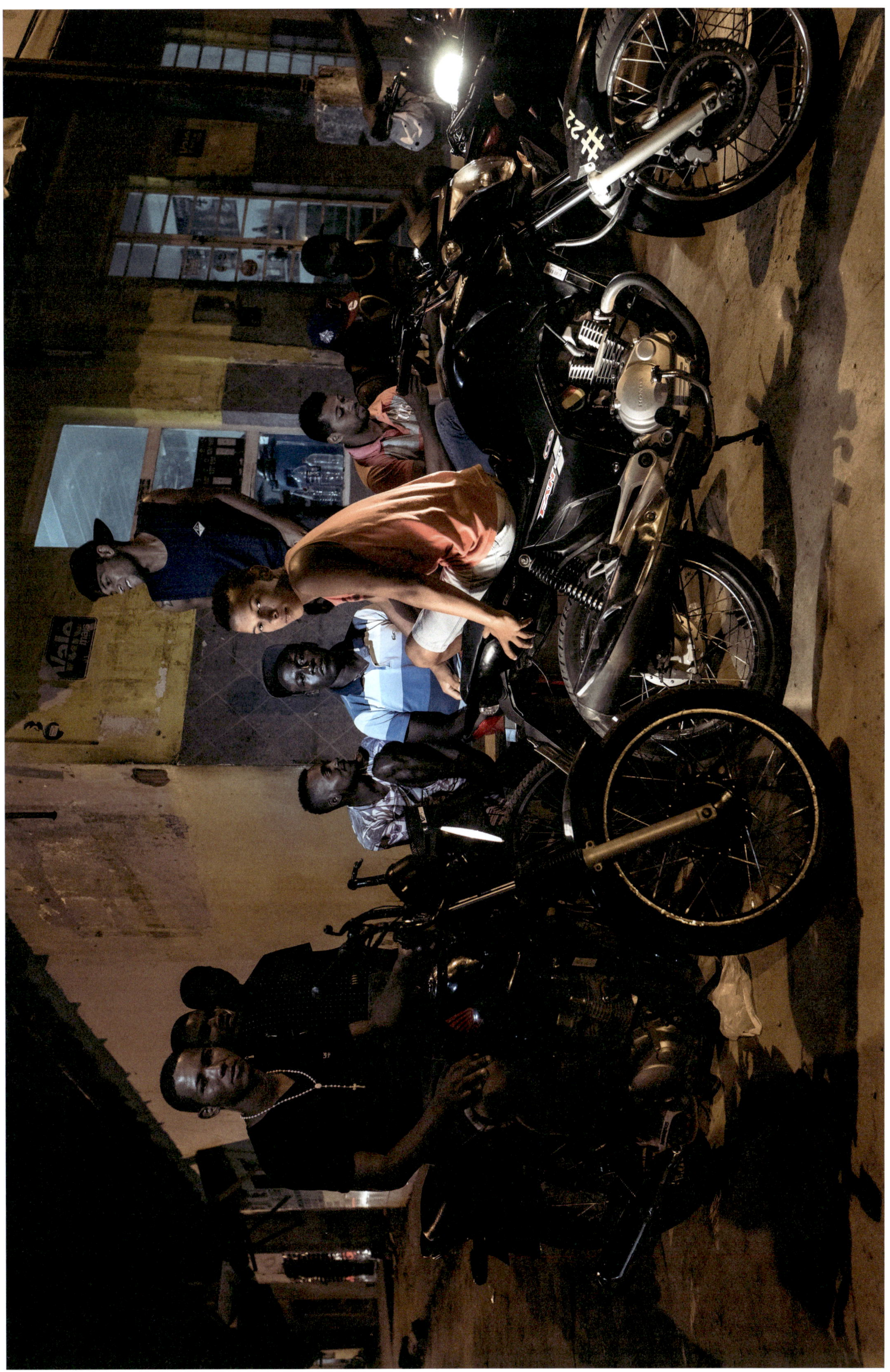

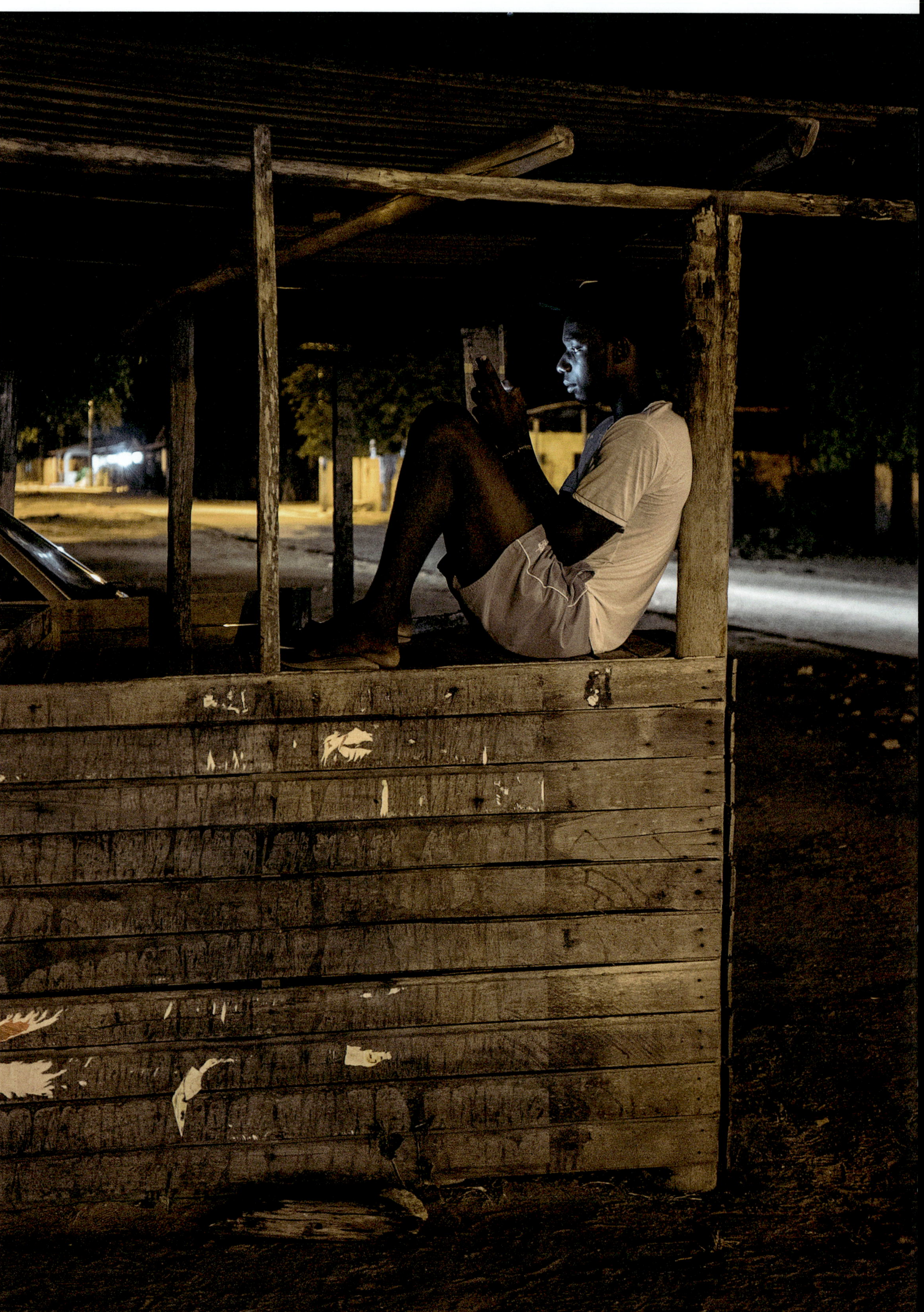

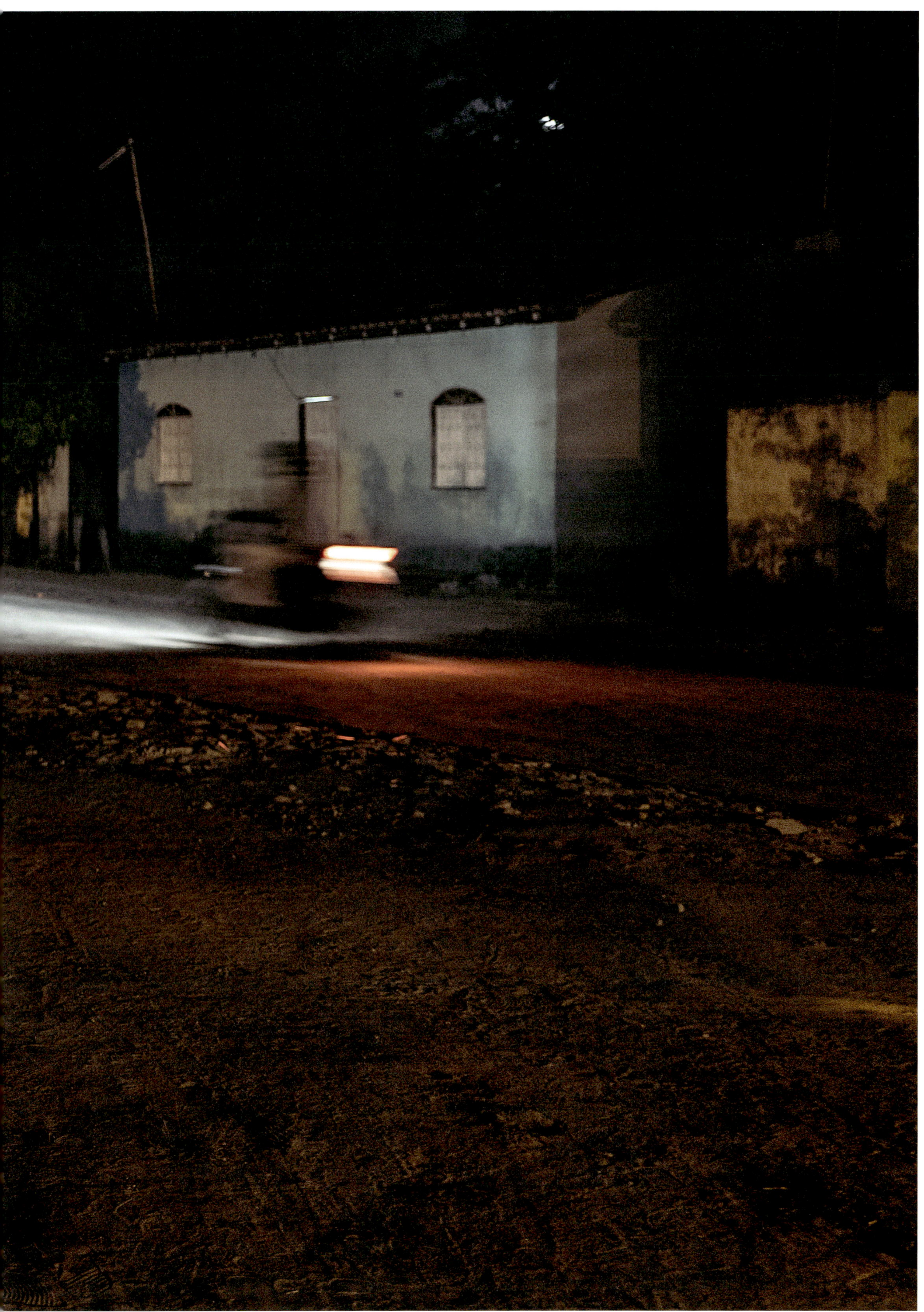

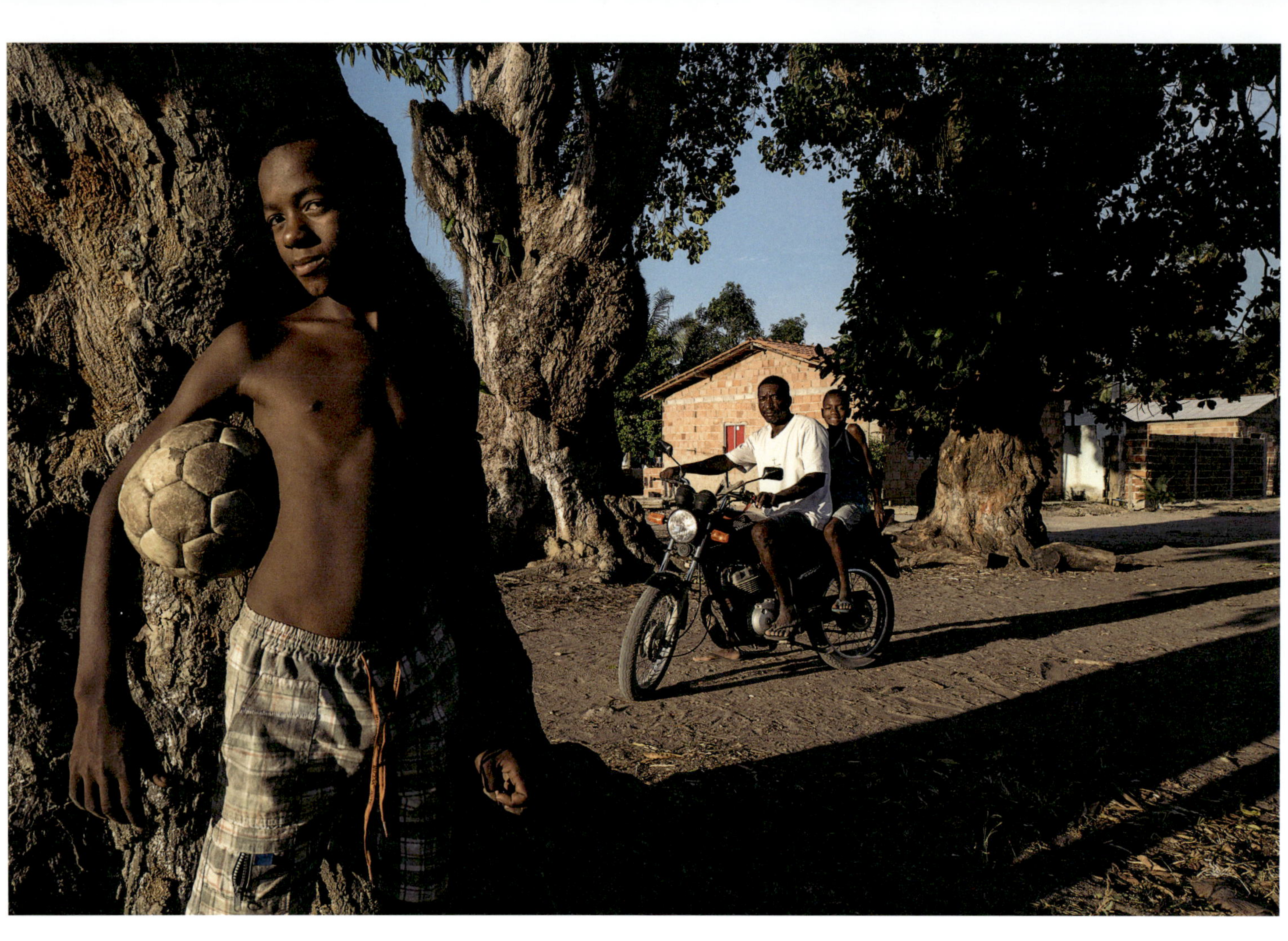

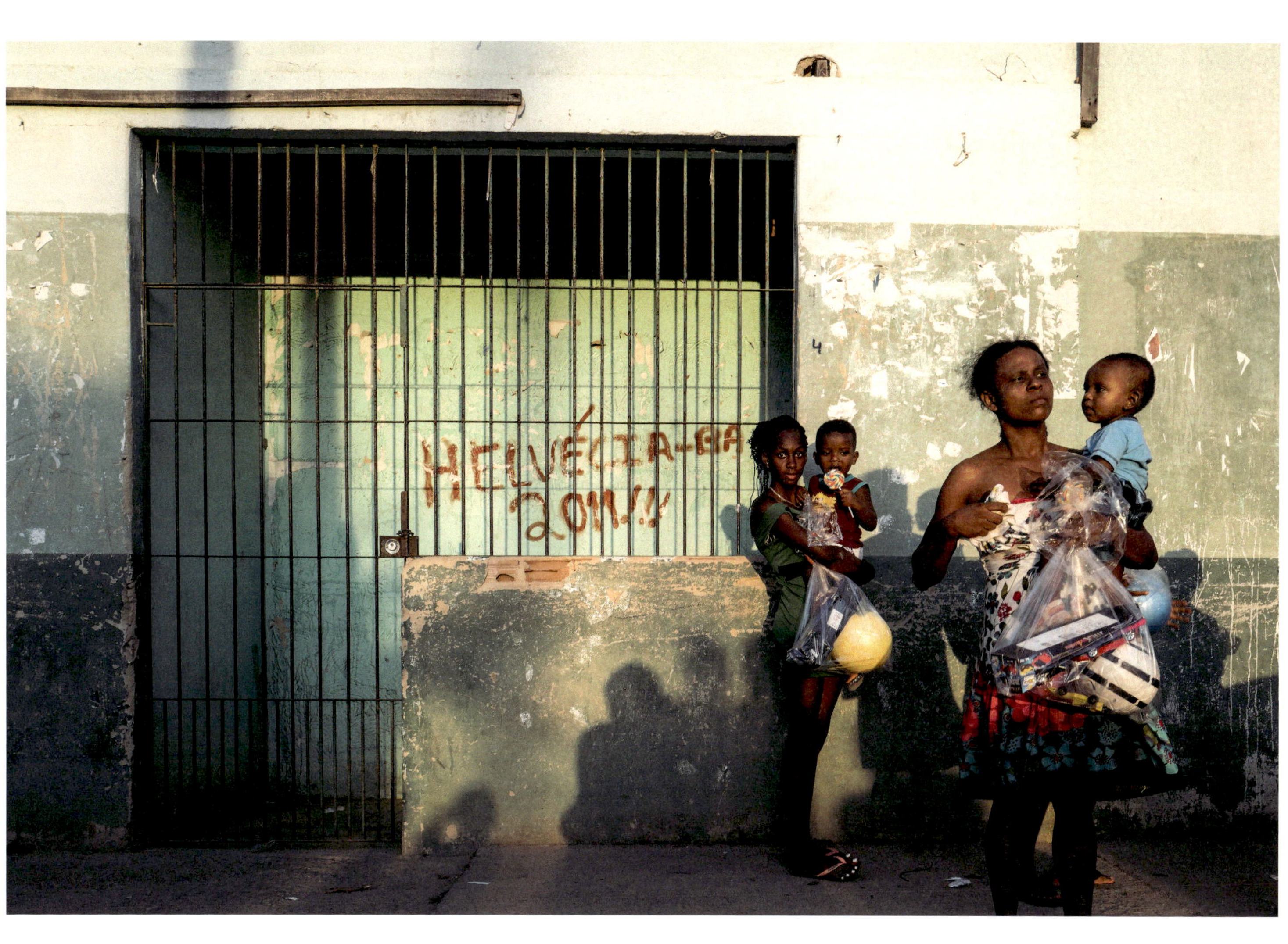

HELVÉCIA-BA
2011!!!

The origins of Helvécia go back to 1818 at least, when a group of Germans, including the naturalist Georg Wilhelm Freyreiss, decided to found a colony on the banks of the Peruípe, a region they had explored earlier during a scientific expedition. They called it Leopoldina in homage to the wife of the royal prince of Portugal. At the time, the prince was looking to people – "whiten," some would say – his vast possessions in Brazil.

In the summer of 1819, Abraham Langhans, a native of Bern, was probably one of the first Swiss to settle in the region. "I thank the Lord I made the decision to come here," he confessed, less than two years after arriving, praising the incredible fertility of his lands, where rice, manioc, oranges, lemons, bananas, and other exotic fruits grew. A veritable Garden of Eden! He hoped and prayed for an influx of colonists from Bern.

Langhans was soon followed by Pierre-Henri Béguin and Philippe Huguenin, natives of Neuchâtel, whose long journey is known to us thanks to the correspondence of the man who sent them there, a certain Charles-Louis Borrel, "They were left at the site on Christmas 1819, alone like Robinson [Crusoe]," Borrel writes. Unlike the Nova Friburgo colony, Leopoldina seems to have prospered in short order, which quickly became known in the Old World, as the *Gazette de Lausanne* of June 16, 1820, reports, "Several persons, on the other hand, speak with approval of the situation of a German colony, placed in the government of Bahia under the protection of the royal princess (Leopoldina of Austria) and where several Swiss, probably from Bern, are gathered. The rivers there are quite teeming with fish; the land abounds in game and fowl; the climate there is mild, the vegetation vigorous, and the coffee trees, planted three years ago, are already offering their bounty to the colonists."

From a document that dates back to 1824, it appears that a certain Baron von dem Busche, Georg Wilhelm Freyreiss, Abraham and Louis Langhans, and David Pache were the five "founders of the colony." Their signatures appear with the "colonists [who] arrived afterwards," including P.-H. Béguin, Ph. Huguenin, and E. Borrel. These natives of Neuchâtel would bring other French-speaking Swiss in their wake, Montandons, Jeanmonods, Jaccards, Maulazes, etc. Surprisingly all of these surnames have since vanished, including that of Johann Martin Flach. This native of Schaffhausen, who was admitted to the royal court of Brazil, managed one of the most extensive farming operations of the colony. Called Helvetia, his property has come down to us as the village that replaced it long ago.

Around 1850, the colony of Leopoldina became one of the most important coffee-growing centers in Brazil. Such was its success that Switzerland deemed it necessary to open a consular agency in the neighboring town of Caravelas. The planters' commercial achievement, however, cannot hide their moral failing; to work their lands, the colonists used human chattel and held in bondage a large number of slaves.* A few quite eloquent accounts of this reality have survived, moreover. In a letter dated 1819, David Pache, a native of the Canton of Vaud, explains to his sister Mélosine that he owns two Negro slaves. He obviously has a hard time seeing their humanity. "These are individuals that can be driven only with the utmost severity. Ours are perfectly kept, well fed and clothed. And yet we can only get something acceptable out of them after thrashing them in a way that they really feel it. They need the blows. I was told this but I wanted to believe none of it." The same lack of misgivings of any sort can be seen in Charles-Louis Borrel. Having reached Rio in the spring of 1827, the native of Neuchâtel tells of the "purchases" he made in this new land. "There was a hangar… holding 500 to 600 Blacks at least… There were handsome men and beautiful women from Congo… For the young negresses, I paid 55 louis each."

Over the years in some farms, the slaves ended up forming large contingents. In 1848, the native of Schaffhausen Johann Martin Flach

* Instead of "slave," some prefer the term "enslaved person" in order to stress the process of reification to which the individual was subjected.

owned 108. In the colony, only the Krull family, related to Peter Peycke, the consul of Hamburg, possessed more. In late 1850, Karl August Toelsner, the colony's physician, recorded that there were apparently two hundred whites for 2,000 slaves, divided among forty plantations. A ratio of one to ten! Which easily explains the complexion of Helvécia's current inhabitants.

Inevitably, the mingling of masters and slaves, and the latter's powerlessness before the former, created the breeding ground of a certain mixing of the races, as this inventory reveals, carried out in 1874 following the death of Henrique Giroud. His union of twenty years with Luiza, his slave, yielded five children. Moreover, it was only when she was widowed that she was emancipated "for the good and faithful services rendered." For the historian Ligia Bellini, these emotional ties were neither disinterested nor devoid of oppression.

The colony's sudden prosperity would only prove a flash in the pan, however. Slave runaways and revolts became increasingly commonplace, like in 1882 on the lands owned by Frédéric-Louis Jeanmonod, the vice-consul of Switzerland. In 1888, the complete outlawing of slavery in Brazil, and the competition that other coffee-producing regions posed, dealt the colony a fatal blow. So much so that in 1895, when Vice-Consul Louis Bornand resigned his post in Caravelas, Switzerland deemed it unnecessary to replace him "in light of the considerably reduced number of Swiss nationals residing in the district in question." Some then left for the mother country. That was notably the case of Edgar Bornand, son of the last vice-consul, who, the Swiss press informs us, was found guilty by a court of law in Paris in 1947 of collaboration with the Nazi enemy.

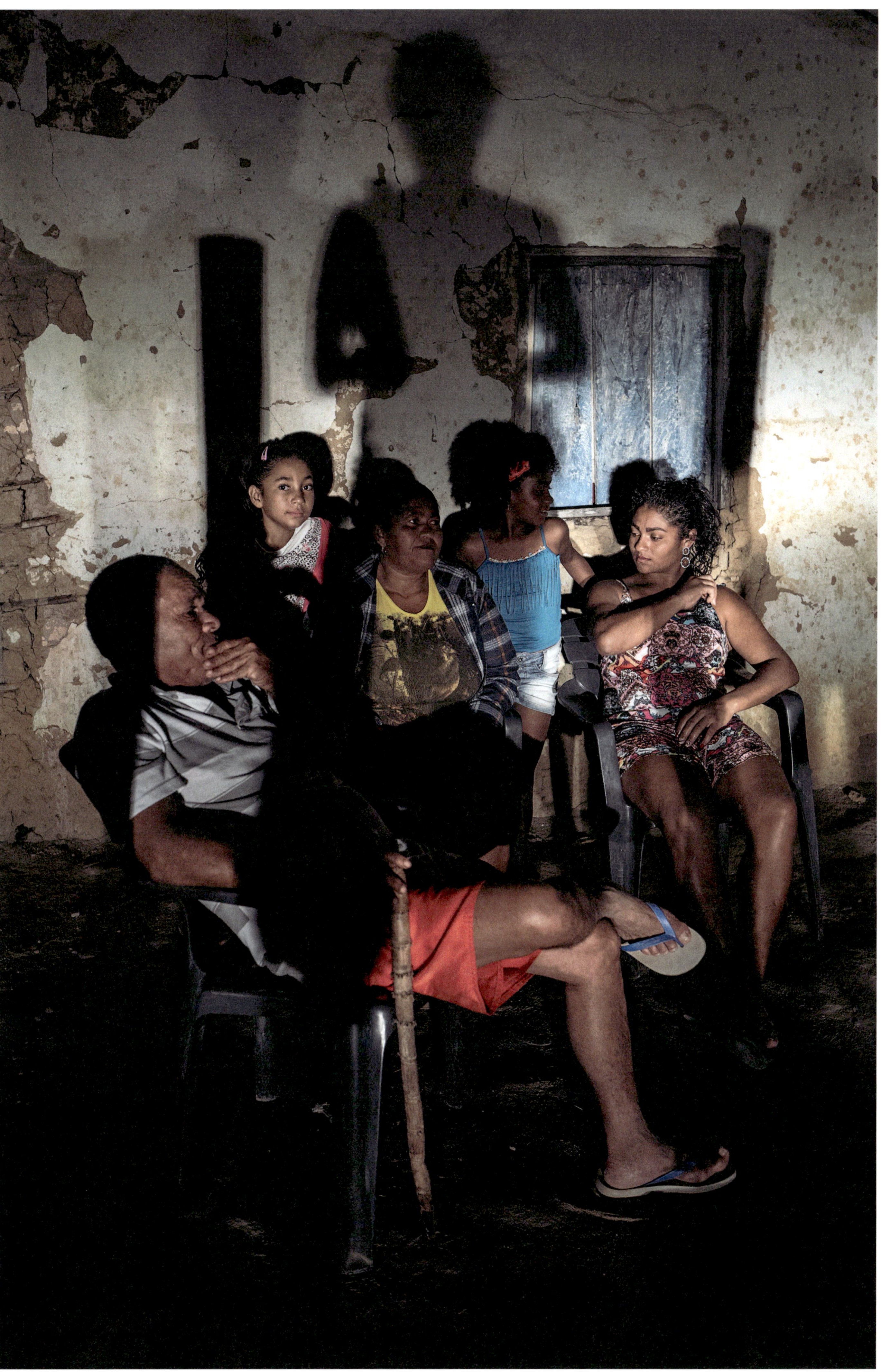

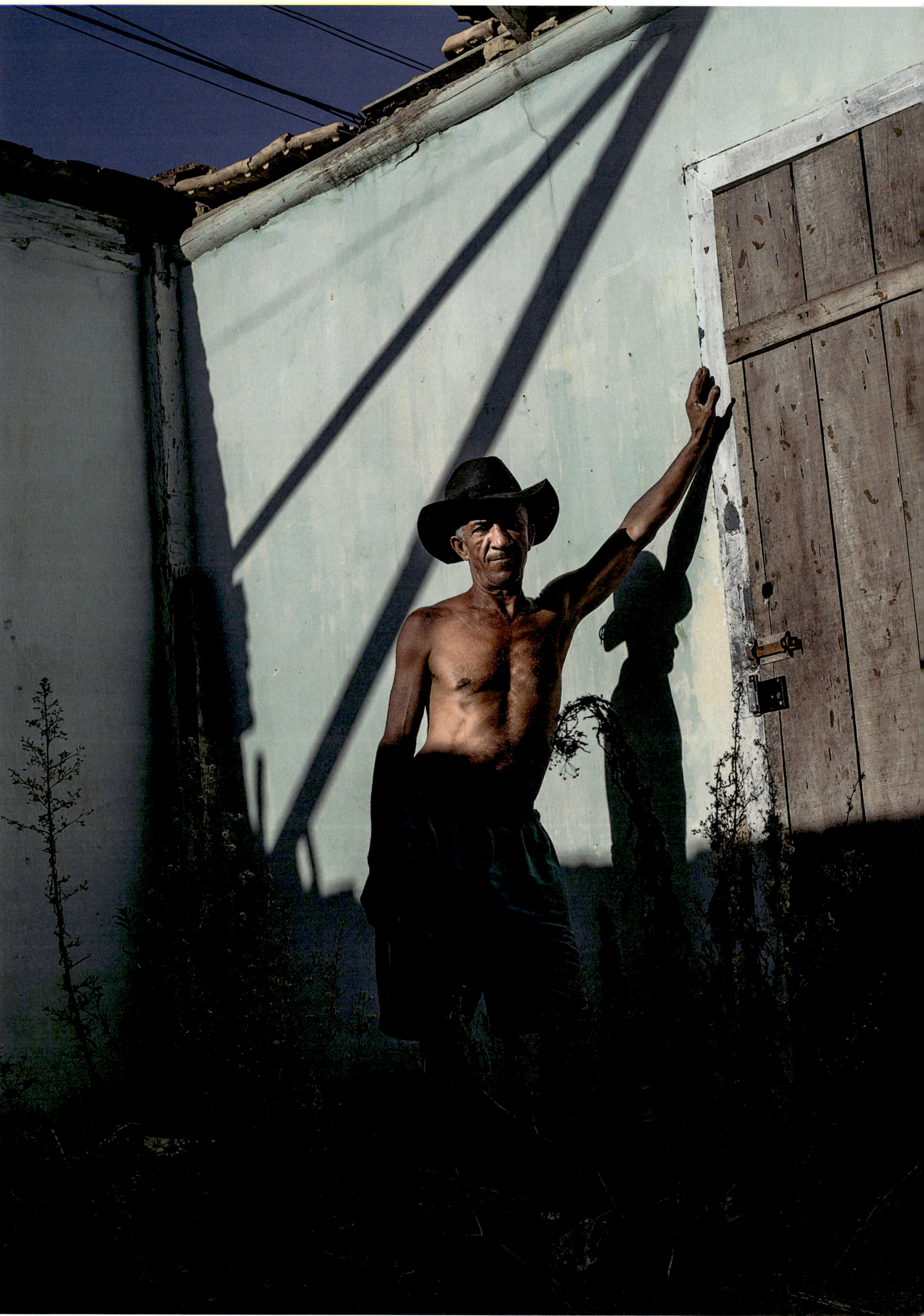

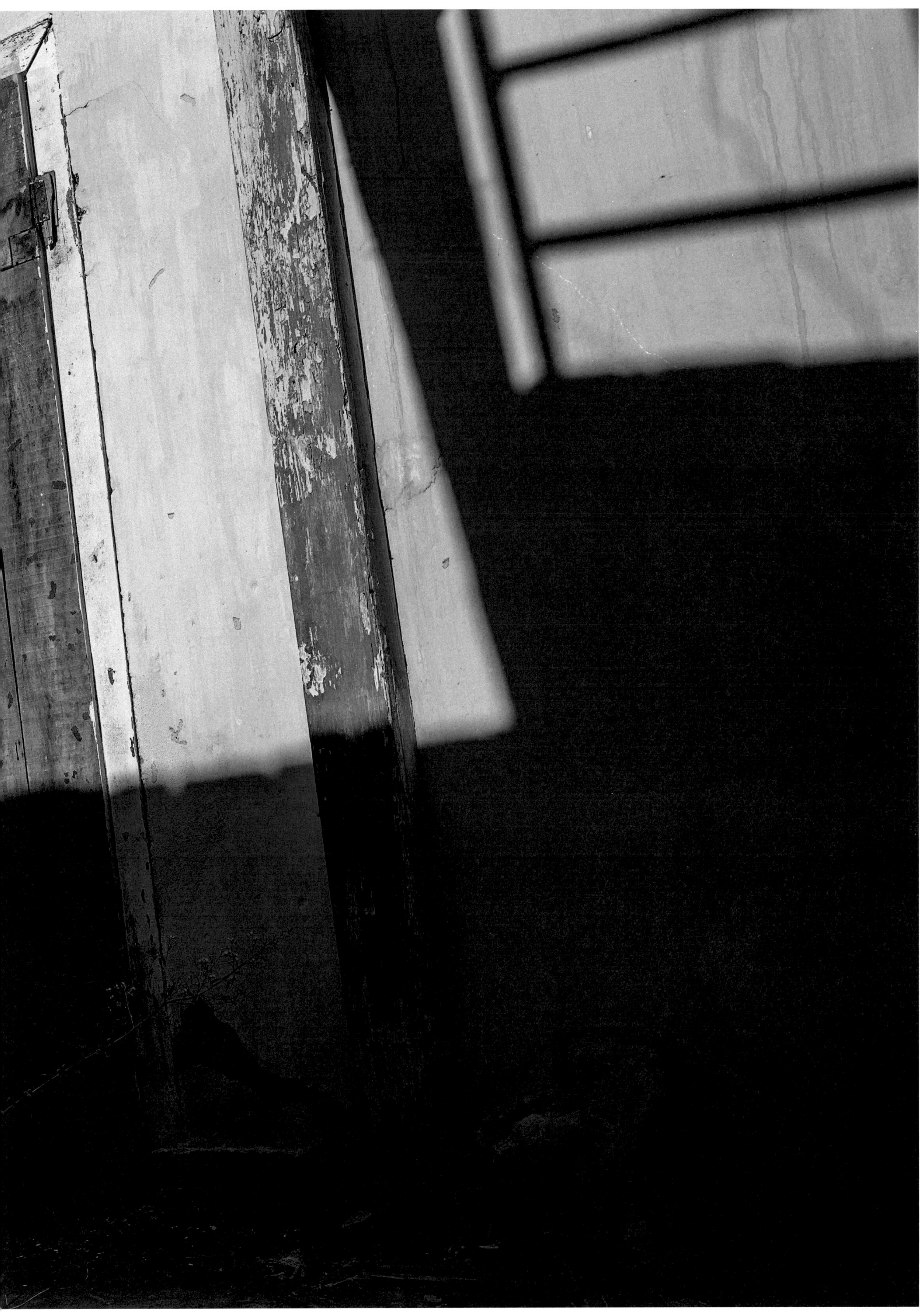

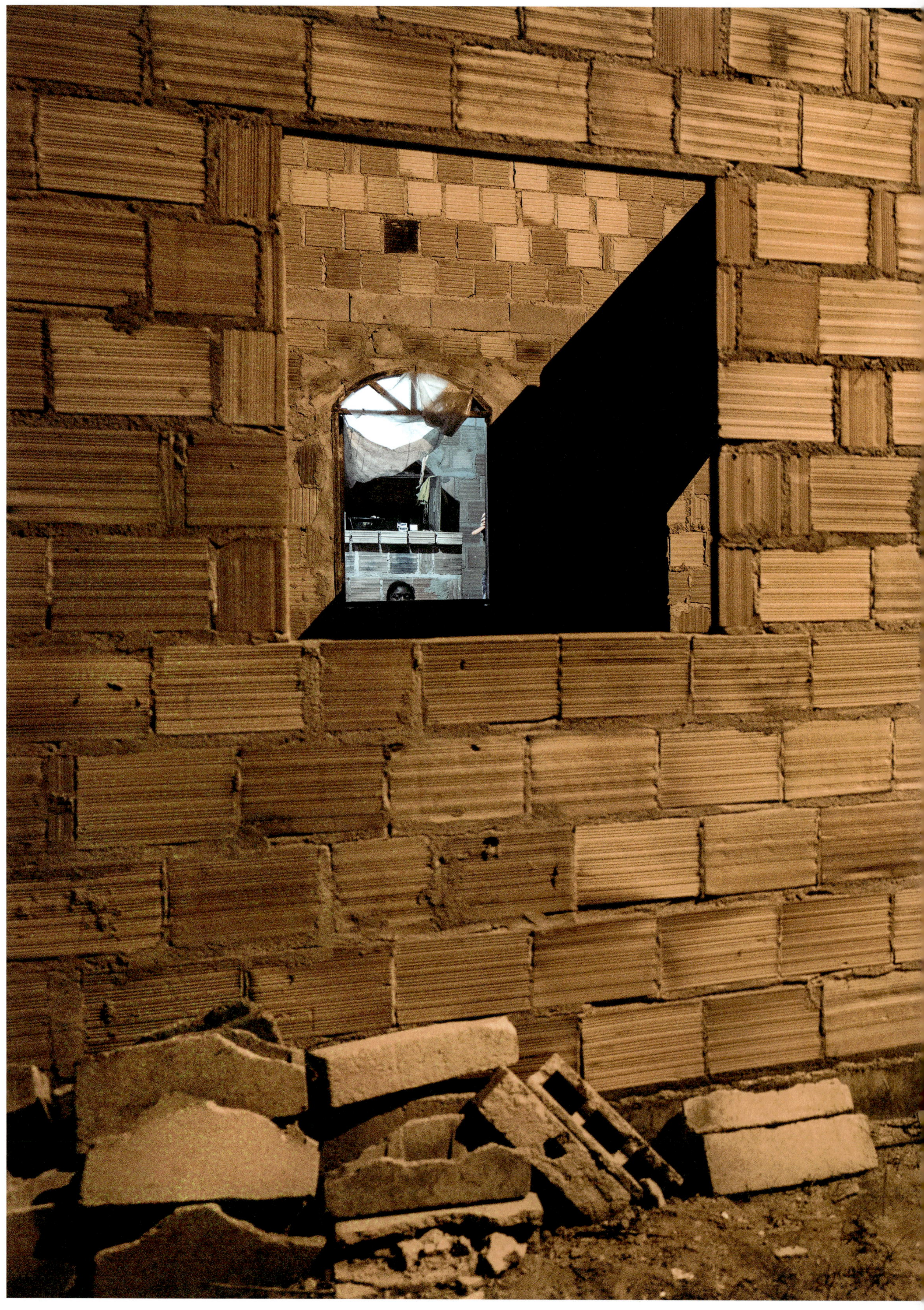

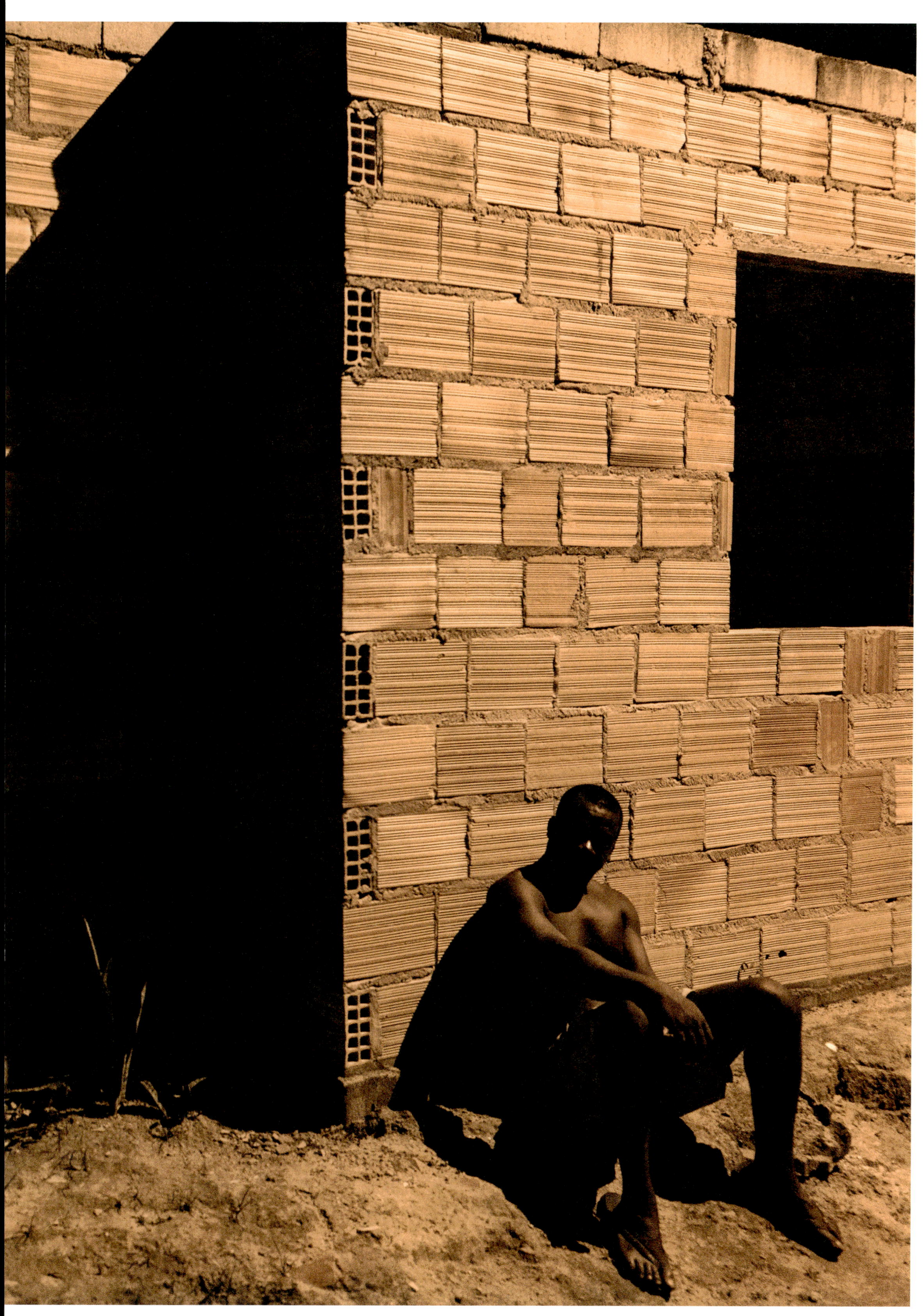

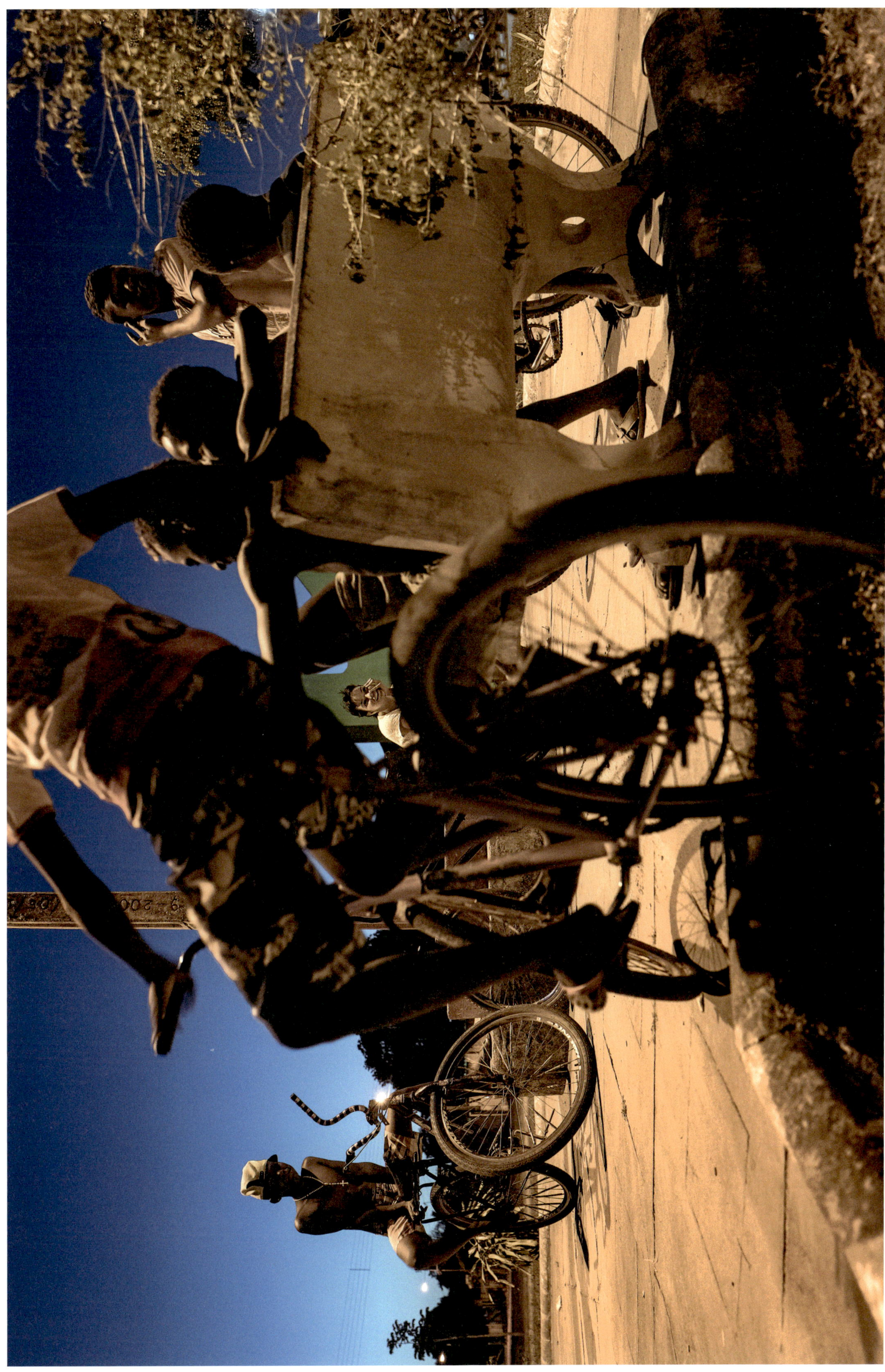

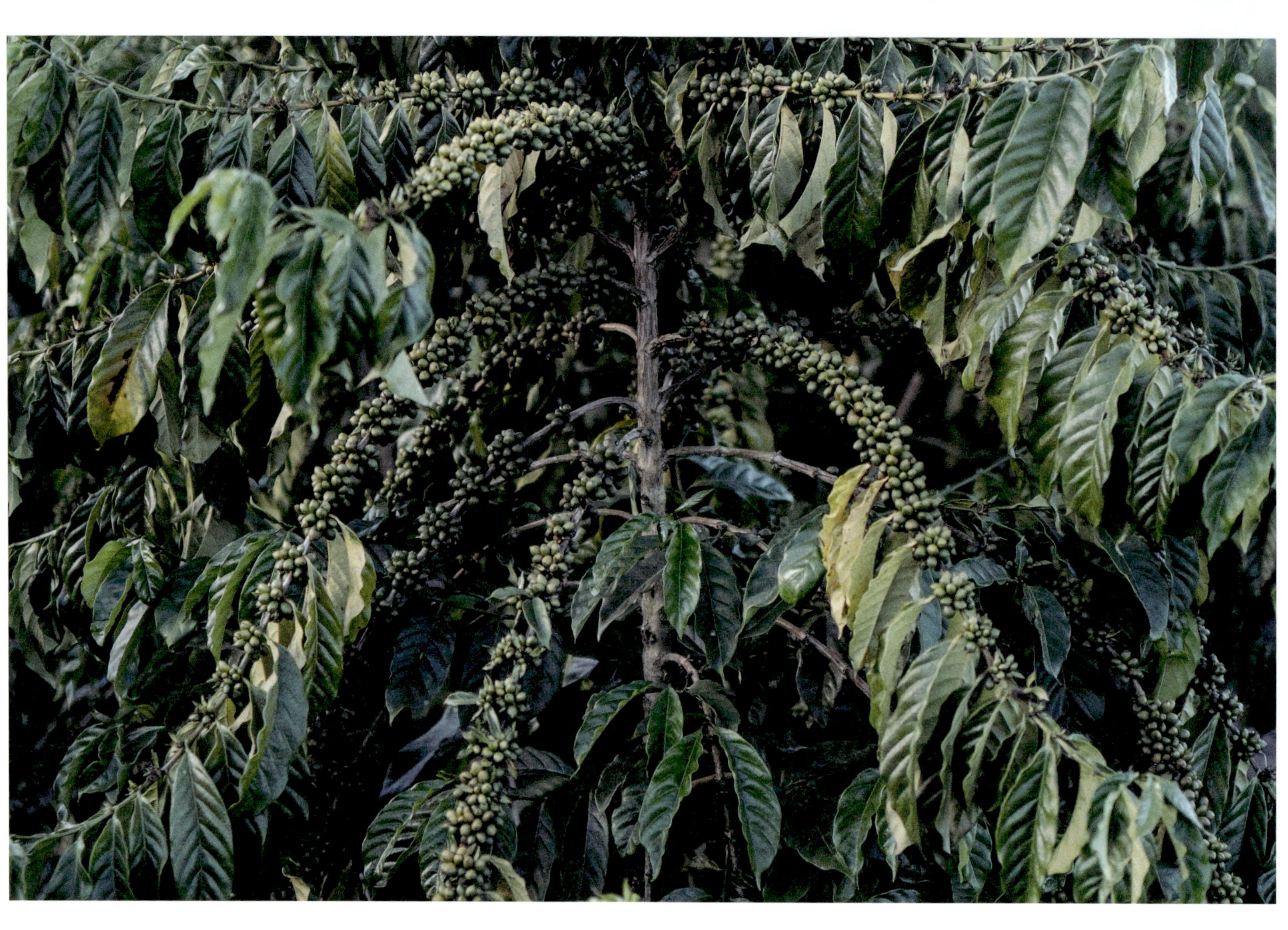

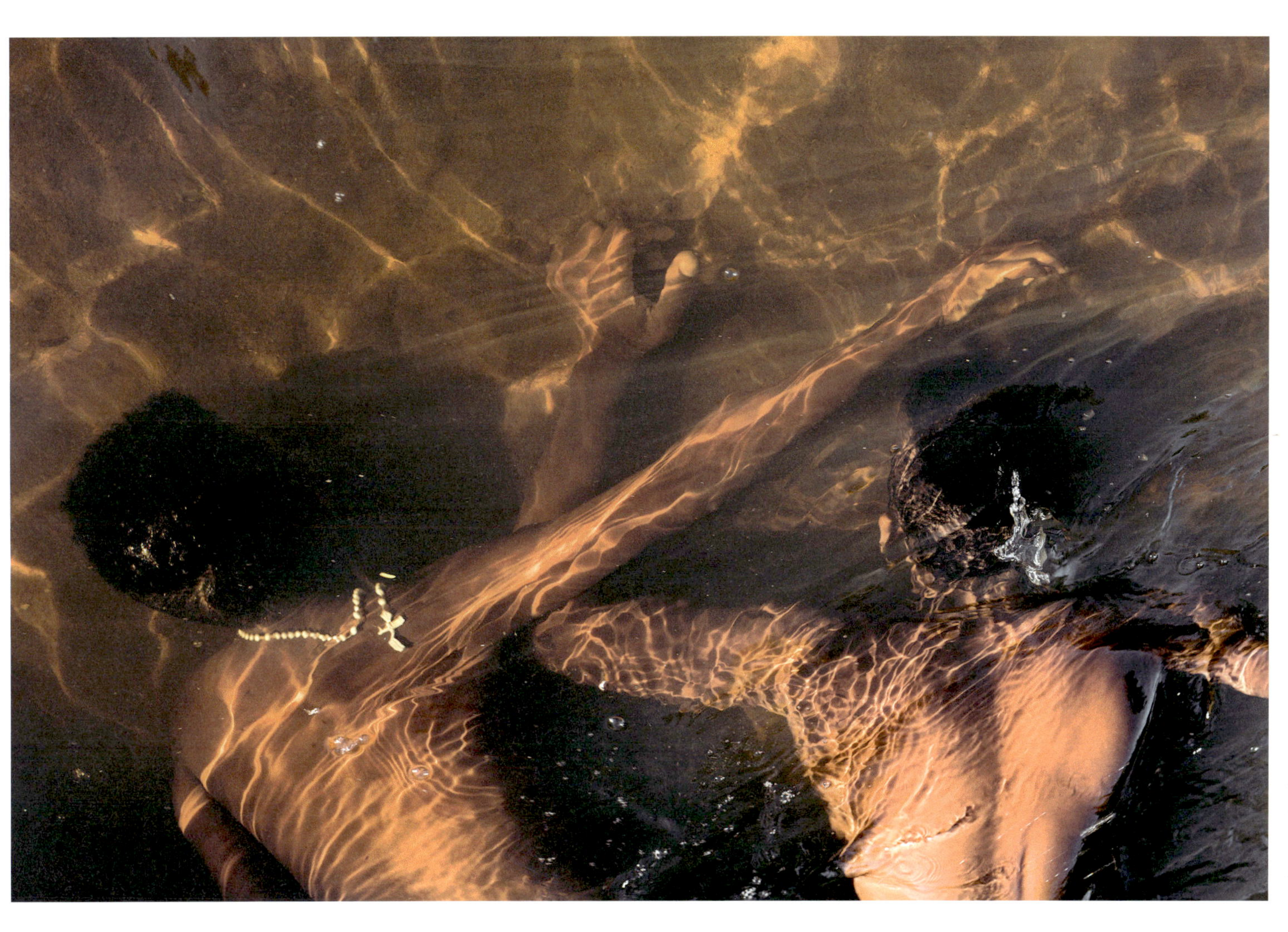

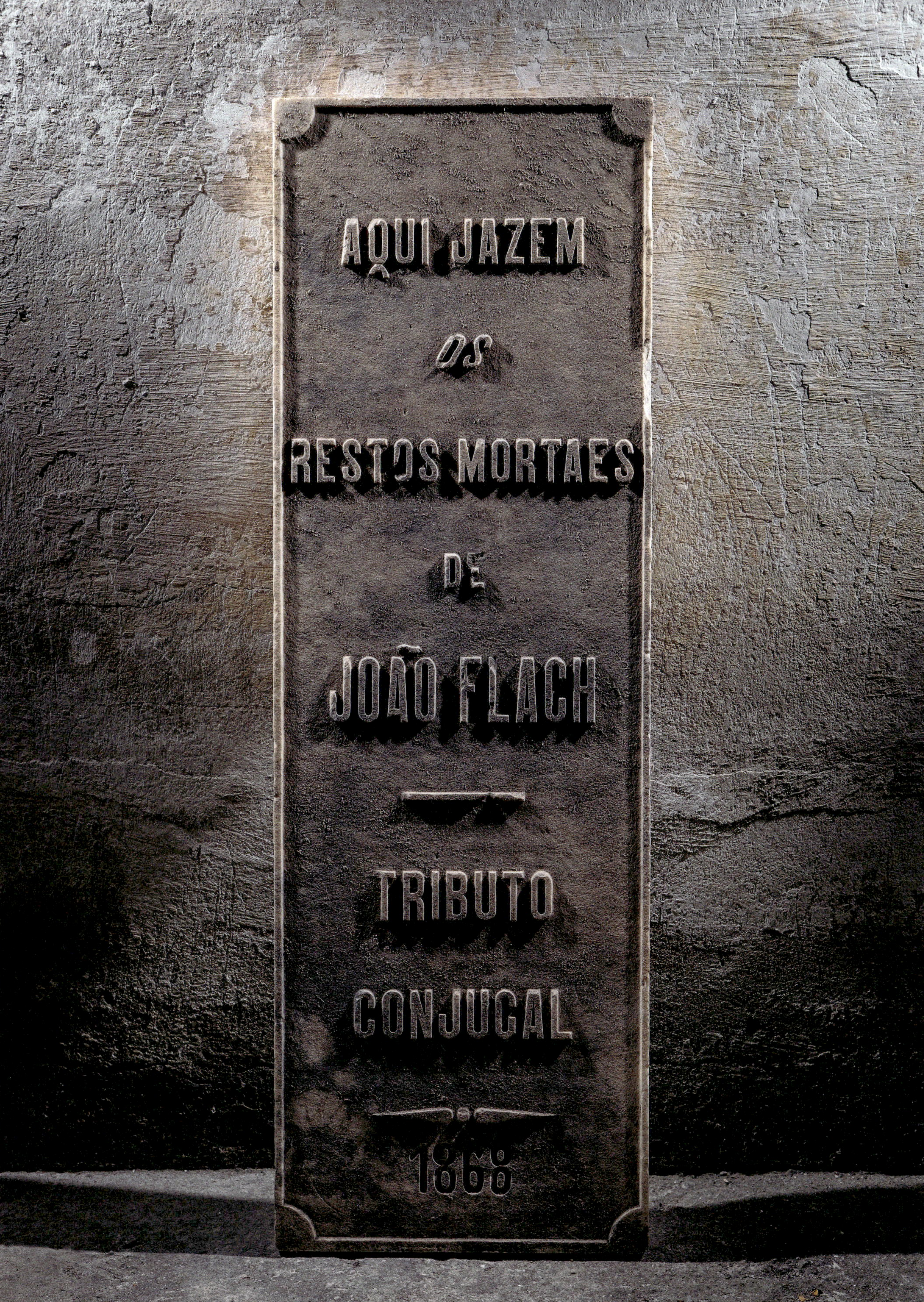
AQUI JAZEM
OS
RESTOS MORTAES
DE
JOÃO FLACH
—
TRIBUTO
CONJUGAL
1868

Nothing or almost nothing remains of this entire history, at least from a material point of view. The museum in Helvécia, located in the former train station, conserves just a nineteenth-century cross that was apparently retrieved from the slave cemetery. There is also a portrait of Henrique Sulz, the first member of the Sulz family to settle in Helvécia. "I had to ask the museum to look after this portrait of my great-grandfather," Rosemar Cerqueira Rafael laughs. "My son Normam had always been scared to death by it. He thought his ancestor was staring at him at night!" Mention should be made as well of the tiles from the oldest houses which, if we are to believe the local inhabitants, were made by slaves after European models. And our inventory would be incomplete if we overlooked the stone memorial to João Flach which Jean Albuquerque, a great lover of local history, made off with like an Indiana Jones. "Stealing tombstones happens all the time. I recovered Flach's before it vanished forever and ever. I'm going to give it back one day!" Ms. Albuquerque promised.

Yielding up few archeological vestiges, the colonial period shows itself just as stinting when it comes to onomastics. In Helvécia, anymore you meet only Sulzes, the lone "Swiss" still around, as well as Krulls, Metzkers, Krygsmanns. The Paches, Borrels, Jeanmonods, Langhanses, Maulazes, and Flaches went off to seek their fortune elsewhere. Here, some claim that only families that hadn't used slave labor put down roots. Local oral tradition doesn't prove much help either for anyone looking to piece together the region's past. Time has had its say, unless the victims of the trade in human beings have repressed humiliating memories to the point where those recollections have indeed become unspeakable.

Less than a century after the founding of the Leopoldina colony, the masters are gone almost without a trace, taking with them their language and customs. Torn from another continent, the slaves remain. Their genes, as well as their culture, tell the story of Helvécia, a village with a Swiss name that has become "African."

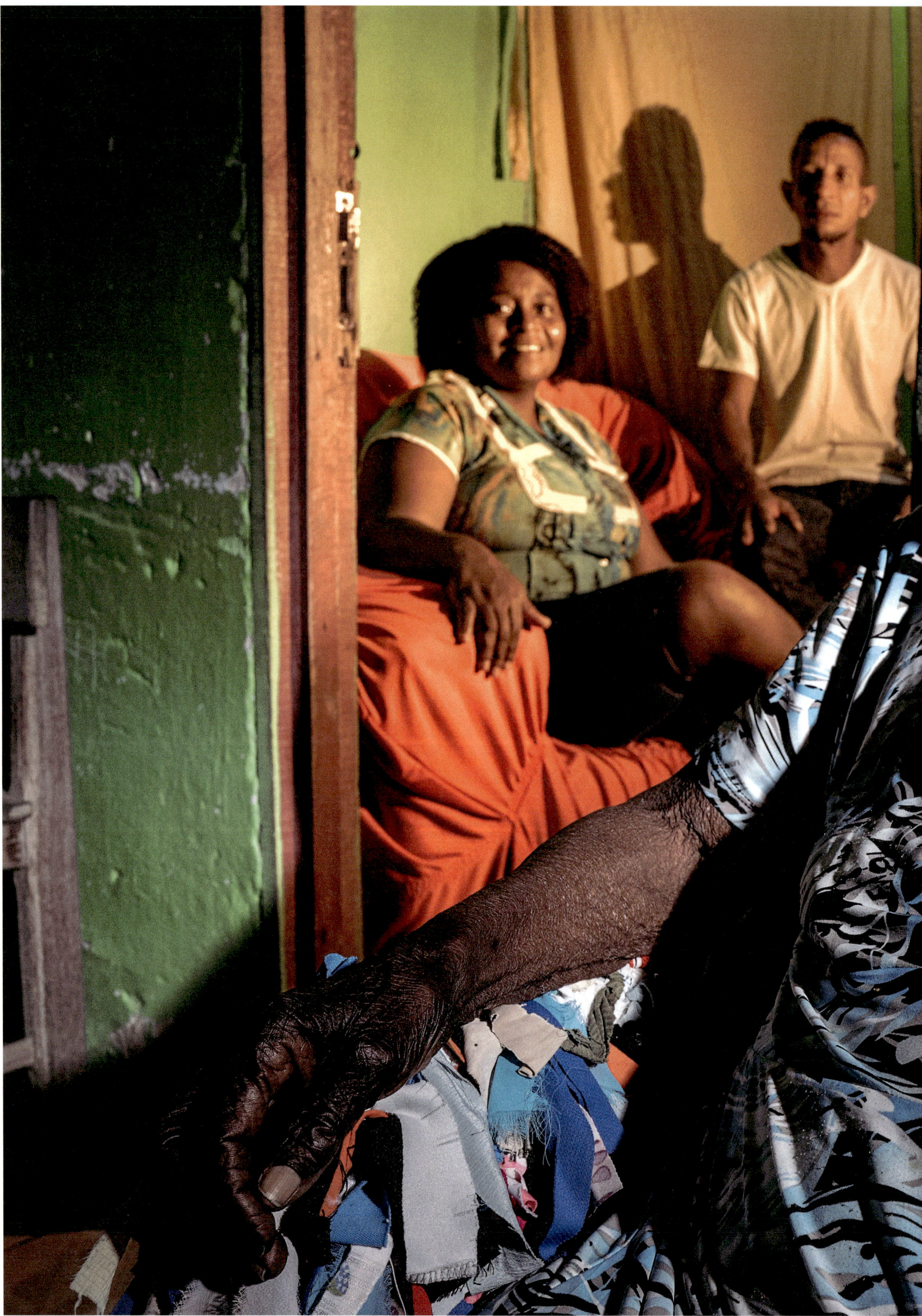

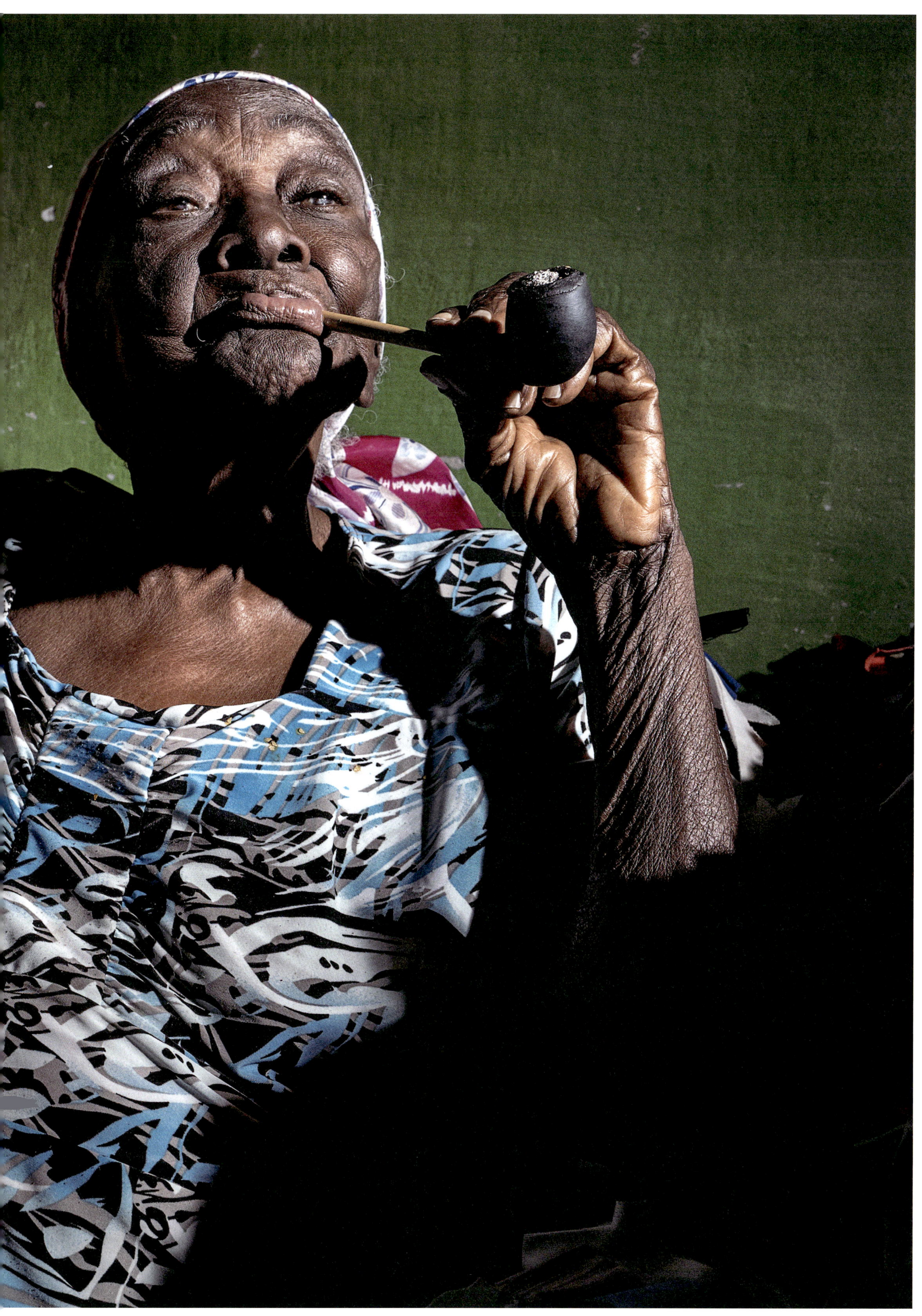

I tell everyone I'm thirty years old, to hang around a little longer… I'm still so young!

My grandfather was the one who raised me. He always told me stories about the hard times. He struggled and suffered a lot, but thanks to God he was always able to bring me up. But life was tough for them back then.

That was the time of slavery. They suffered a lot. He told me about their lives. My grandfather told me family stories, like the day they snatched a child off his mother's back and threw him into the oven… to burn him. And his mother still had to carry on toasting flour there.

Once my grandfather showed me: "Look at this dance, this dance, where the people work, and the whip does the talking." That wasn't a life for humans. It was a dog's life. When the ship came to Caravelas and everyone disembarked, that was the start of the problems around here… A bunch of foreigners arrived but people never knew which country they had come from.

When I was ten, I was already a girl who worked to eat. No one gave me anything. I was thirteen when my grandfather died. I had to work hard if I wanted to eat.

I've been a Roman Apostolic Catholic ever since the day I was born.

One day I went with my mother to my aunt's house. When I got there, she began moaning and my mother asked me to help her and to stay close to her. I gave her company and stayed at her house for more than a year… That aunt died in my arms at the age of 115. Here, in my house.

Whoever arrives at my house, is my son, but my pipe comes first. Only God can take it away from me. I smoke it all day. I just sit here smoking, whenever I want.

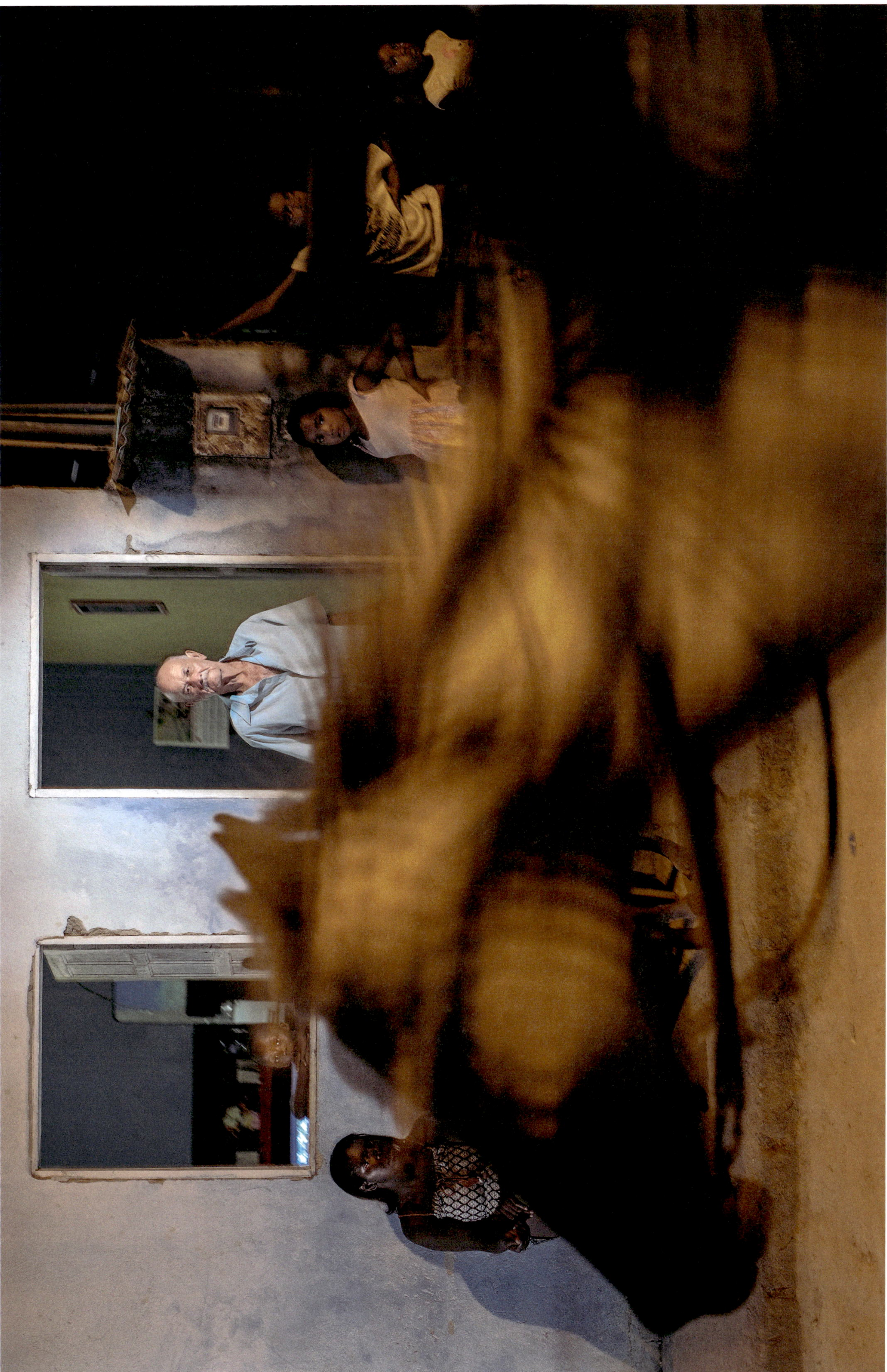

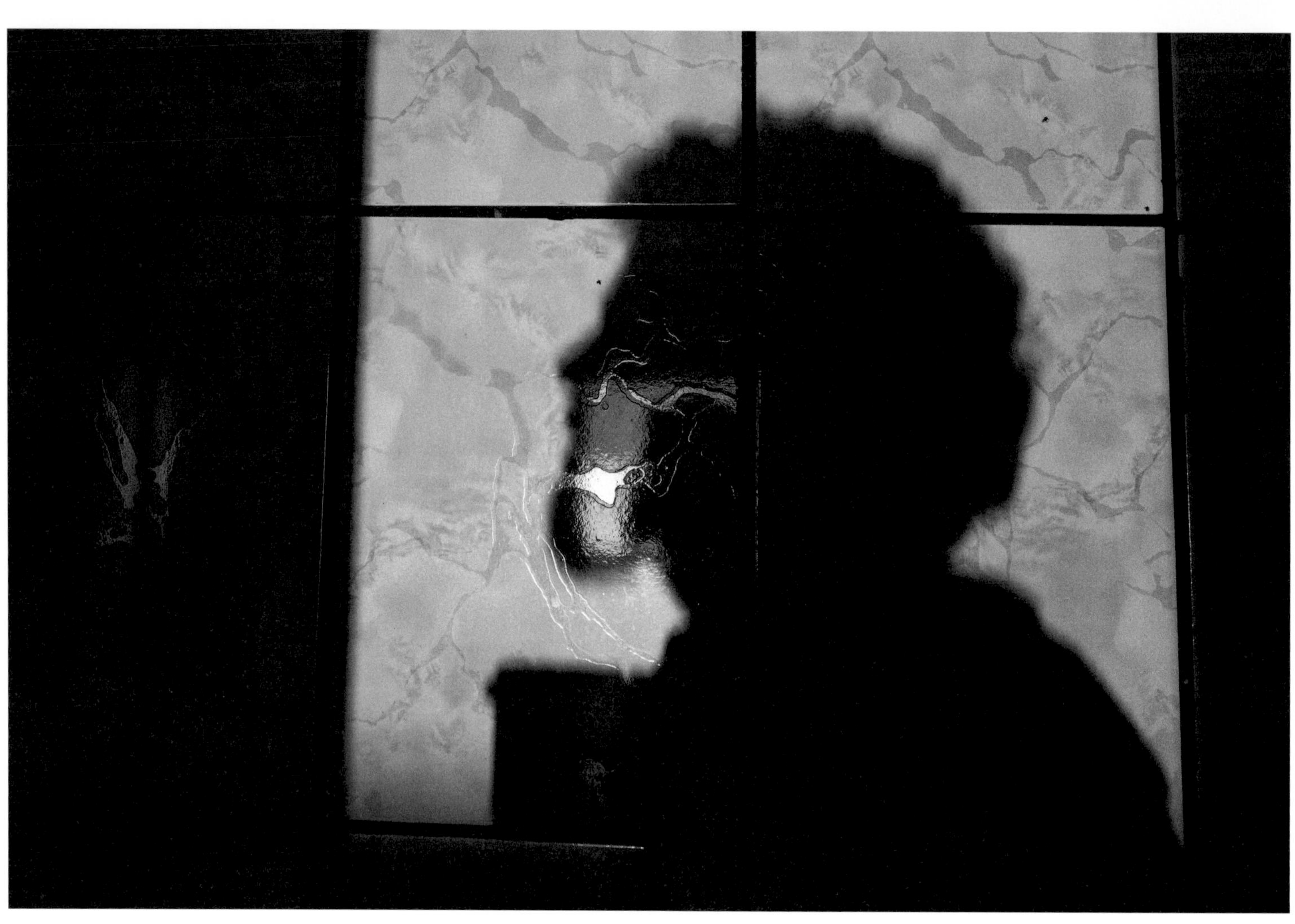

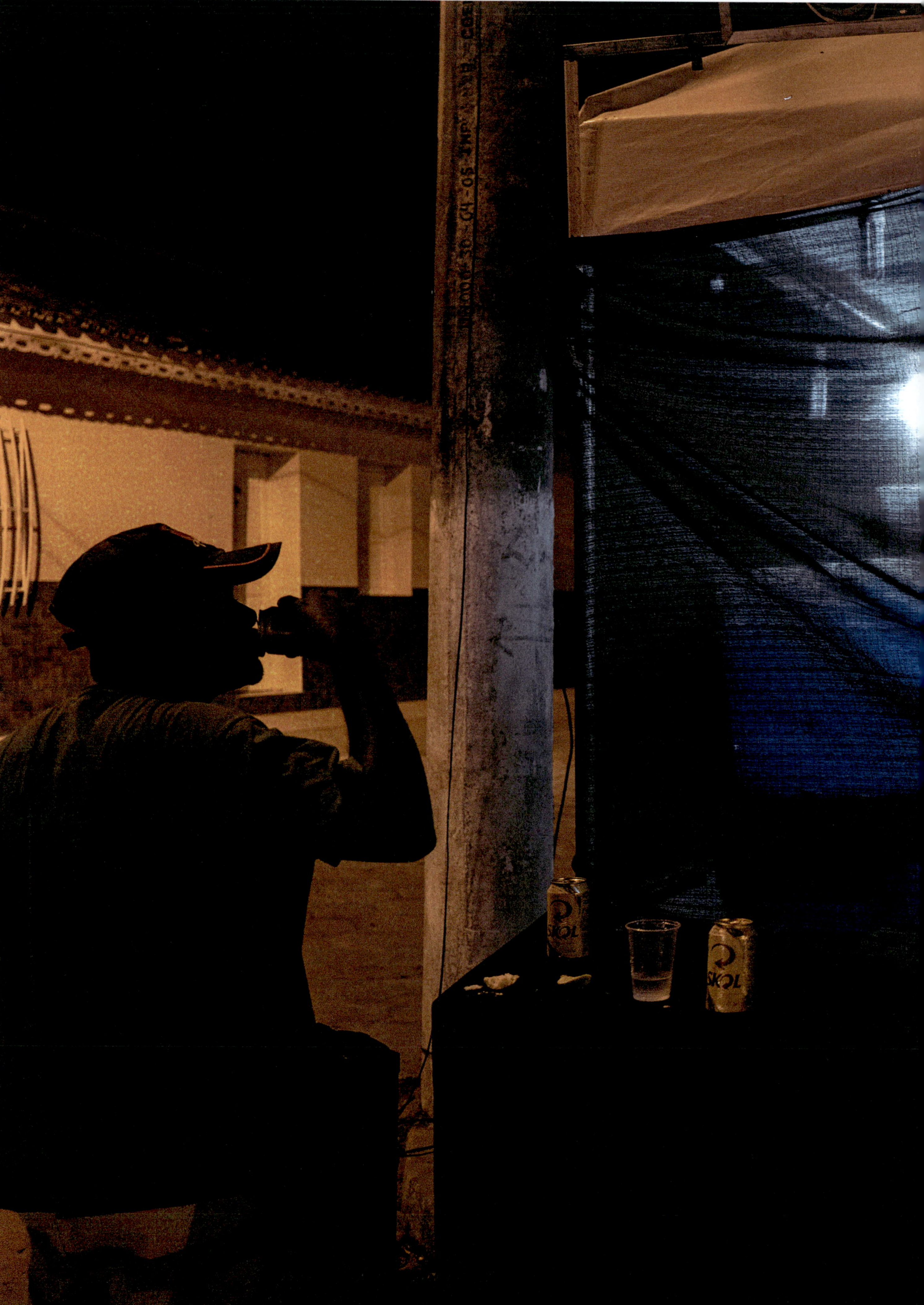
SKOL
SKOL

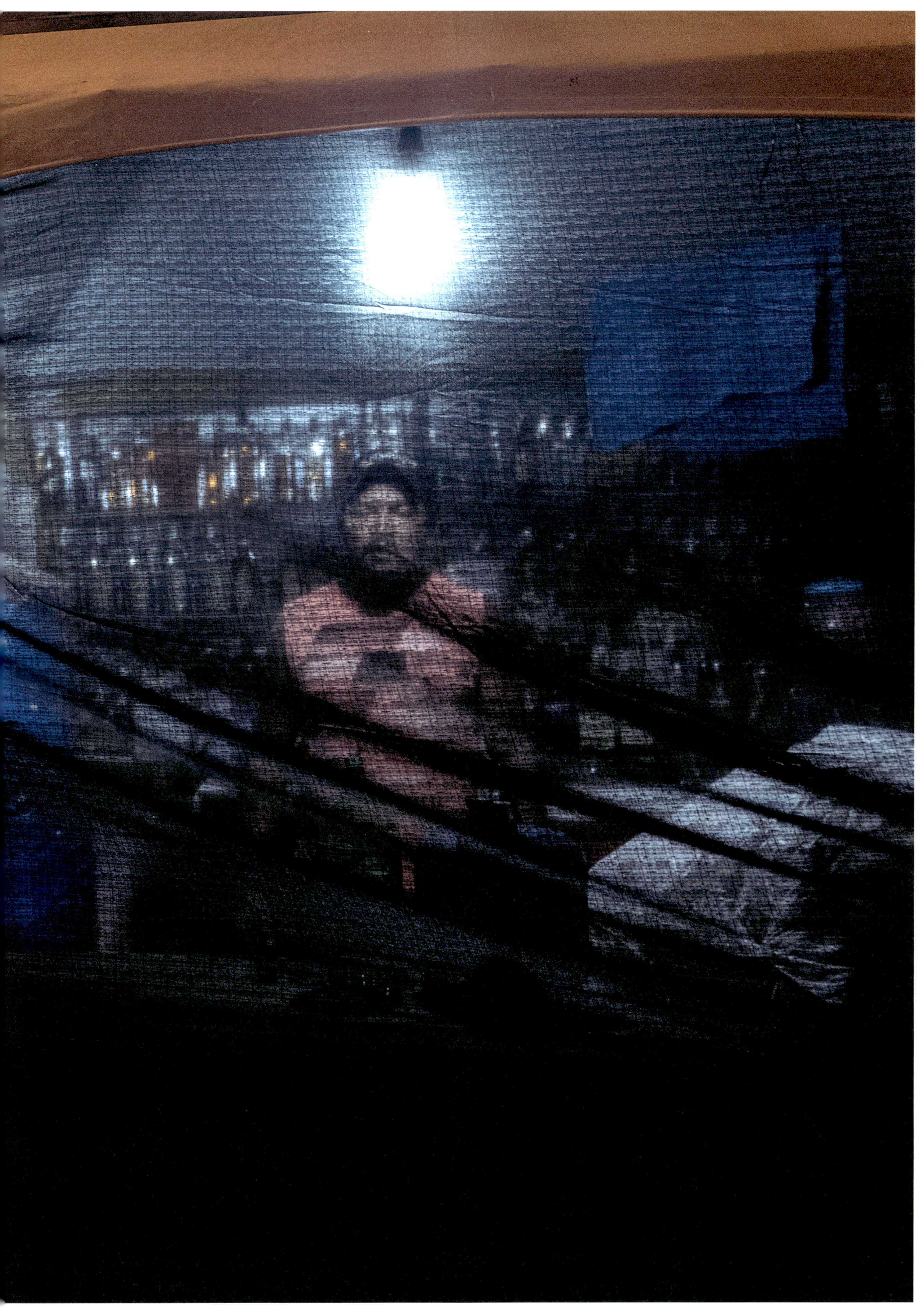

I was born here in Helvécia. I lived for a while in Posto da Mata,[1] but then I came back here. I've got no plans to leave again. With seven children my family isn't that large, but it's a reasonable size, and I now have eleven grandchildren.

My family is originally from Germany on my grandfather's side, and from Africa on my grandmother's. My grandfather himself, Walter, was the first person to come. He had to flee because of a war and came here by foot. He met my grandmother, and moved here, living here until he died.

I inherited my grandfather's blue eyes, see? I get my strong blood from my grandmother because she is Black and with strong blood. Do you know that Africans have stronger blood than the white folk? Much stronger, thicker. Africans are more at risk of suffering greater sicknesses because of their stronger blood. Germans' blood is calmer, less thick.

Speaking of the Krulls, there's one that lives nearby, another one in Posto da Mata, in Rio de Janeiro, scattered all over the place. But they aren't my grandfather's grandchildren. I think they're the grandchildren of one of his cousins. I don't know them directly.

I don't know much about Helvécia's history. It was a plantation. People settled here and the place grew over the years. It used to only be a plantation and farms. I've no idea why it's called Helvécia!

I don't know much about the stories of other families. I only know that my grandfather Walter Krull married my grandmother Bela Sofia, and that they had five children, and so here we are. There is one who had already left because God needed to have him back.[2]

1 A town about twenty kilometers from Helvécia.
2 Domingo's brother, Ednilson, died in 2018. The photograph shows the brothers together.

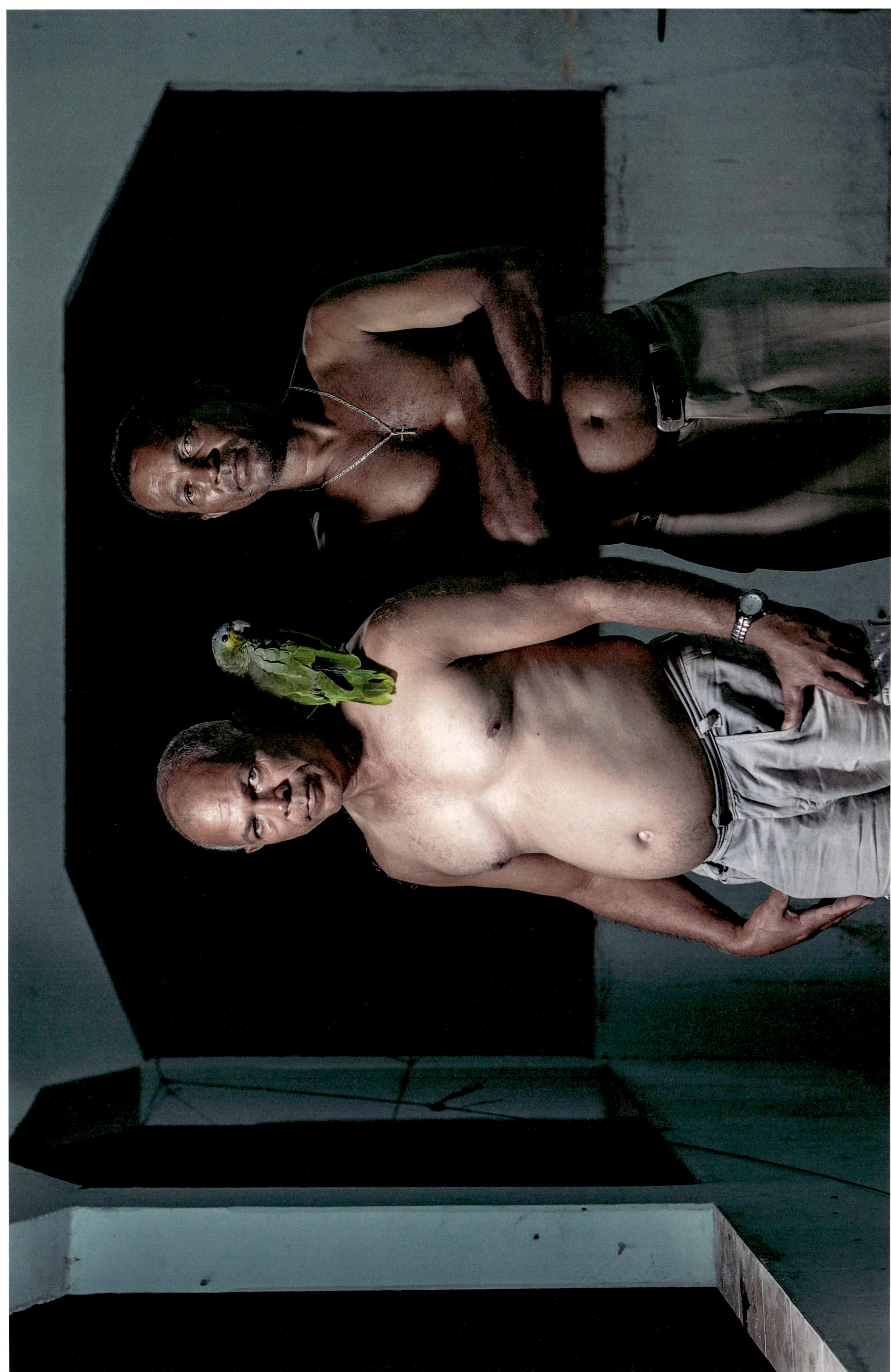

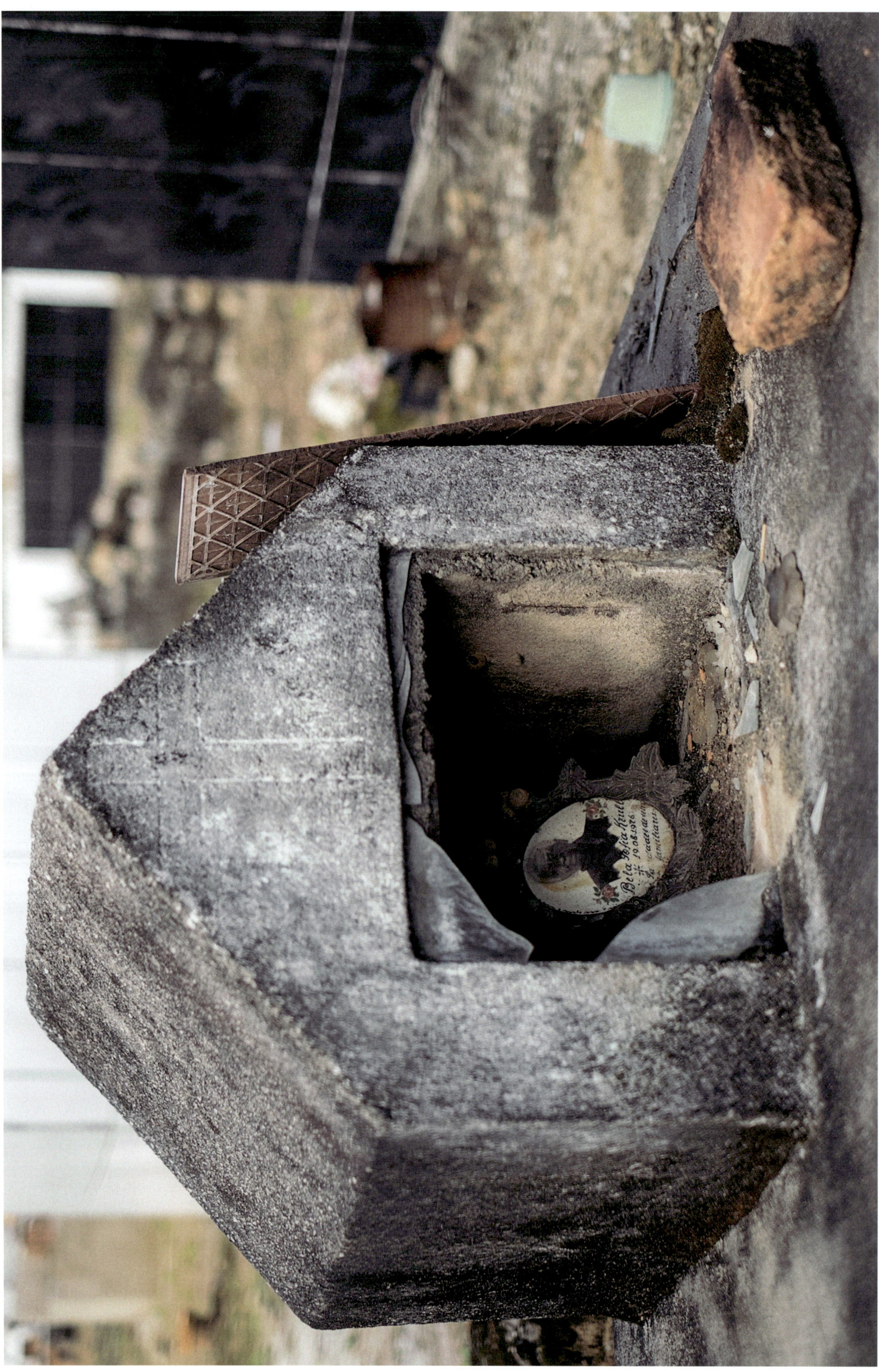

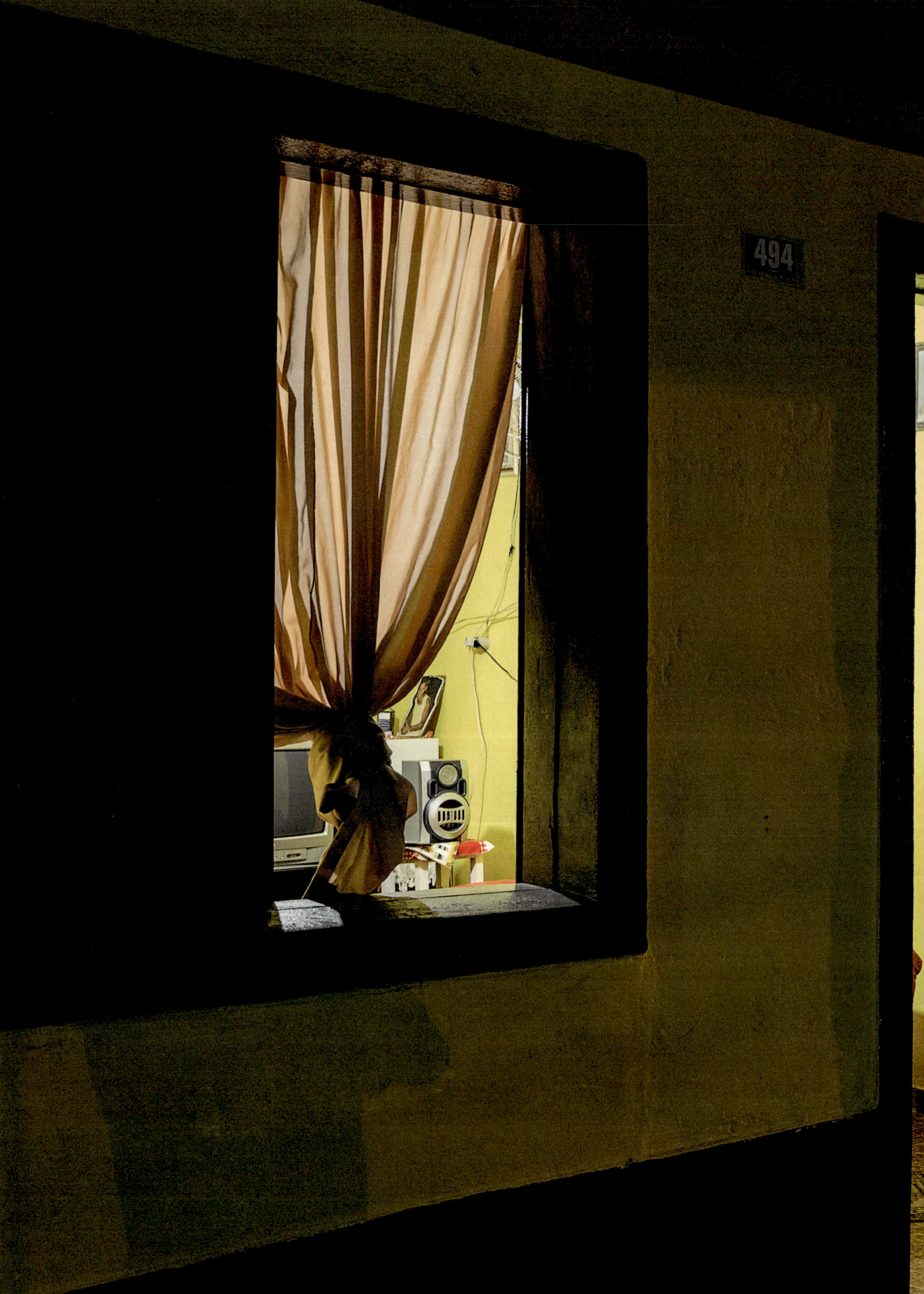
494

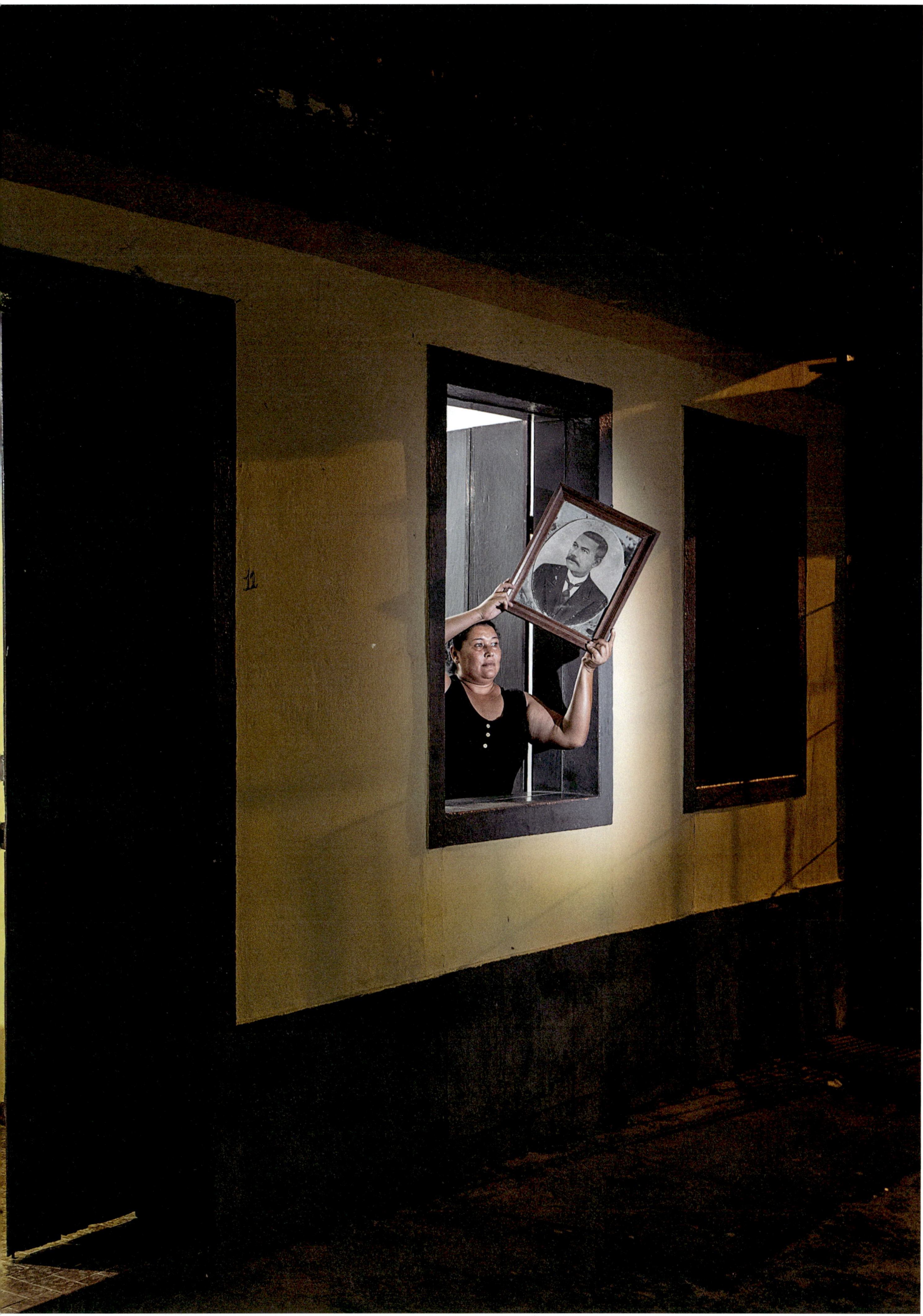

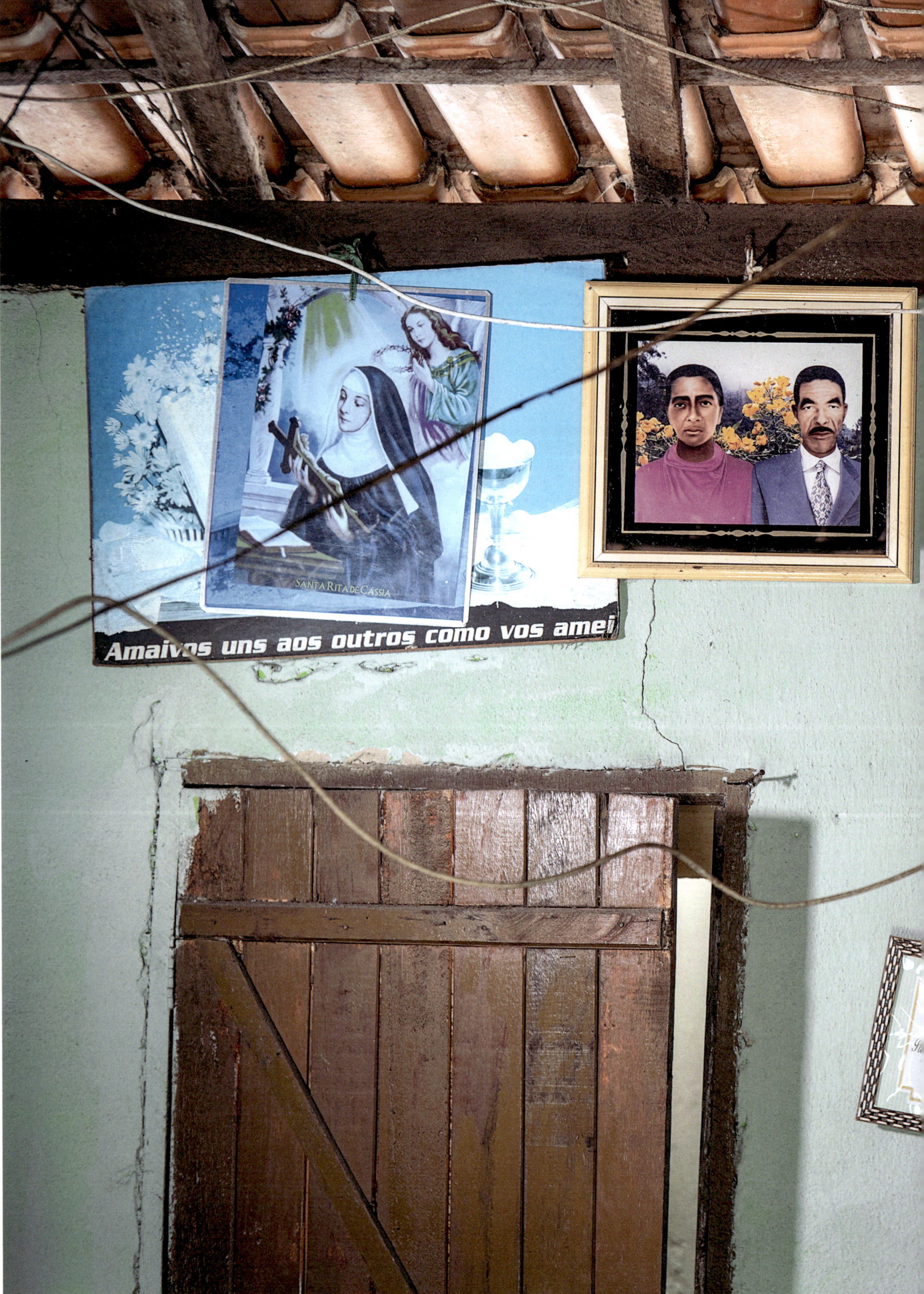

SANTA RITA DE CÁSSIA
Amaivos uns aos outros como vos amei

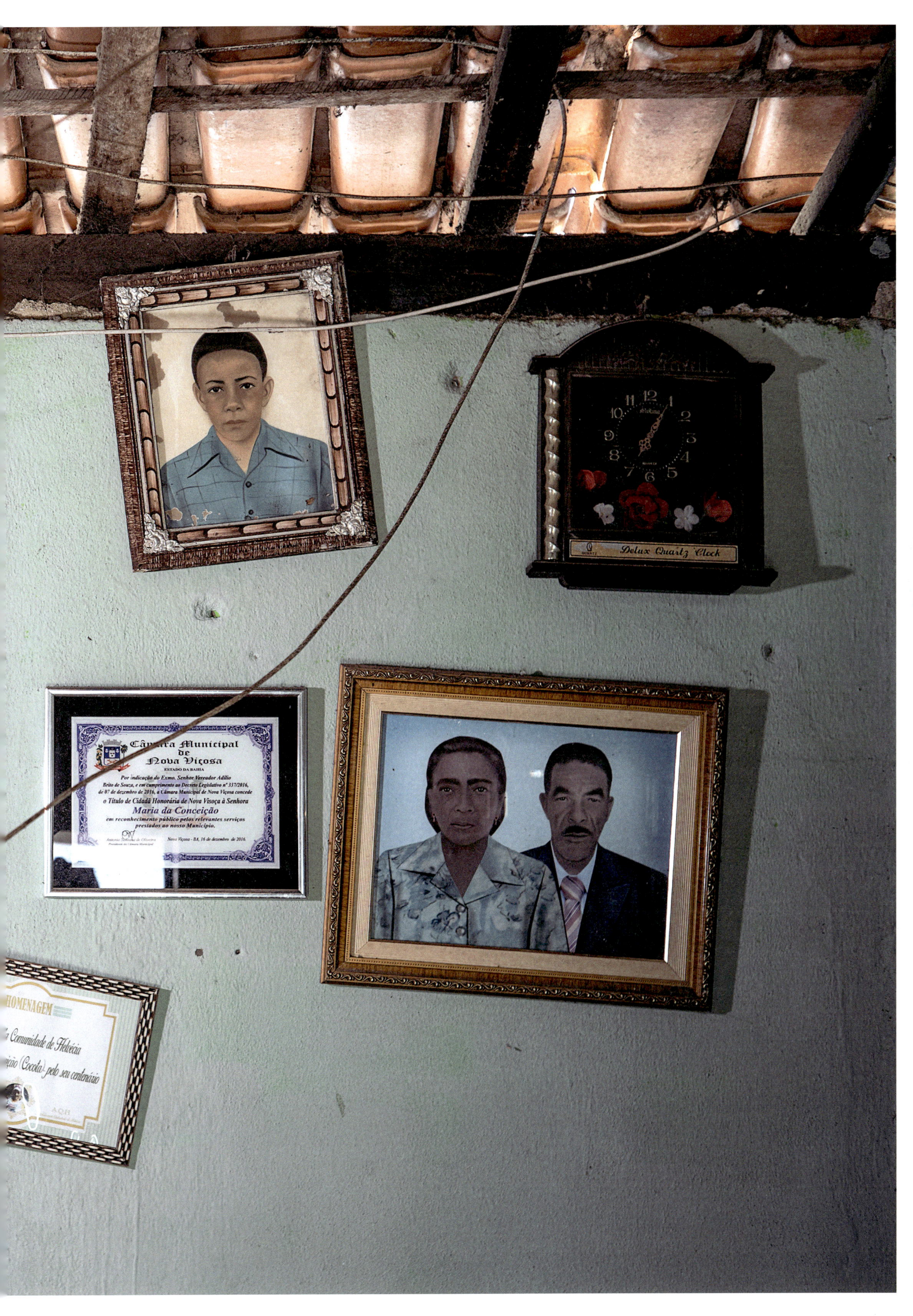

Câmara Municipal
de
Nova Viçosa
ESTADO DA BAHIA
Por indicação do Exmo. Senhor Vereador Adílio
Brito de Souza, e em cumprimento ao Decreto Legislativo nº 337/2016,
de 07 de dezembro de 2016, a Câmara Municipal de Nova Viçosa concede
o Título de Cidadã Honorária de Nova Visoça à Senhora
Maria da Conceição
em reconhecimento público pelos relevantes serviços
prestados ao nosso Município.
Antonio Santana de Oliveira
Presidente da Câmara Municipal
Nova Viçosa - BA, 16 de dezembro de 2016.

Delux Quartz Clock

HOMENAGEM
à Comunidade de Helvécia
ição (Cocota) pelo seu centenário
AQII

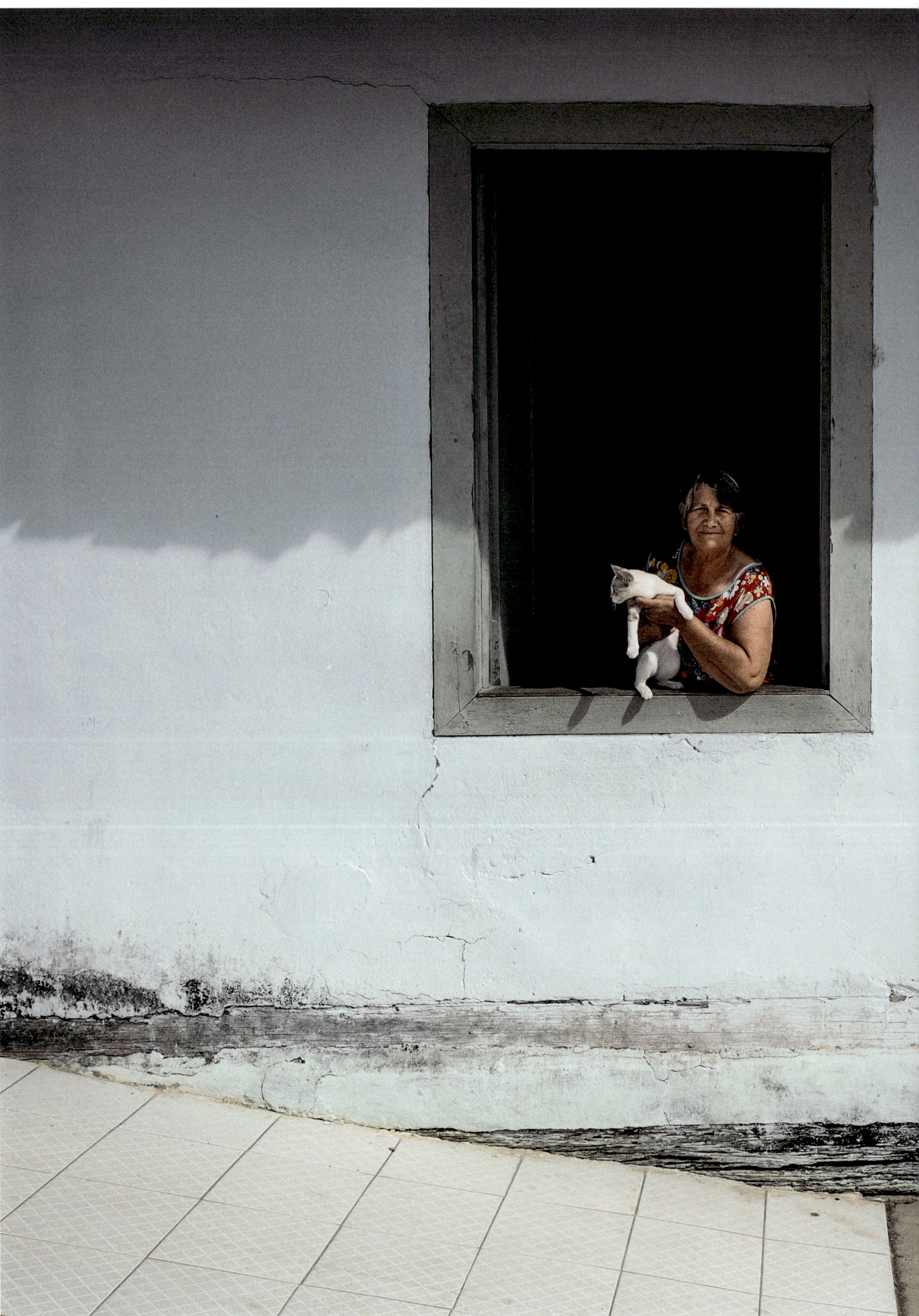

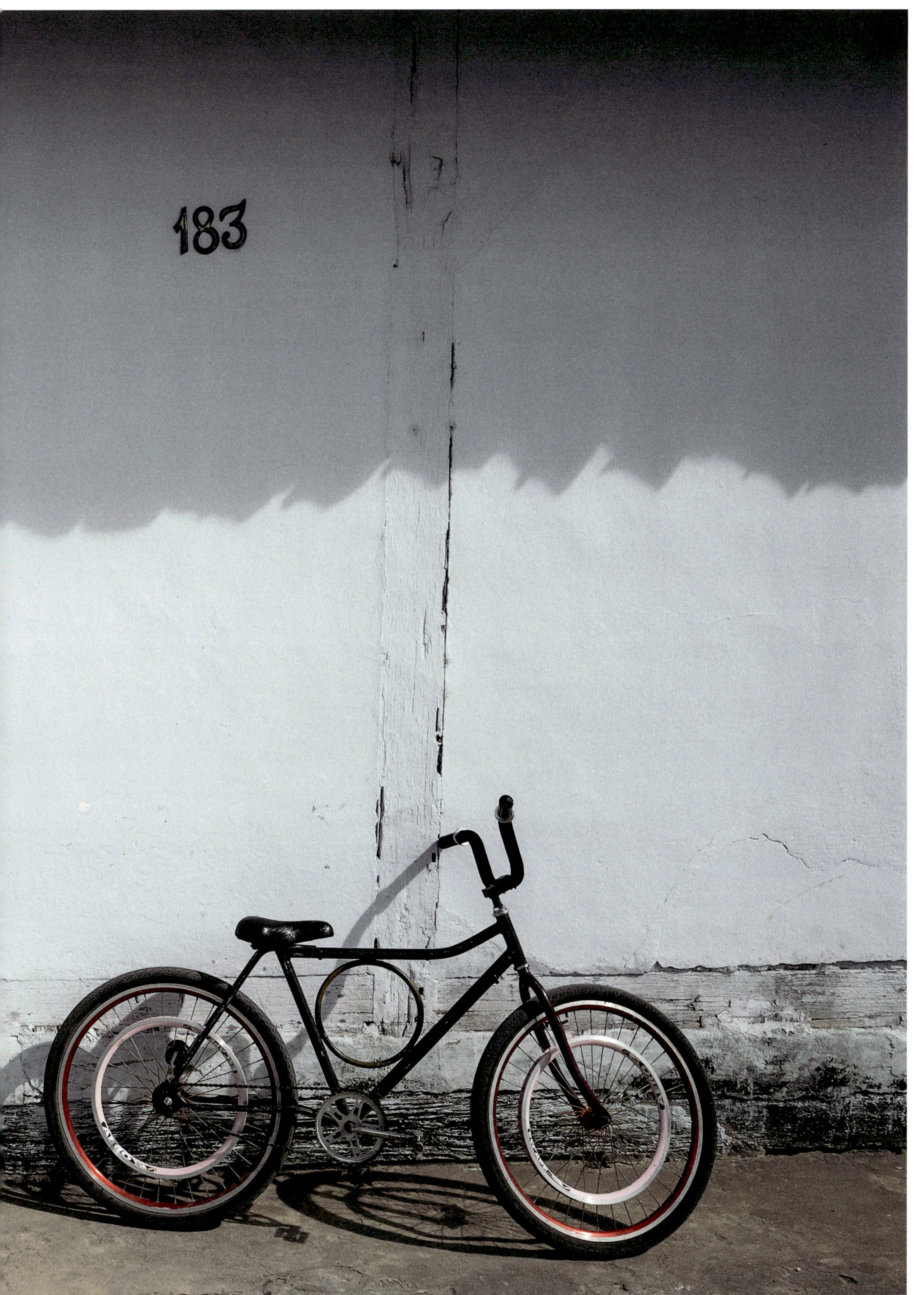
183

My surnames, Sulz and Metzker, are German. They come from the same place. I just found out that one of them also comes from Switzerland, but I don't know which one. My cousin, who knows, didn't say this to me, but told someone else.

When these folk came to Brazil, people didn't know how to spell Schulz and wrote Sulz instead. That's why it's now Sulz. I was once in line to inherit something, but we didn't receive anything because in Brazil there's no record of that name, Schulz.

They say that I've got blue blood, that I'm the only one with it here in Helvécia. I told them that my blood was red, that I don't understand. But they said, "no my child, you're a Metzker from your father and a Sulz from your mother, that's how it is." Recently I cut myself here while prizing open a coconut with my knife. I tried to see if my blood was blue, but I didn't see anything [laughter]. It was red! I think it's all a load of rubbish, but that's what they say. What can I do?

The road opposite is named after my grandfather.[1] There's another road with his name in Posto da Mata! I have an uncle, my mother's brother, who's also called Henrique Sulz. They were distinguished gentlemen! But there's no one still alive to tell the story. I longed to know my father. I never met him. I was only a year old when he died.

I know that Helvécia used to be called the Leopoldina settlement. I even have some papers about it, but I can't show them because I don't know where they are. The person who knew everything was this uncle of mine who died, and his daughter, who has passed away too. They have grandchildren and great-grandchildren, but they don't know anything.

My mother told lots of stories about the slaves, but I didn't listen. My sister, who paid more attention, knows more. That pink house next door belonged to my uncle and there was a chain, or some kind of device, that was fastened to slaves. But I don't know where it ended up because the owner, poor old Dona Cirlene, died. Her son, Bruno, is the only one there, and I don't know if he knows or not, or whether he threw it out.

I only agreed to this interview to get some Swiss chocolate. I've never even seen it, let alone eaten it [laughter]. It's a good thing I don't have any more teeth, because that way they can't fall out anymore. I'm only joking, I'd love to know those places… Switzerland!

That house where I live was originally on the plantation. It was completely taken apart and my grandfather rebuilt it here. Oxen carried this house from the plantation. Those tiles [pointing to the tiles on her house], do you know where they come from? From Germany!

They aren't from Brazil. They were brought here by boat. The boat moored on the sand, and then they sent them to the plantation and eventually here. There was a lot of cattle, and one thing came after the other, in succession, a yoke and a whole load of tiles.

My grandfather owned all of this, in Helvécia. He was known as Colonel Bêlica, you can ask any of the elderly folk around here. He had a large store and sold medicines. People from Rio do Sul[2] came for his potions. People didn't know how to write and said: "bili mandy mucie poti." Did you understand that? "Don Bêlica, send me a bottle of that 'Escotchi' potion." My grandfather knew everything because he understood the language of the swarthy people, the Black Nagô descendants.[3]

I traveled a lot by train. I'd go to Caravelas and stay there for thirty days at a time. The station was over there. I sat on a seat and the journey would take ages. You could even go to sleep. When I was born, the railway already existed, but my daughter never saw it, because they came and just took away the whole railway.

I think that on my grandfather's farm they had slaves, but he treated them as employees. Because people did terrible things to the slaves, didn't they? My mother told me, she said that there was a man who beat a slave to death with a stick on the street. I knew his name, but now I've forgotten it.

I'm proud of being Brazilian, a Sulz and a Metzker. When someone says you're a Metzker I go up to heaven and then come back to earth. My dead God! I've inherited it! At least I inherited that. Isn't that the best thing? The money's all gone, but the name survives. I'm so proud of it that when I got married, I didn't get rid of the Sulz or the Metzker. My sister lost them, but I never did. I get a buzz when people say my name.

1   Henrique Sulz Street.
2   A neighboring community.
3   The name of Black people from Nigeria, Benin, and Togo, who speak the Yoruba language.

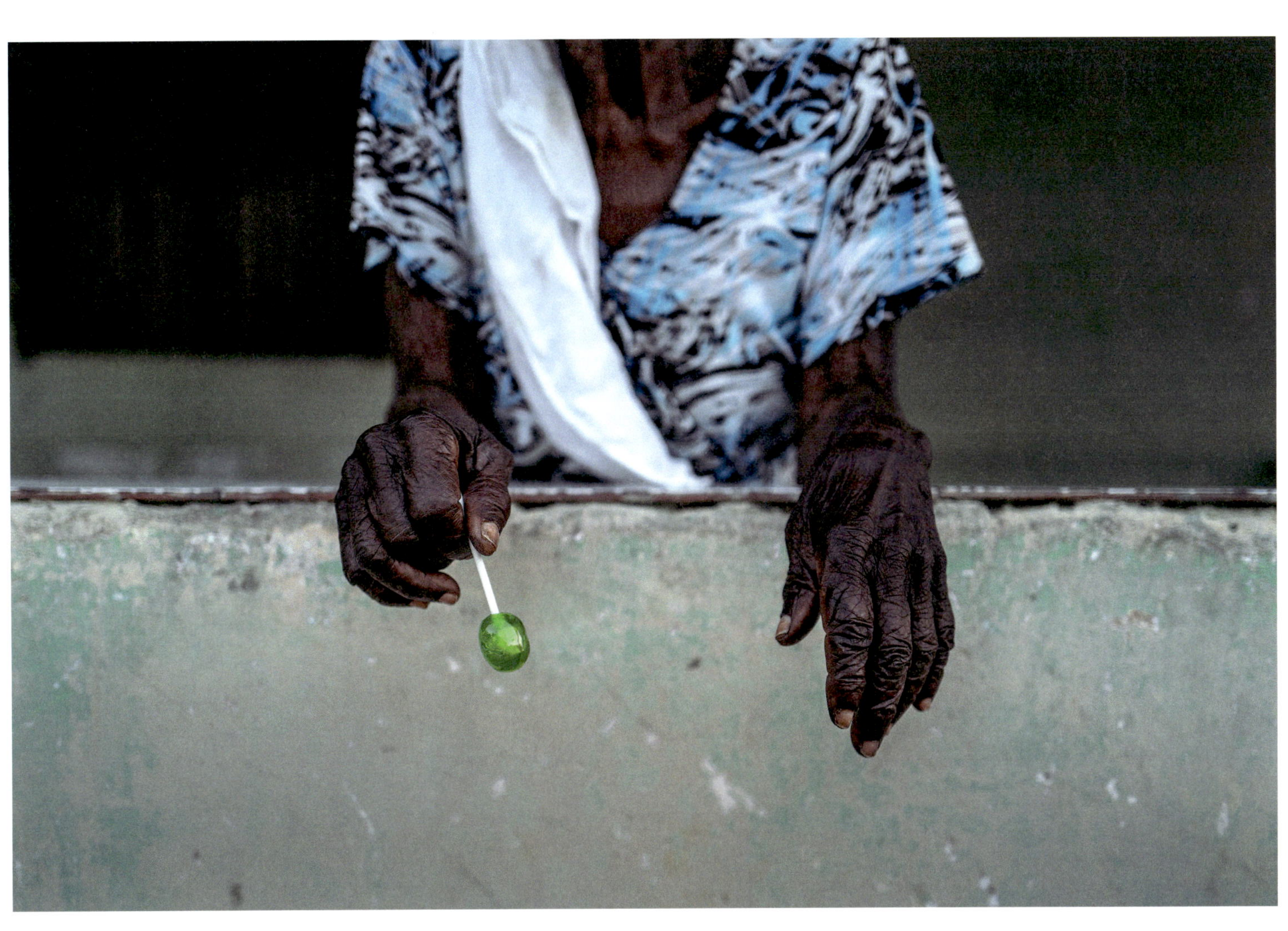

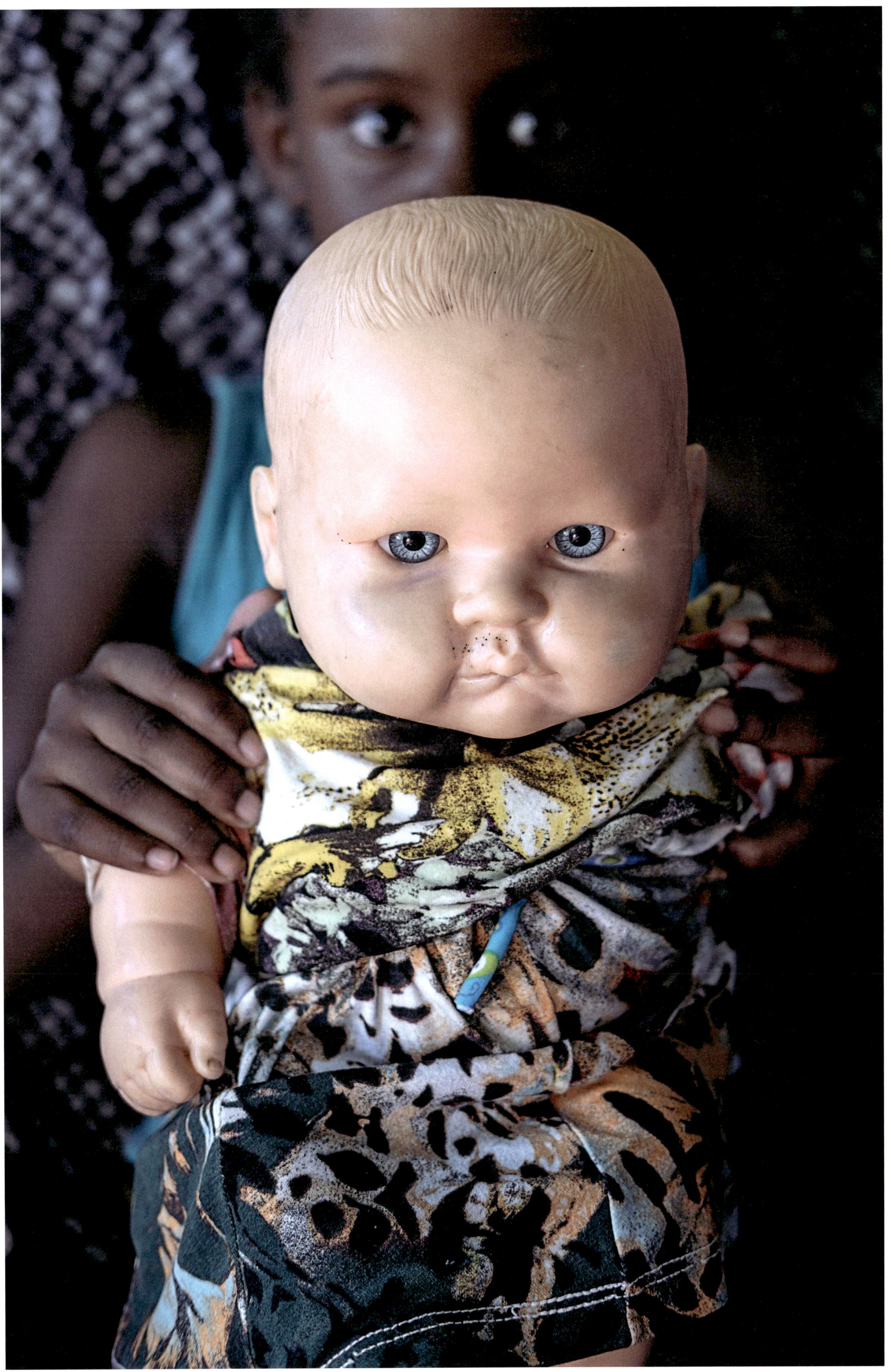

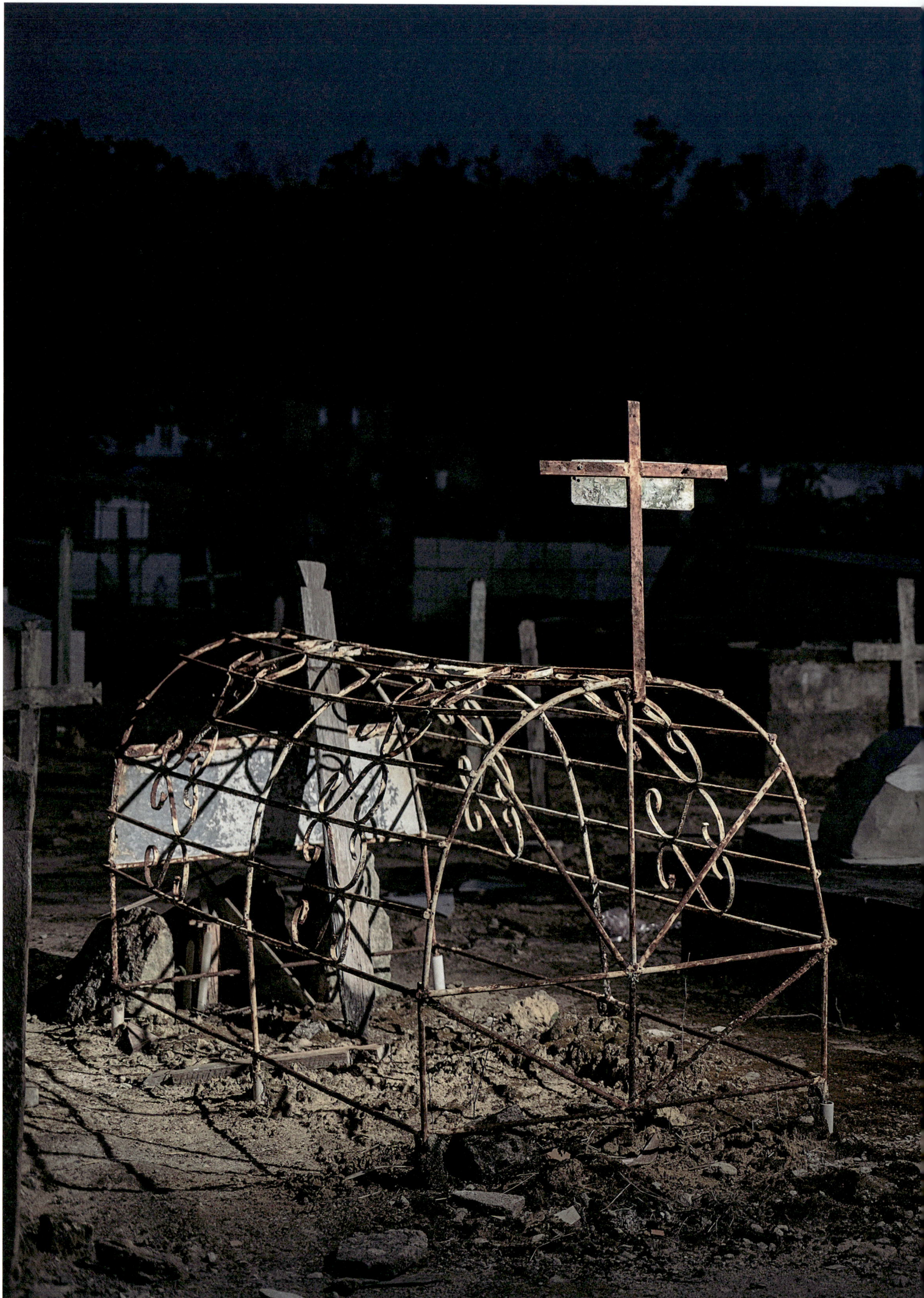

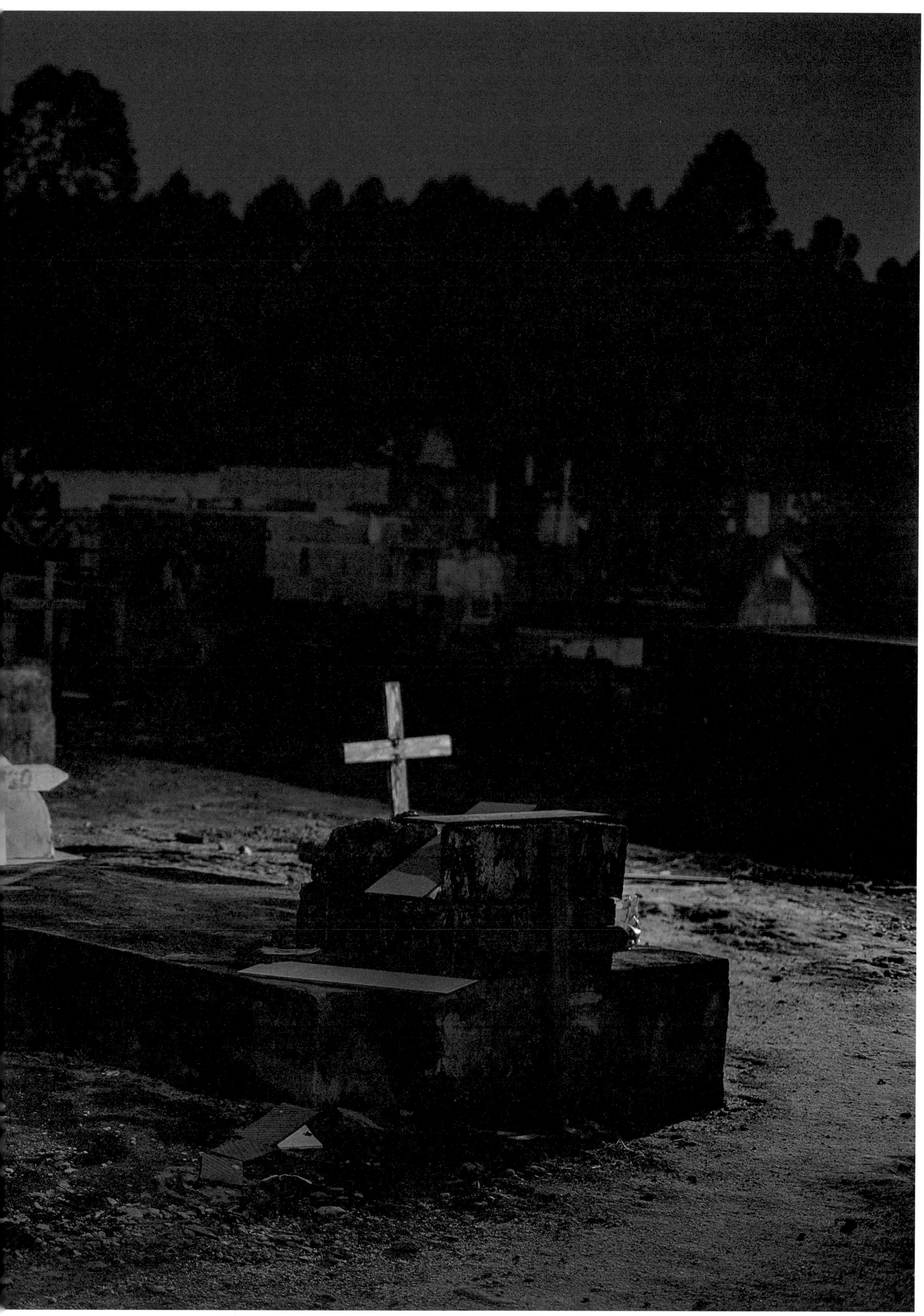

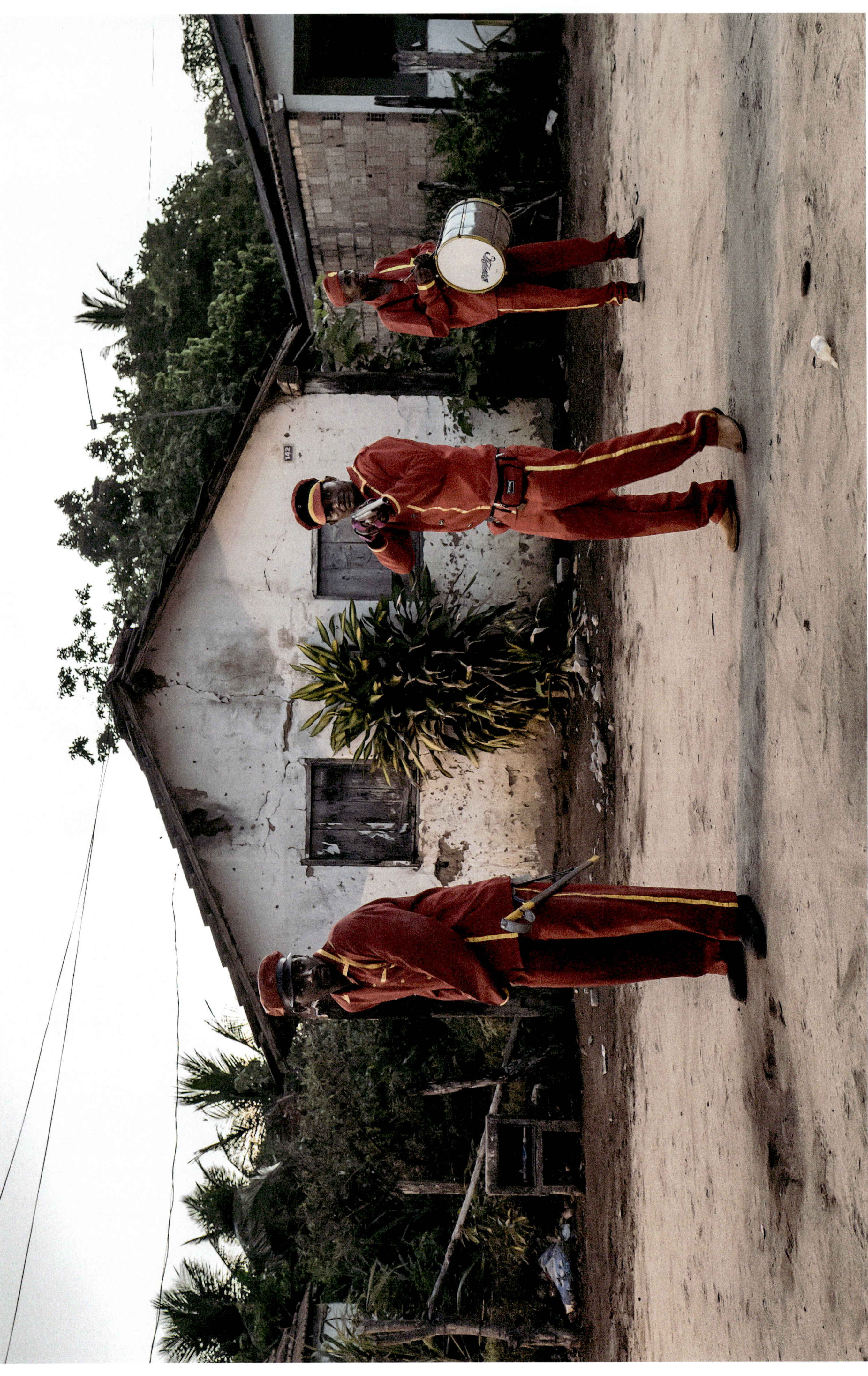

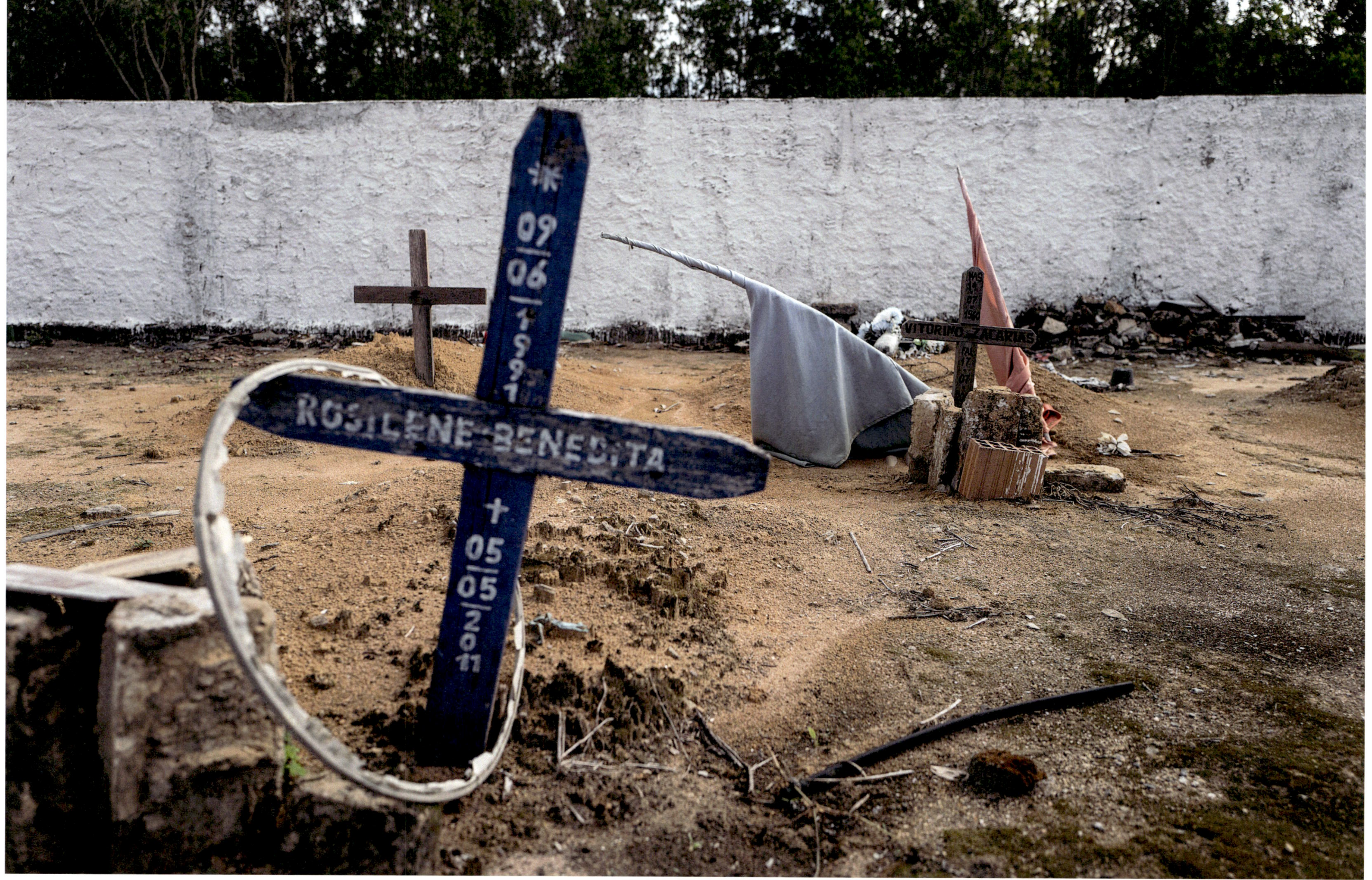
ROSILENE BENEDITA
✳ 09/06/1997
† 05/05/2011
VITORINO ZACARIAS

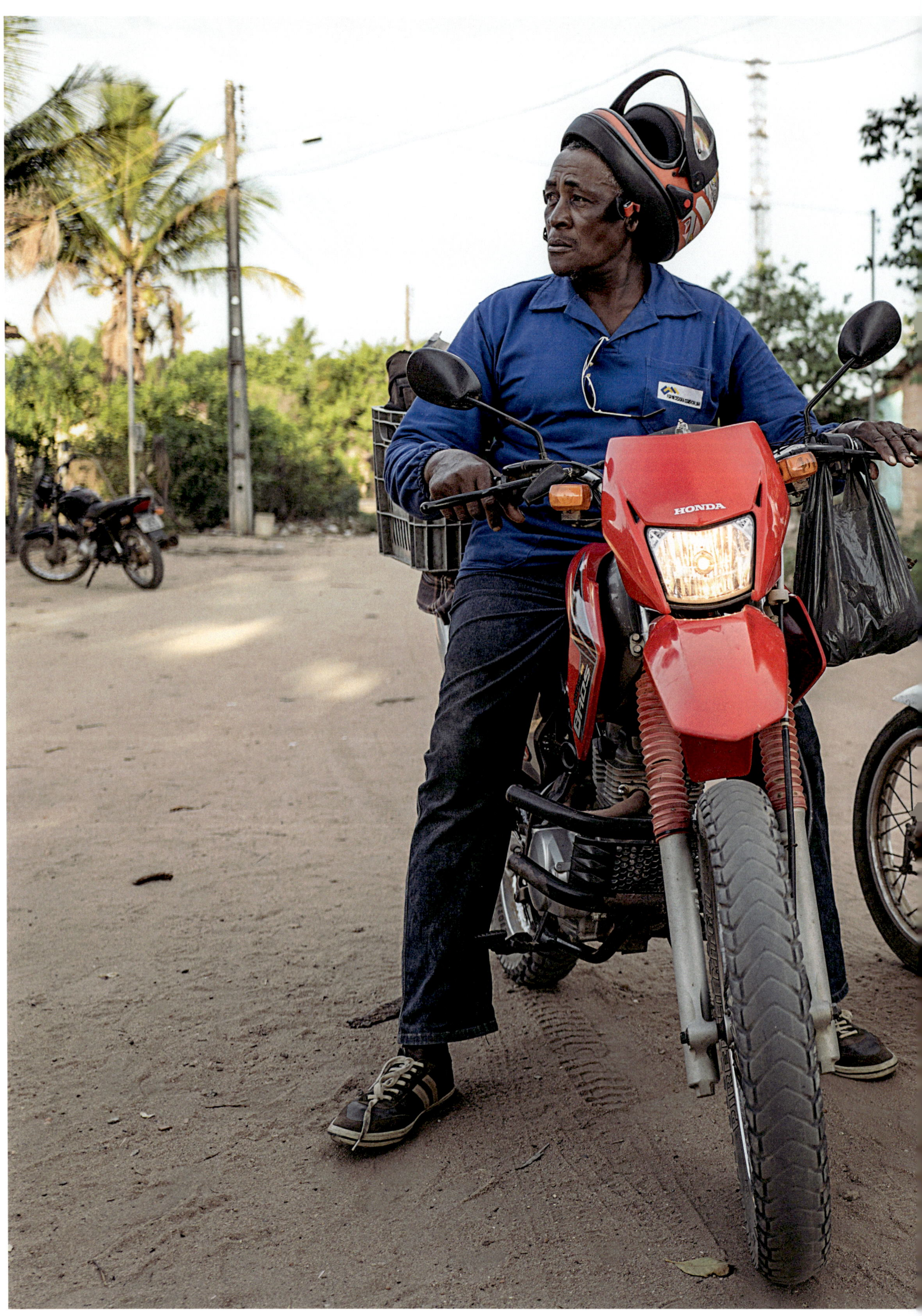

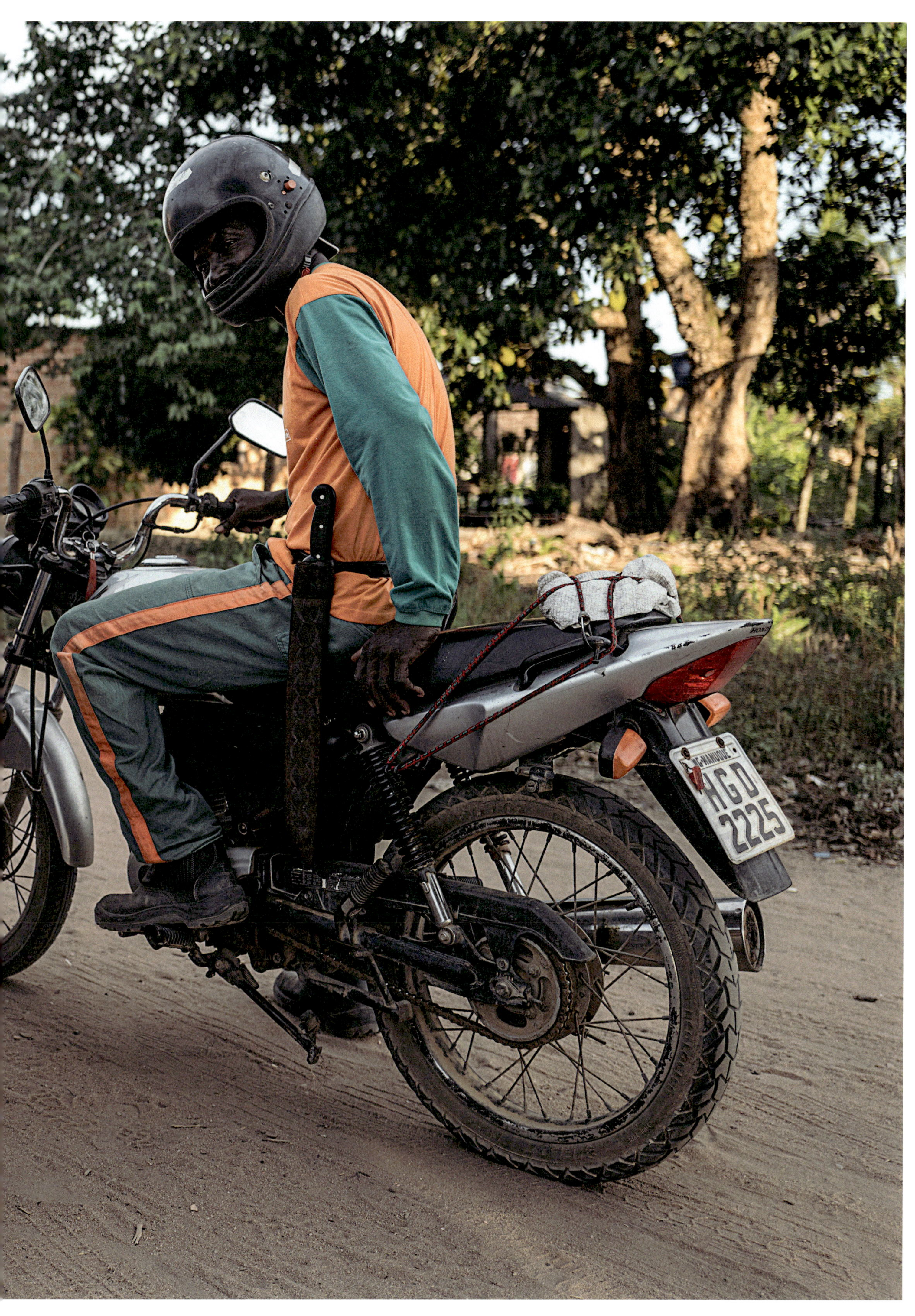

MOÇAMBIQUE
HGD
2225

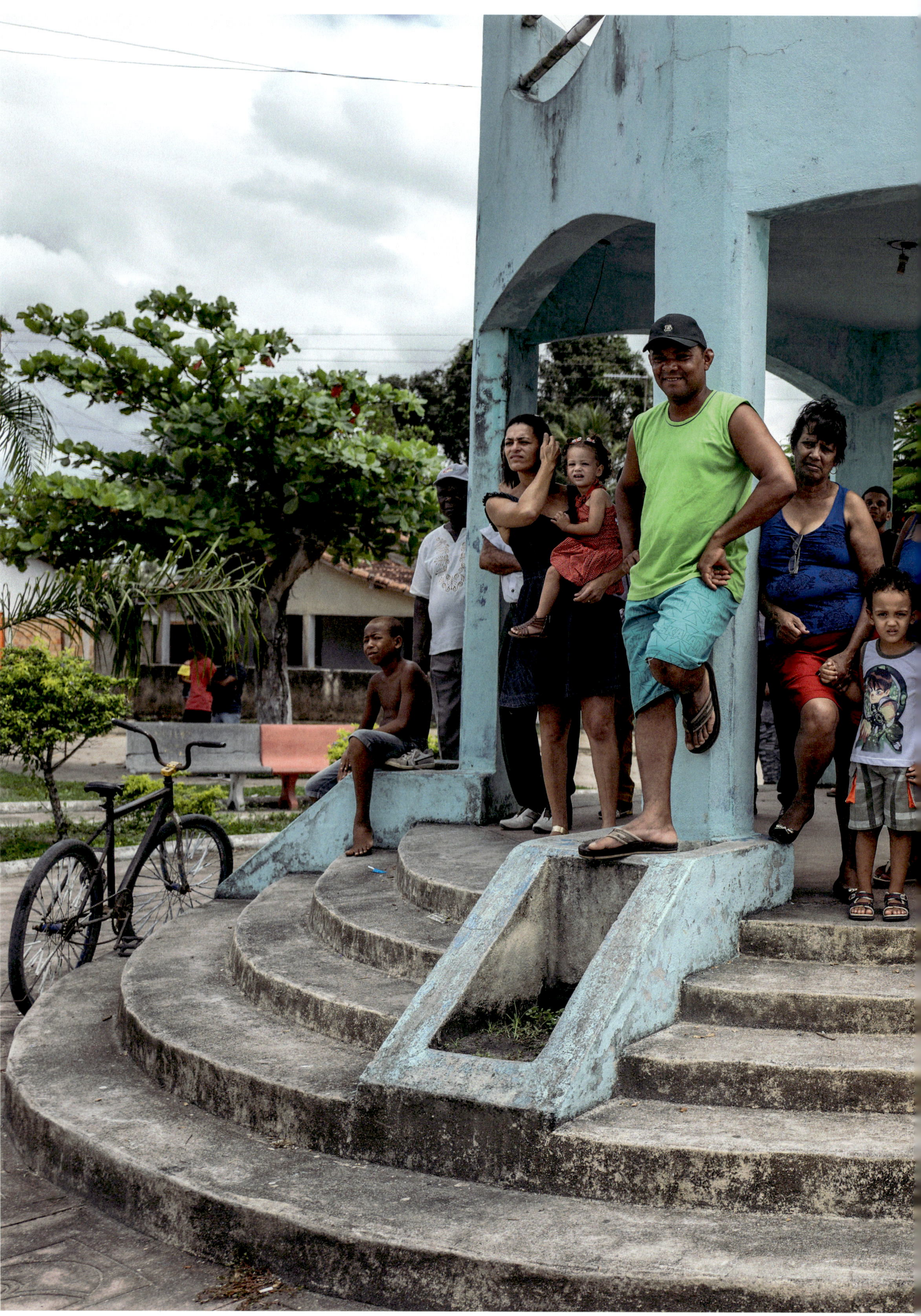

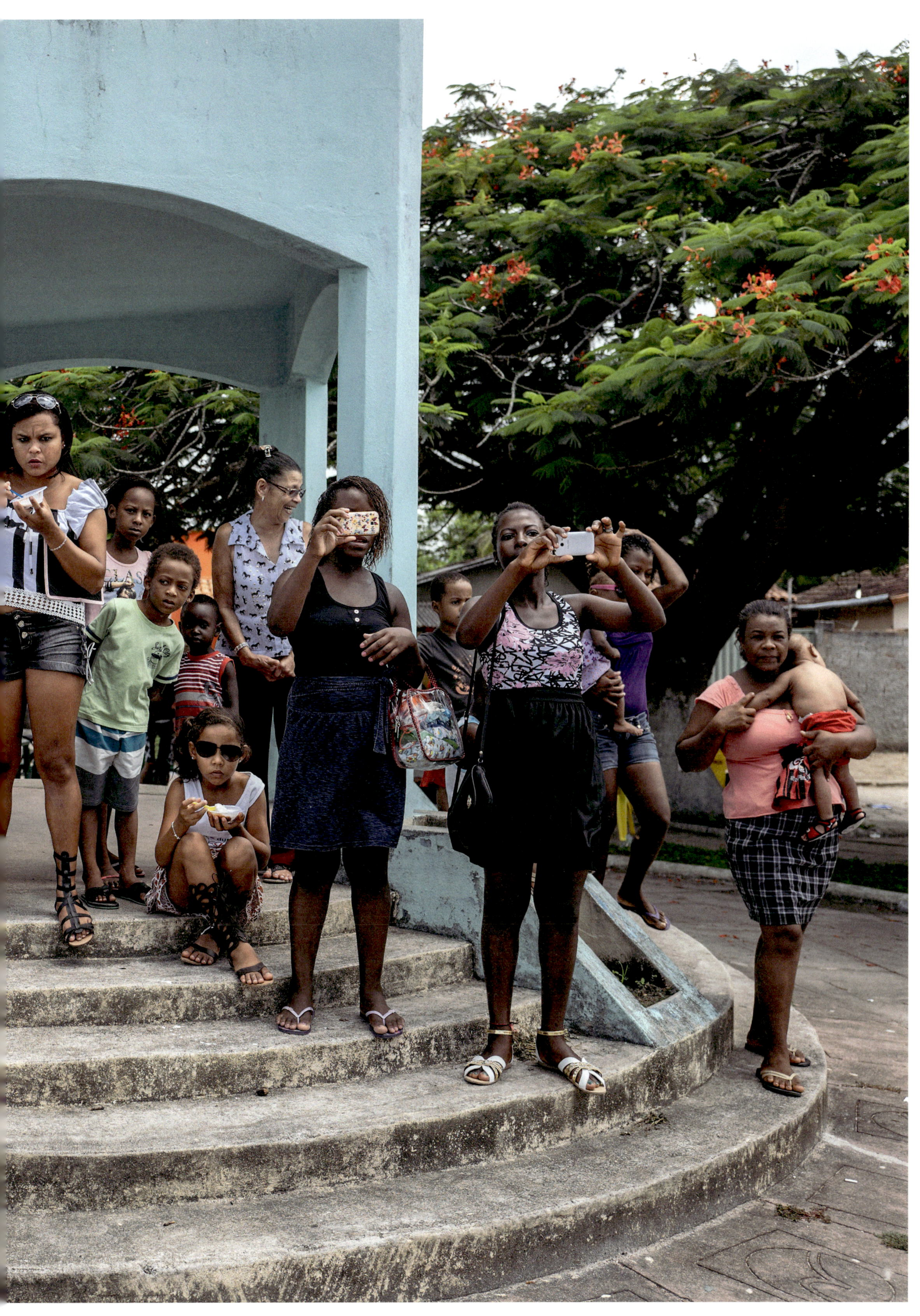

There's a crowd on Helvécia's central square. While the villagers, celebrating the feast of São Sebastião, throng around the front of the Catholic church to the sounds of a band playing, Vinicius stands off at a distance, proudly posing in front of his car. In the trunk, enormous loudspeakers are pumping out what Brazil calls funk *carioca*, the electronic music that was born in the favelas of Rio. Having long kept to the fringe of prevailing fashions and the usual communication networks, the little community can no longer escape the assaults of global culture. Yet this veneer of modernity cannot make a clean sweep of a past that is still very much present. Black people constitute Helvécia's population, and Black is its culture, despite everything. *Umbanda*, *capoeira*, and *bate-barriga* are proof of that – and in the most beautiful of ways possible.

The *terreiro* of Mãe Maria, the village's place of worship, looks like a real shambles. A little army of statues of Christ and the Virgin Mary clutter the furniture. On the wall hang two bath towels, completely out of place, one showing an animated film heroine in a come-hither pose, the other very likely depicting Princess Aurora. We are decidedly not in a Catholic chapel but a place of worship dedicated to *Umbanda*, an Afro-Brazilian religion. In the middle of this setting and dressed in green Mãe Maria proudly stands, the holy hostess presiding over all of it: "I am a practicing Catholic, but that doesn't stop me from taking care of my *orixás*.*" A perfect example of syncretism, *Umbanda* is a mix of Christianity and African spirituality crossed with Amerindian elements. A religion of slaves, *Umbanda* was, and still is, frequently despised. Nowadays evangelical movements, flourishing in Brazil, are aggressively opposed to this faith. In one instance when the local believers were practicing their religion on the village square, an evangelical minister dared to yell out, "Everything coming from Blacks is the work of the devil!"

In the streets of Helvécia, you still often hear the twang of the berimbau, an instrument that is closely associated with *capoeira*. A martial

** Orixás* are African-American divinities originally from Africa, specifically from the Yoruba religious traditions. They are the most important spiritual forces in the *candomblé* tradition.

art that has been listed as an intangible cultural heritage (ICH) by UNESCO since 2014, *capoeira* has indeed become a true national emblem of Brazil. This combat sport, however, with its roots in Africa, was in fact banned for many years. From the time when slavery was legal, *capoeira* gave voice to a form of resistance – in the guise of dance – by slaves with regard to their masters. Moreover, for Reginaldo, the village's *capoeira* teacher, practicing his art means quite simply cultivating his roots, "My ancestors were African. Their blood flows in me. Through *capoeira*, I defend their culture. It's my heritage."

"Learning that slavery had been abolished, in 1888, the slaves were elated," Faustina Zacharias Carvalho says. "Joyously the women began to wiggle and dance, rubbing up against each other. Others sang and yelped, while others beat on boxes. Because they were knocking each other on the belly, they decided to call this dance *bate-barriga*, literally the belly-beat."

For the anthropologist Valdir Nunes dos Santos, this dance, like *capoeira*, channels a certain cultural resistance. "It's a way of telling the younger people about the struggles of the past. I am convinced that this dance can reinforce the self-esteem of Afro-Brazilian communities, in Helvécia and elsewhere."

Daughter of the slave trade, today Helvécia enjoys a special status, that of a *quilombo* community, the recognition on the federal level of the village's past and roots in Africa.

"Until recently in Brazil, the descendants of Africans had to give up everything that formed their identity," Benedito dos Santos, a history teacher in Helvécia, explained. "Our traditions were forbidden, our rights were ridiculed. To be recognized as a *quilombo*, that is, as a community of the descendants of fugitive slaves, restores to us our lost pride."

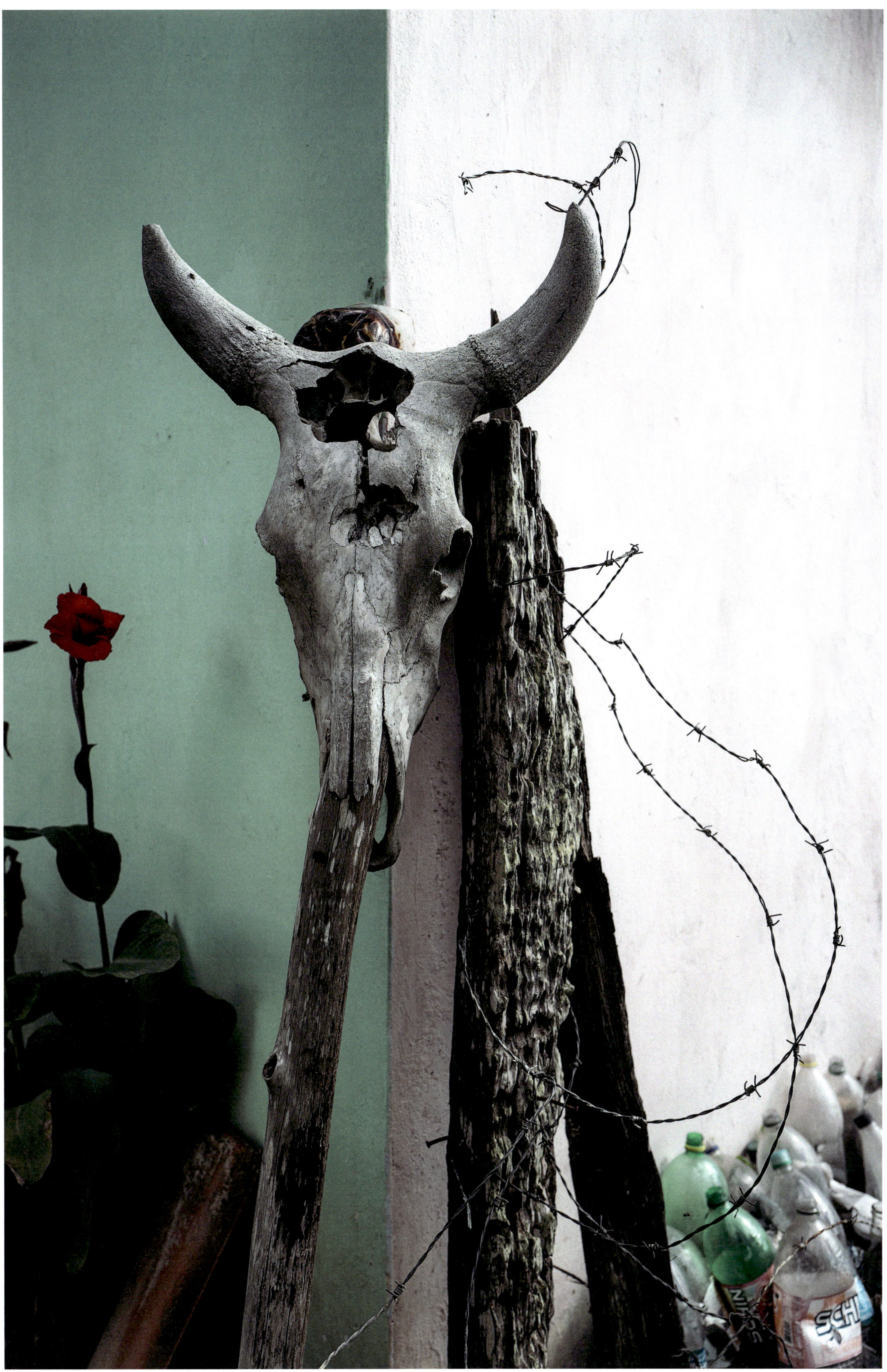

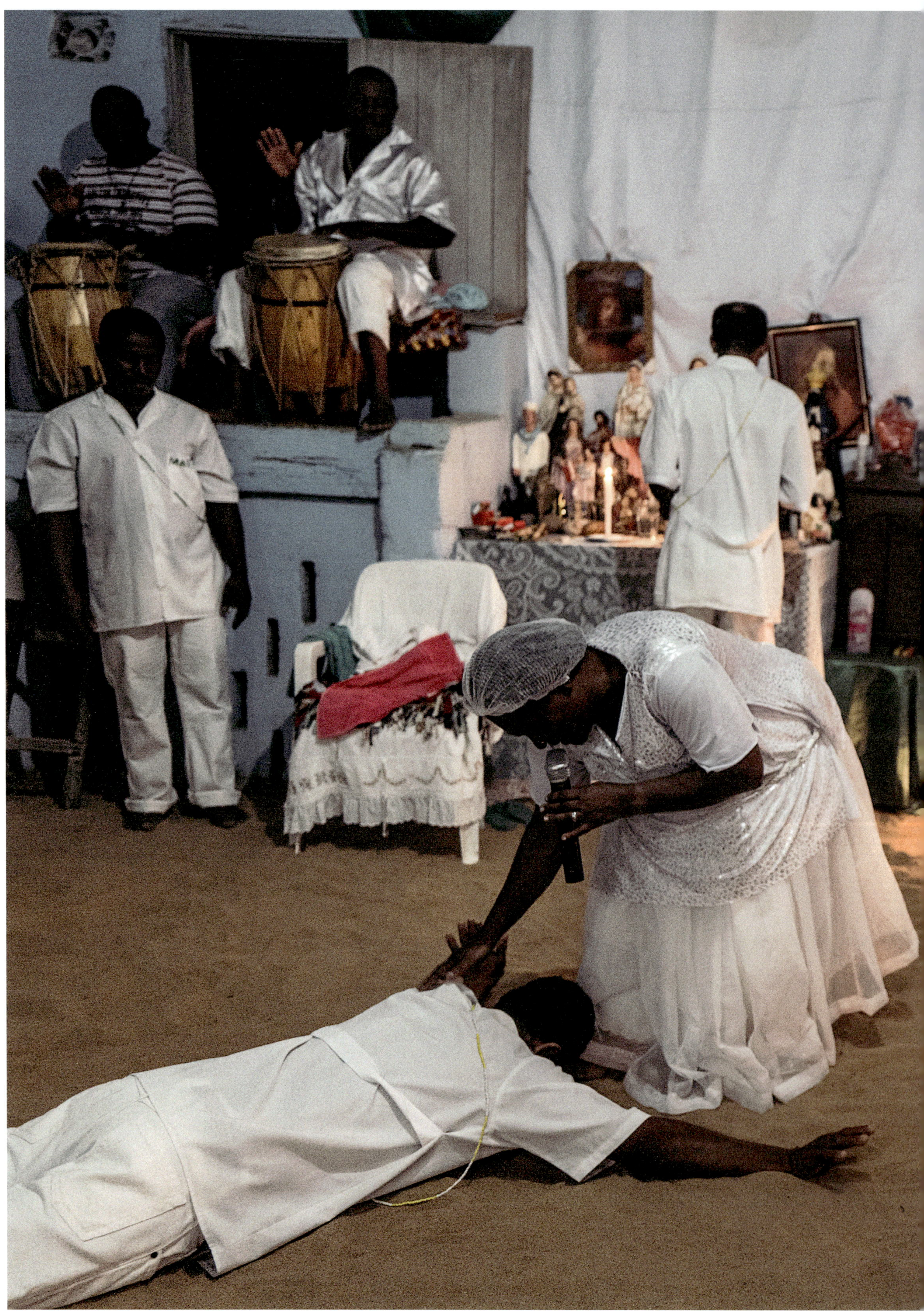

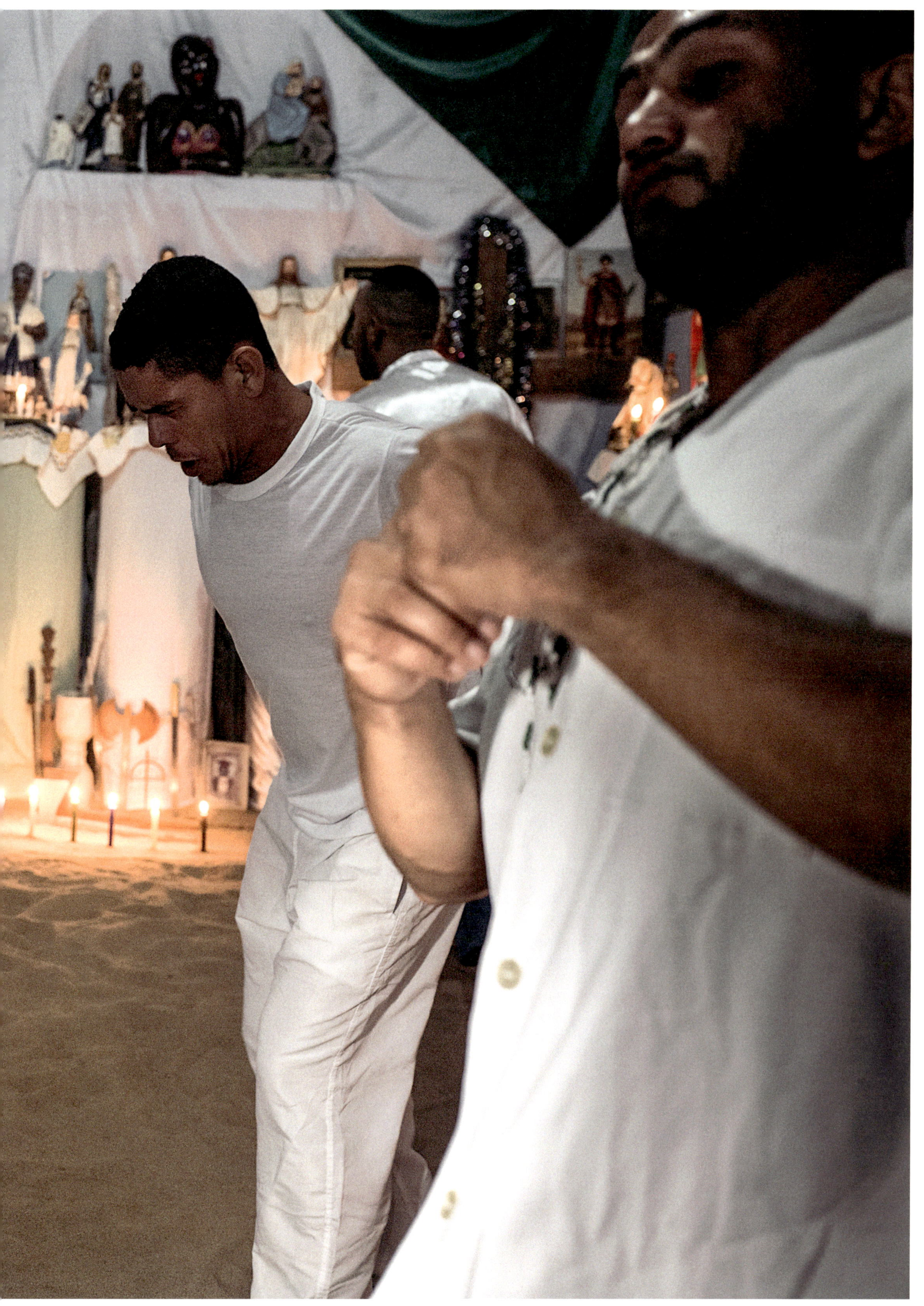

My name is Fabio Teixeira de Jesus and I work independently and I'm an evangelical Christian. In the church I attend, the Madureira Assembly, I'm the deacon and generally I'm also the sound engineer and *Levita*. Deacons help out the church by serving water, cleaning. And the *Levita* is a worshipper who says prayers and sings to the Lord.

I have been an evangelist for twenty-two years. When I accepted Jesus, I belonged to a different ministry, I was a baptist. There are many churches here. Generally, when we go and listen to God's word, the Holy Spirit touches us.

There are about eight churches in Helvécia. The importance of Helvécia's churches is in relation to the family. To accept Jesus, the young give up their vices, so that the family doesn't fall apart. That's the point of being an evangelical. It's about bringing peace, joy, and love. The worshipping takes place every fifteen days in the town square. It's an open-air workshop and brings together the different churches. It's evangelical, and focused more on people's souls, for people who don't go to church. Every minister comes from a different church.

It's really hard to talk about culture, isn't it? Because there used to be a lot of bad stuff going on, and people in the old days talked about those things coming mainly from Black communities. Not only back in the day, but there are still people who set out to curse others. Preachers shouldn't be hypocritical. The kingdom of darkness shouldn't get mixed up with the kingdom of light. We accept their religion, but the way they practice it contradicts the word of the Lord and of the Bible.

I hardly know anything about the history of Helvécia. There's been a lot of research into the history of the train, for example, but I don't know anything about it. Those who know are the elders, and I'm only thirty-two. Nor can I explain why Helvécia is a *quilombo*. Perhaps it's something to do with skin color because many people say that there were a lot more Black than white people living here.

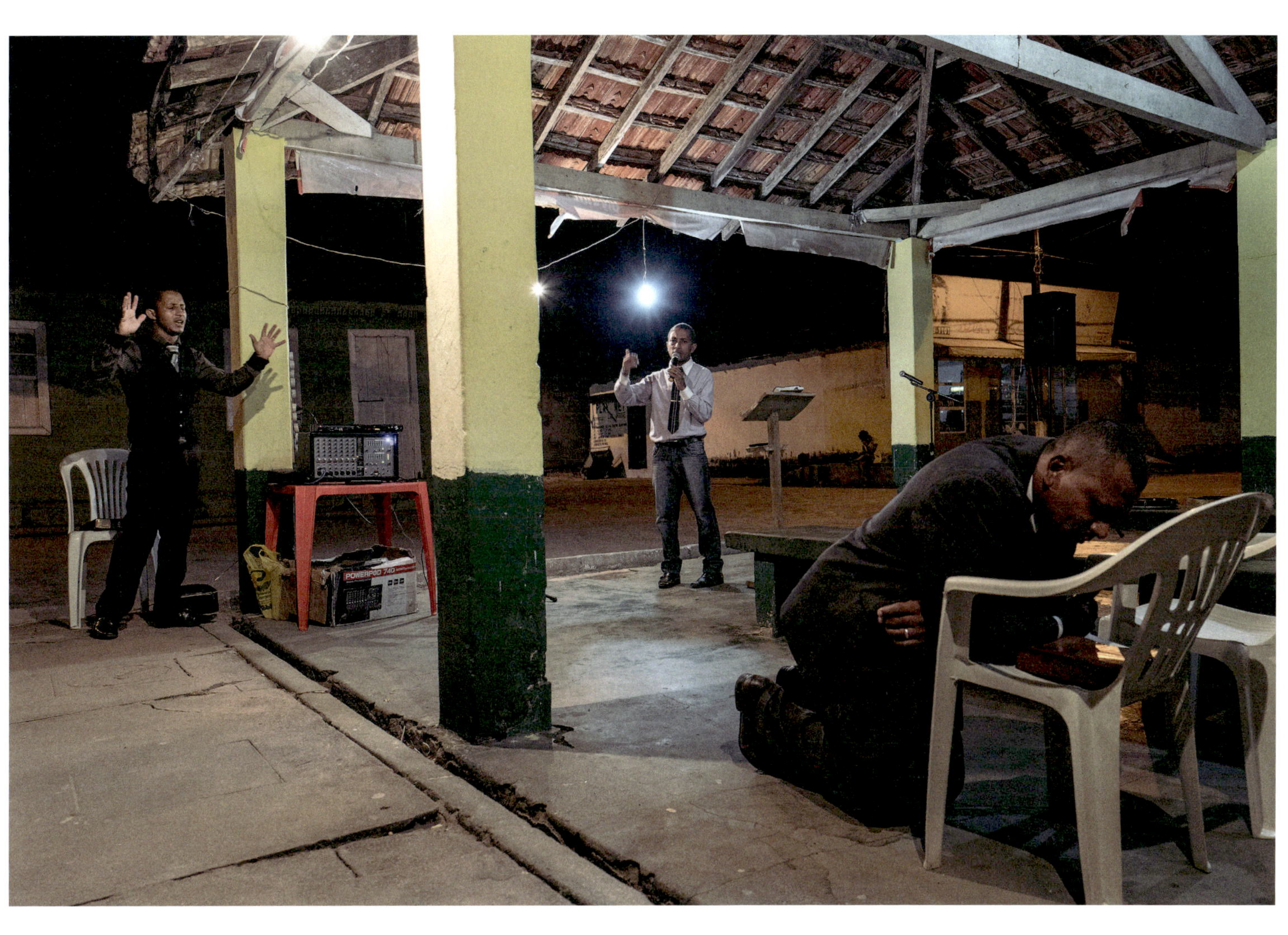

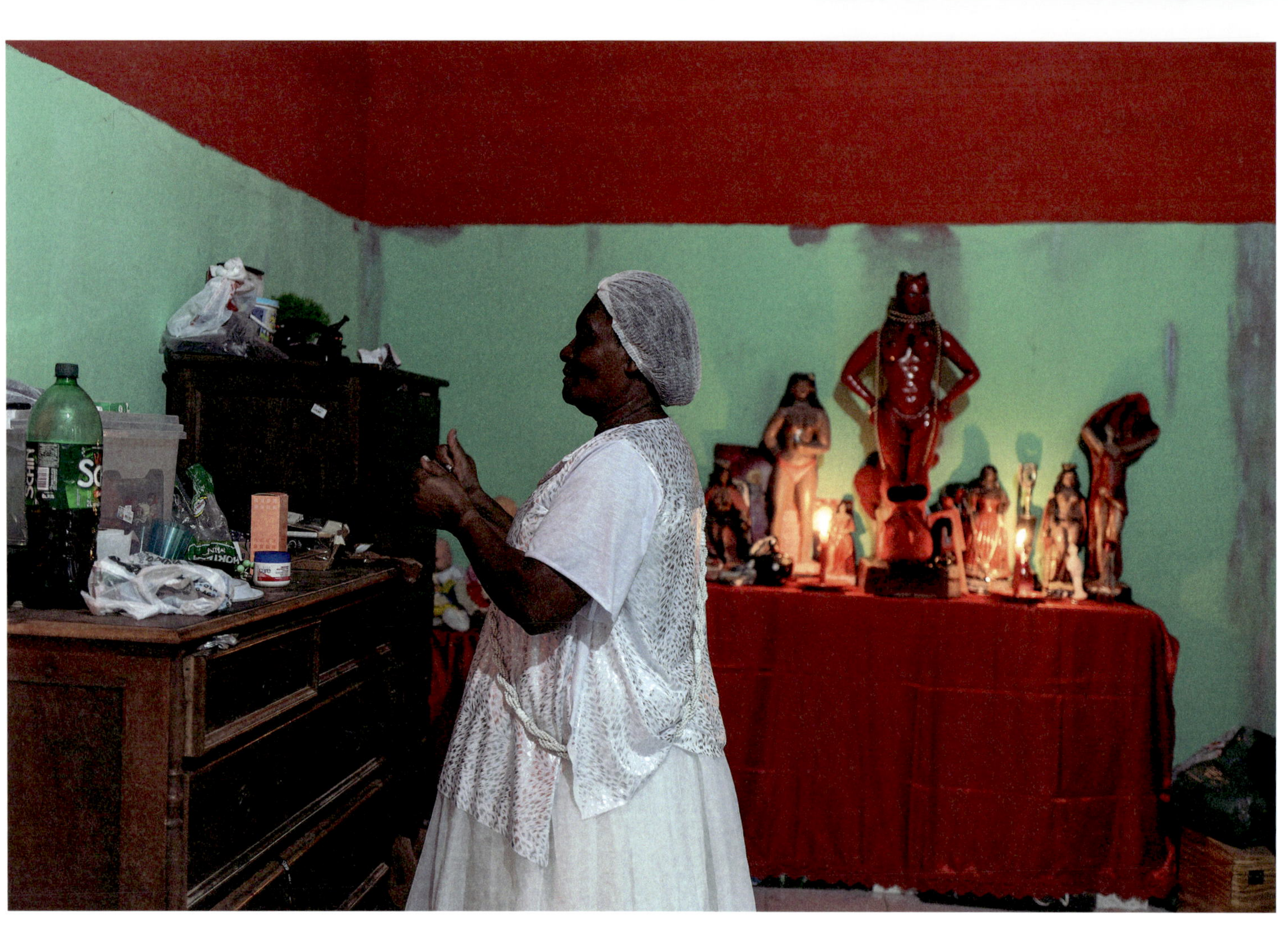

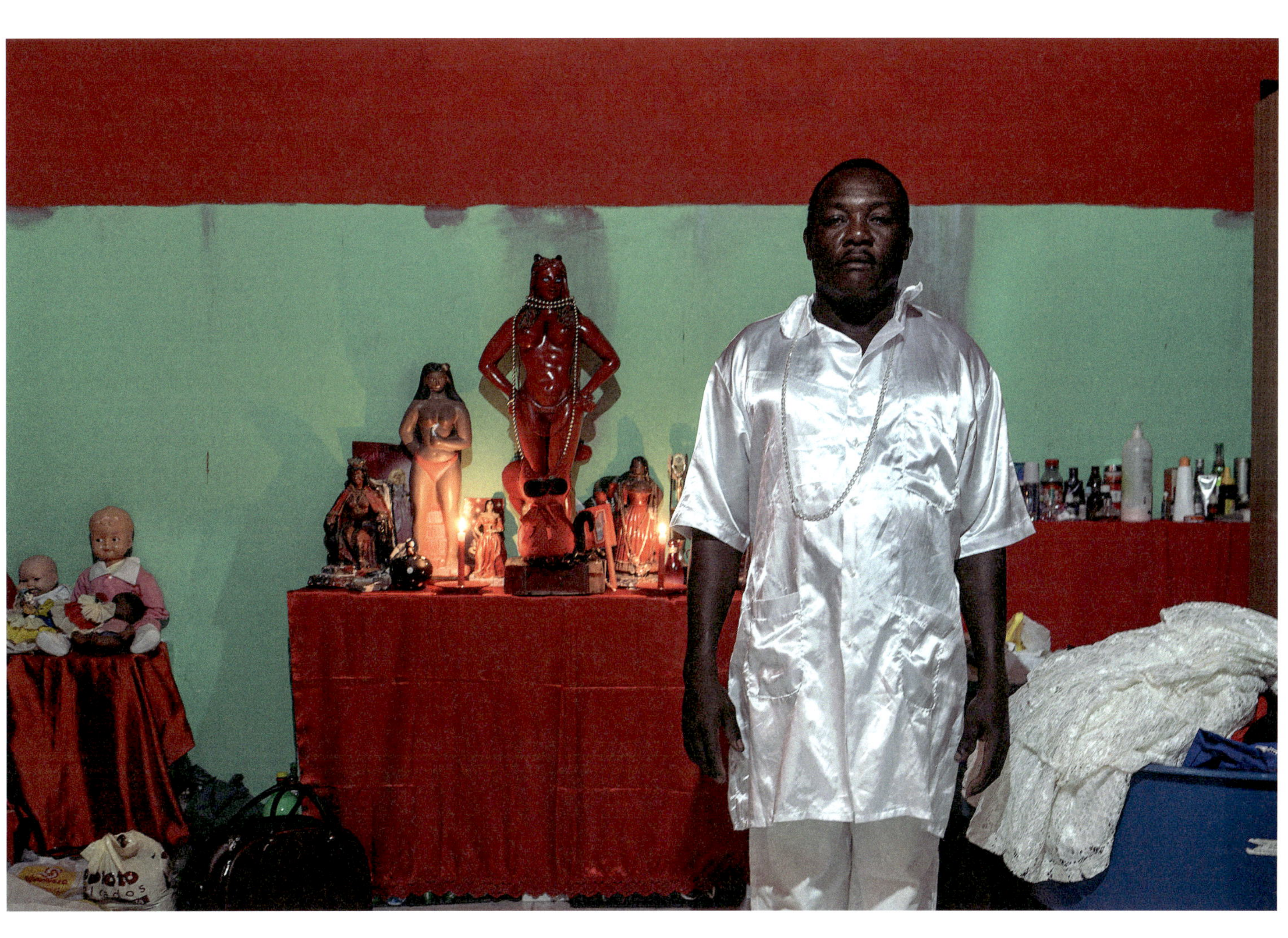

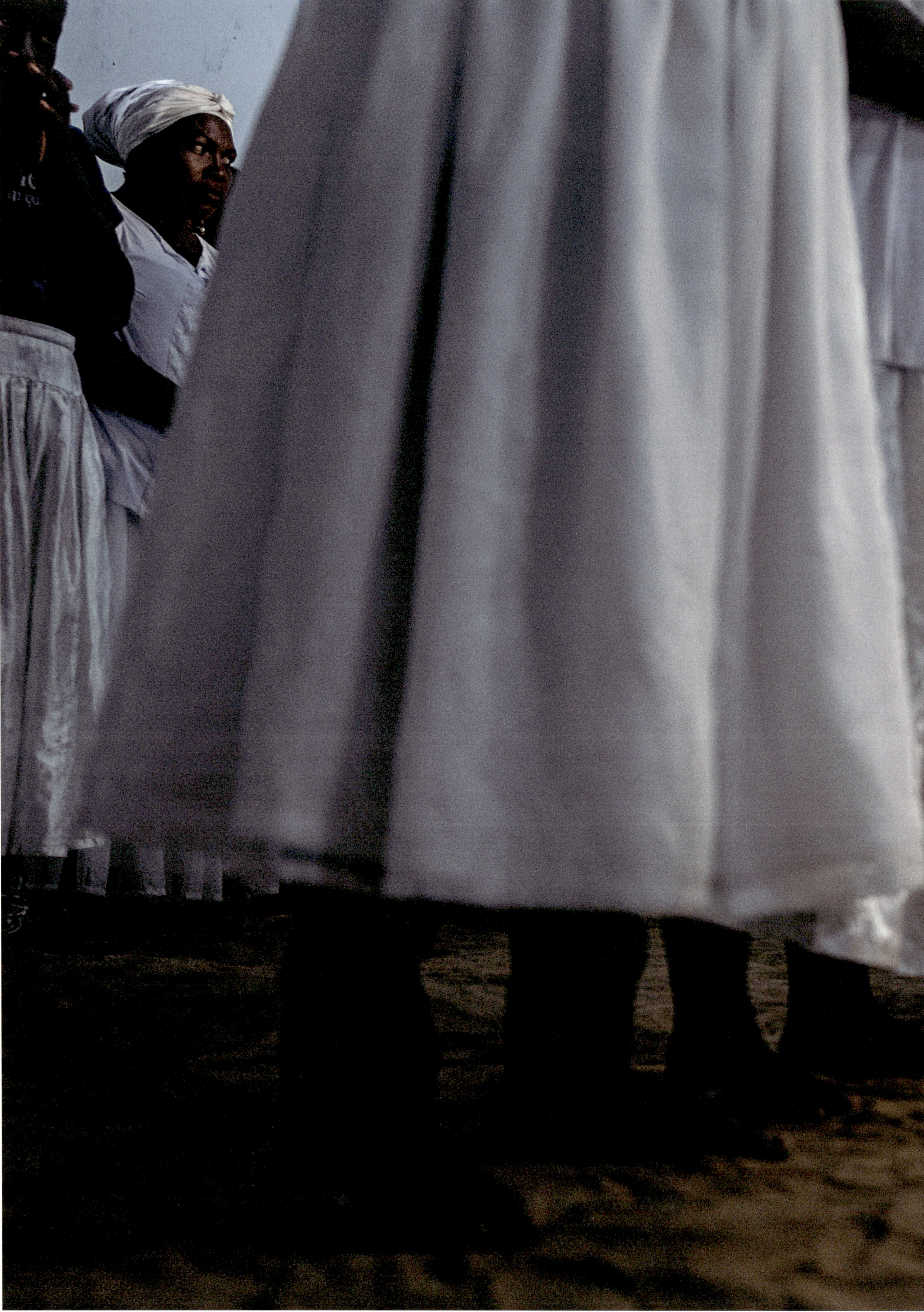

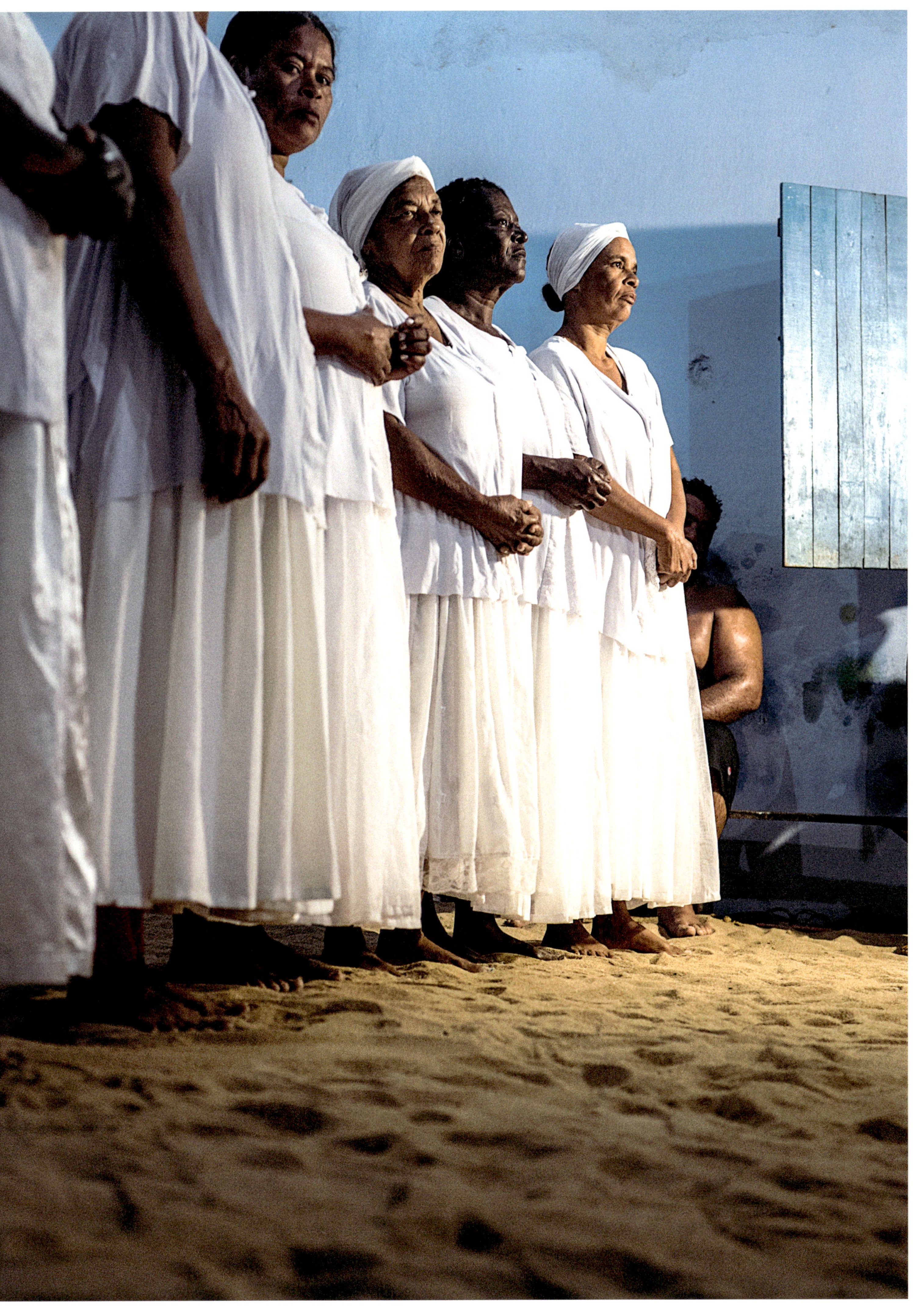

My whole life has been here. I always dreamed of becoming a soccer player, but after something that happened here, I believe that God came into my life and I became religious… I began singing in the choir, and then started playing an instrument… and then God somehow came and touched my heart.

The thing is that I began shoplifting from a supermarket. One time the owner caught me stealing and kept me in the shop. This incident made a big impact on me. Nothing like that had ever happened in my family. My father always worked, and gave me money. I had the money to buy the biscuit, but even so I still ended up stealing…

And so I persevered. I still wanted to become a soccer player, but with my heart set on serving God. To start with I wasn't interested in becoming ordained as a diocesan priest, but to serve the Church. Only after some time, when a deacon came to invite me to join the diocese. That's how I started the process of becoming a diocesan priest.

Clearly very few Black people become professionals, either in the Catholic Church or in schools and universities. Having a Black person in a profession is a big deal for the community, and a Black priest is a big deal because it's not only a privilege but has special importance for all of us.

From what I've read about the community it was once called the Leopoldina Settlement before it became known as Helvetia–a Swiss-German name if I'm not wrong. Then it was Portuguese-ified as Helvécia. I think it was founded by Swiss-Germans. We have a tomb, and I even visited one here, "John Flater" one of the settlement's founders. The story goes that Black people came here from Africa, and after the settlers left, the Black people took over possession, and Helvécia became one of the last communities where they received freedom. We remained slaves for a long time, even after the Golden Law[1] was passed.

The Christian churches are more popular here, I think. That began with the evangelicals… they aren't more numerous than the Catholics, but I think their way of evangelizing caused a split from the African religions. Before, a lot of people went to the *terreiros* of the *umbanda*. Since I was a child, I remember people began to convert to Christianity, which then grew. Now it's the religion that watches over Helvécia.

1   See the "Chronology of Leopoldina (Helvécia)" in this publication, p. 168.

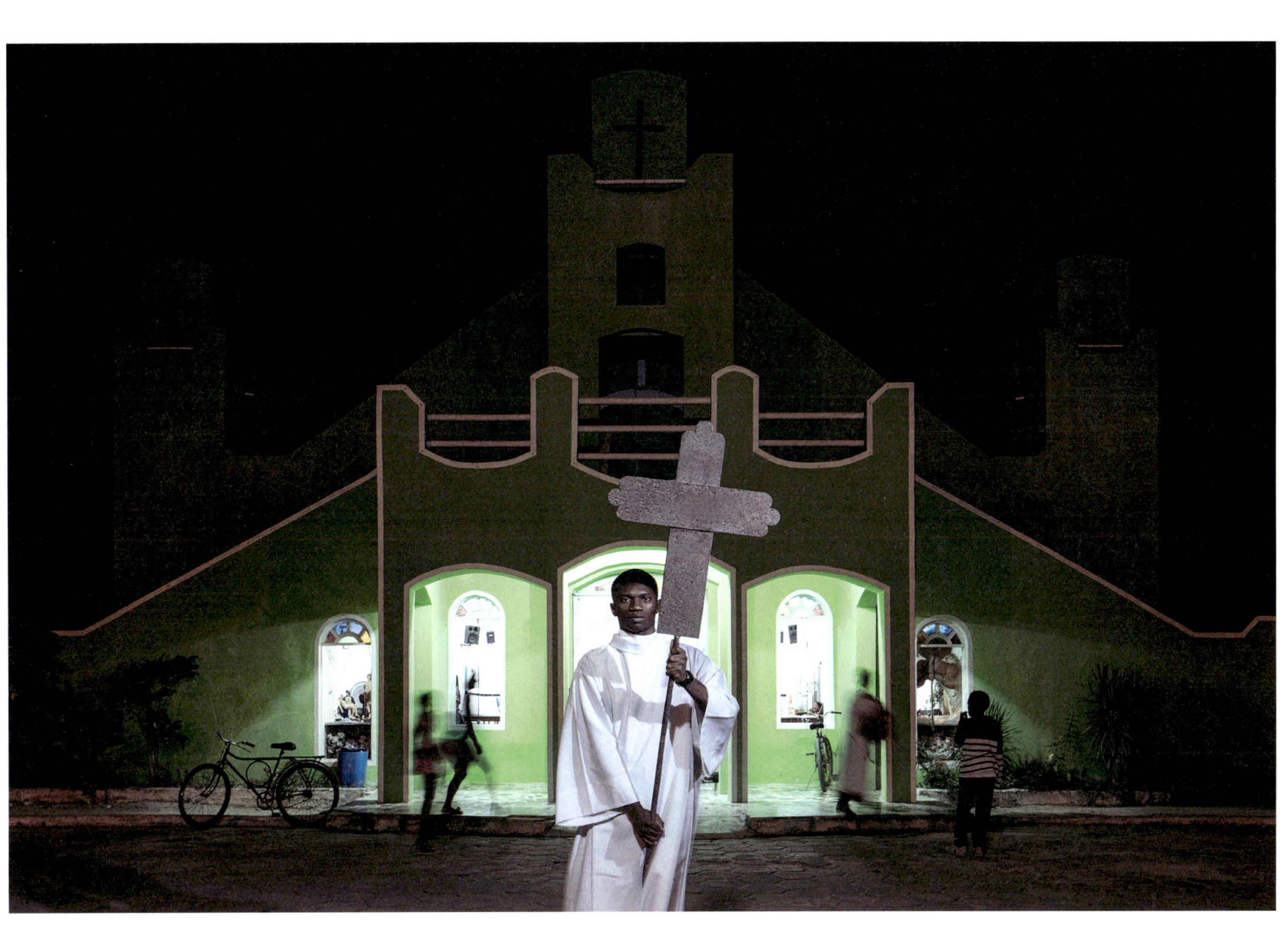

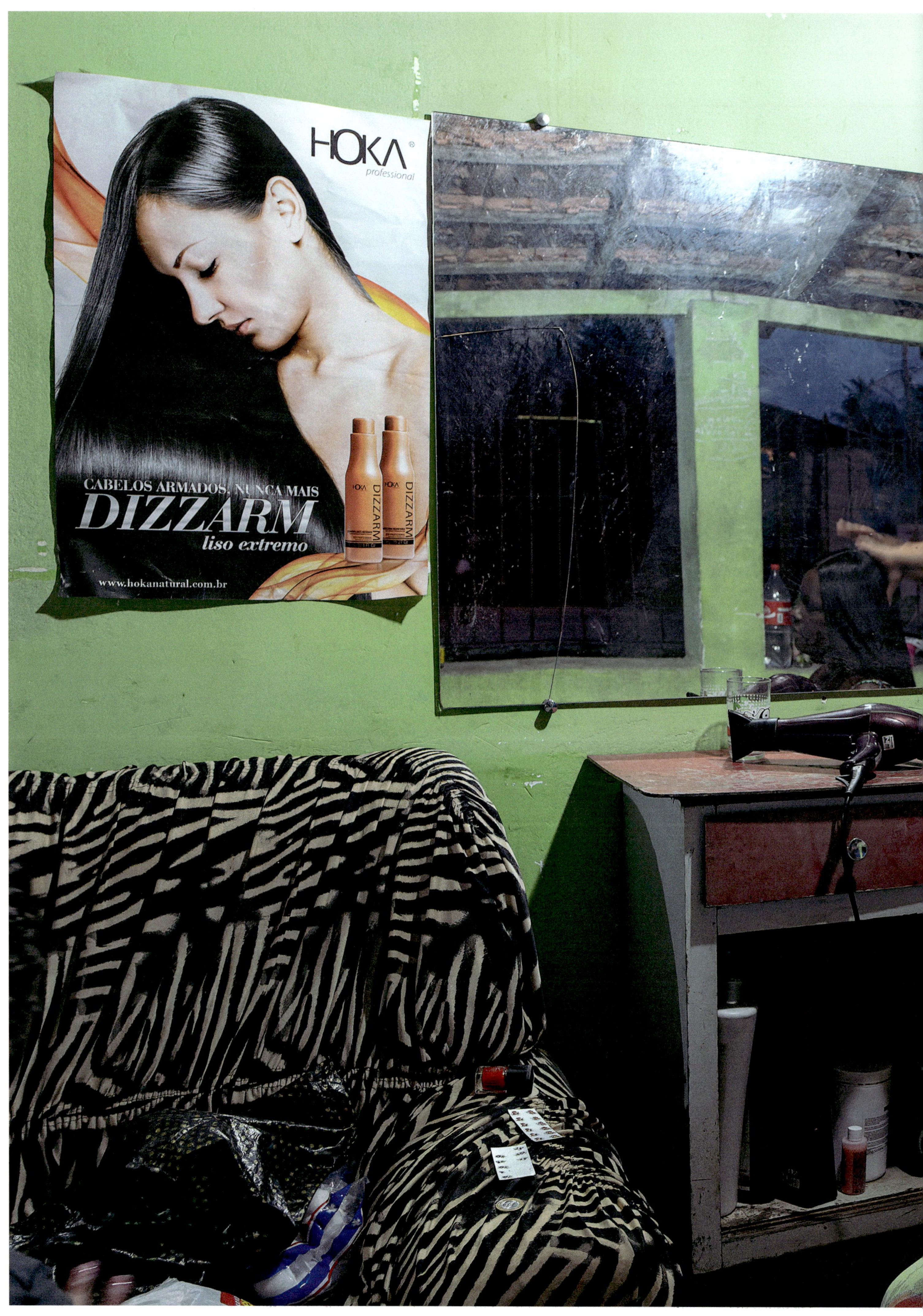

HOKA
professional
CABELOS ARMADOS, NUNCA MAIS
DIZZARM
liso extremo
www.hokanatural.com.br

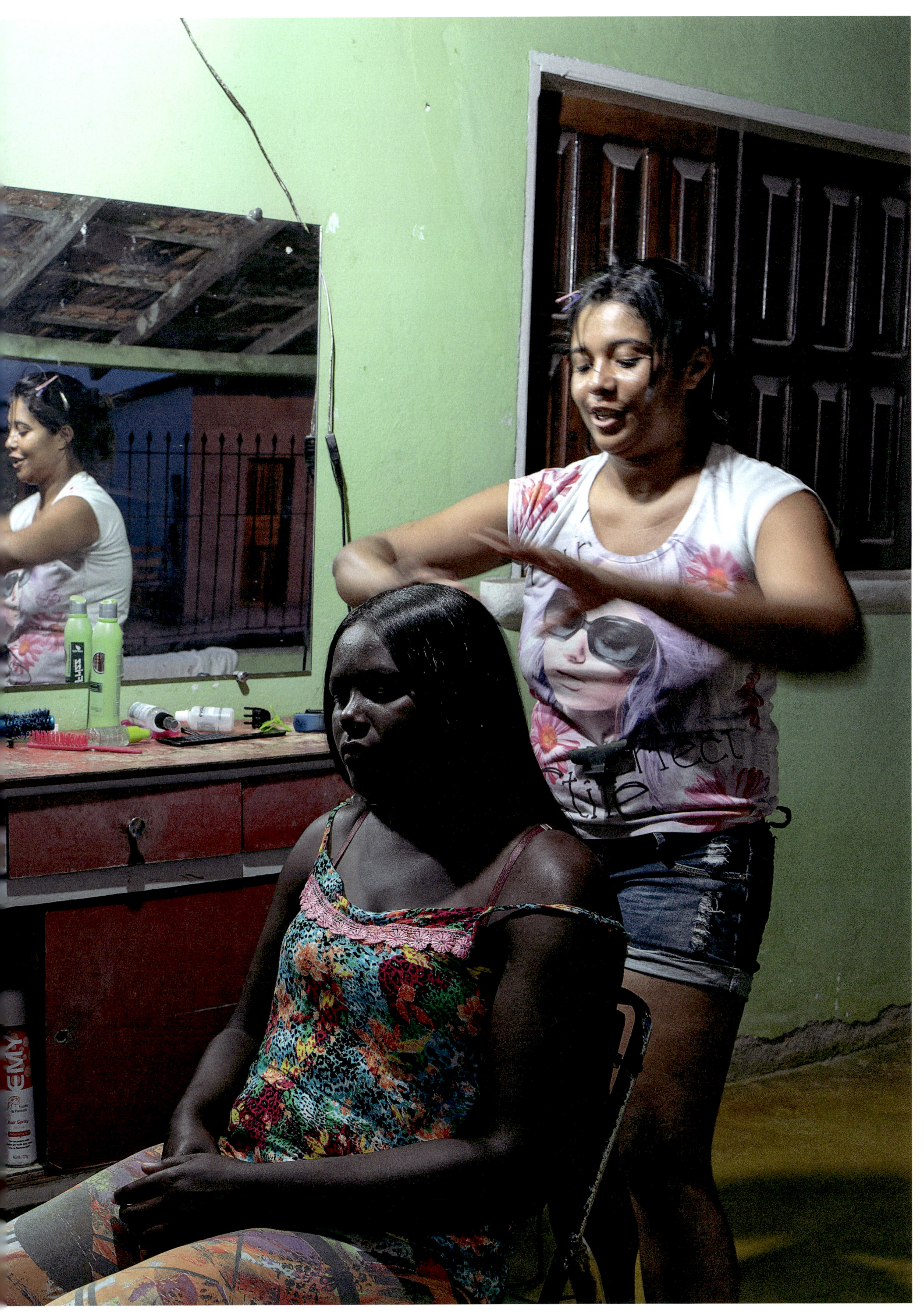

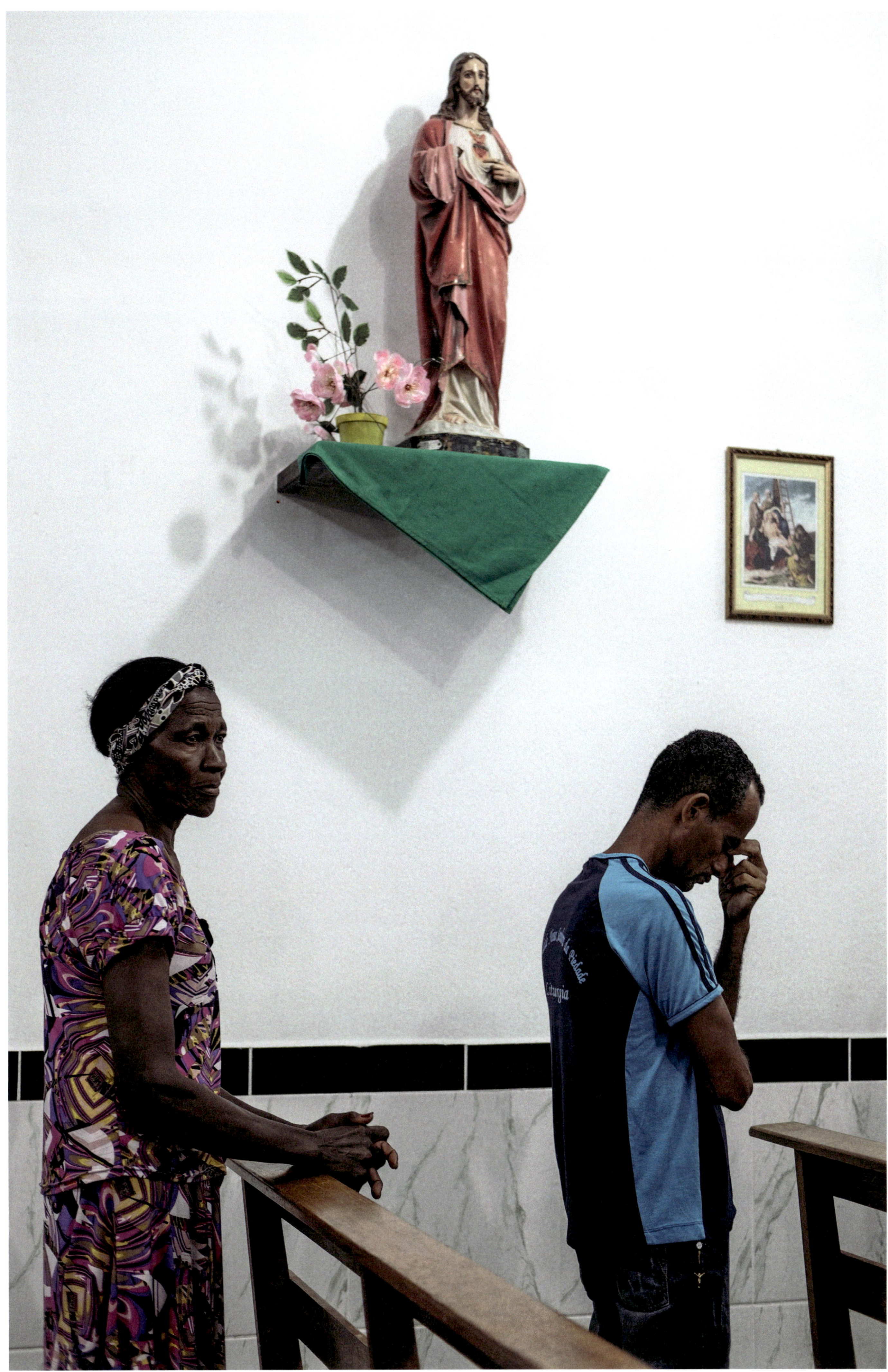

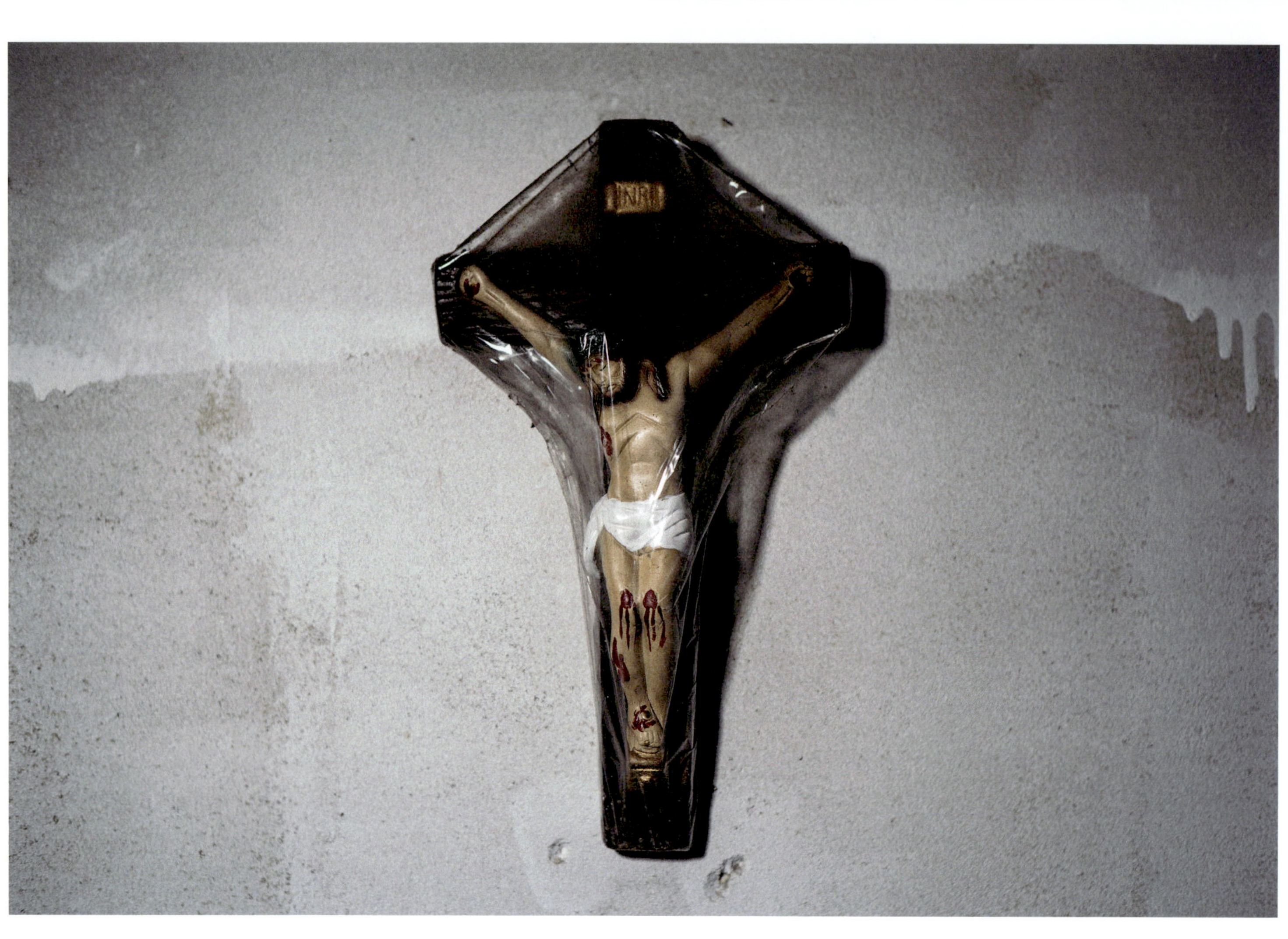

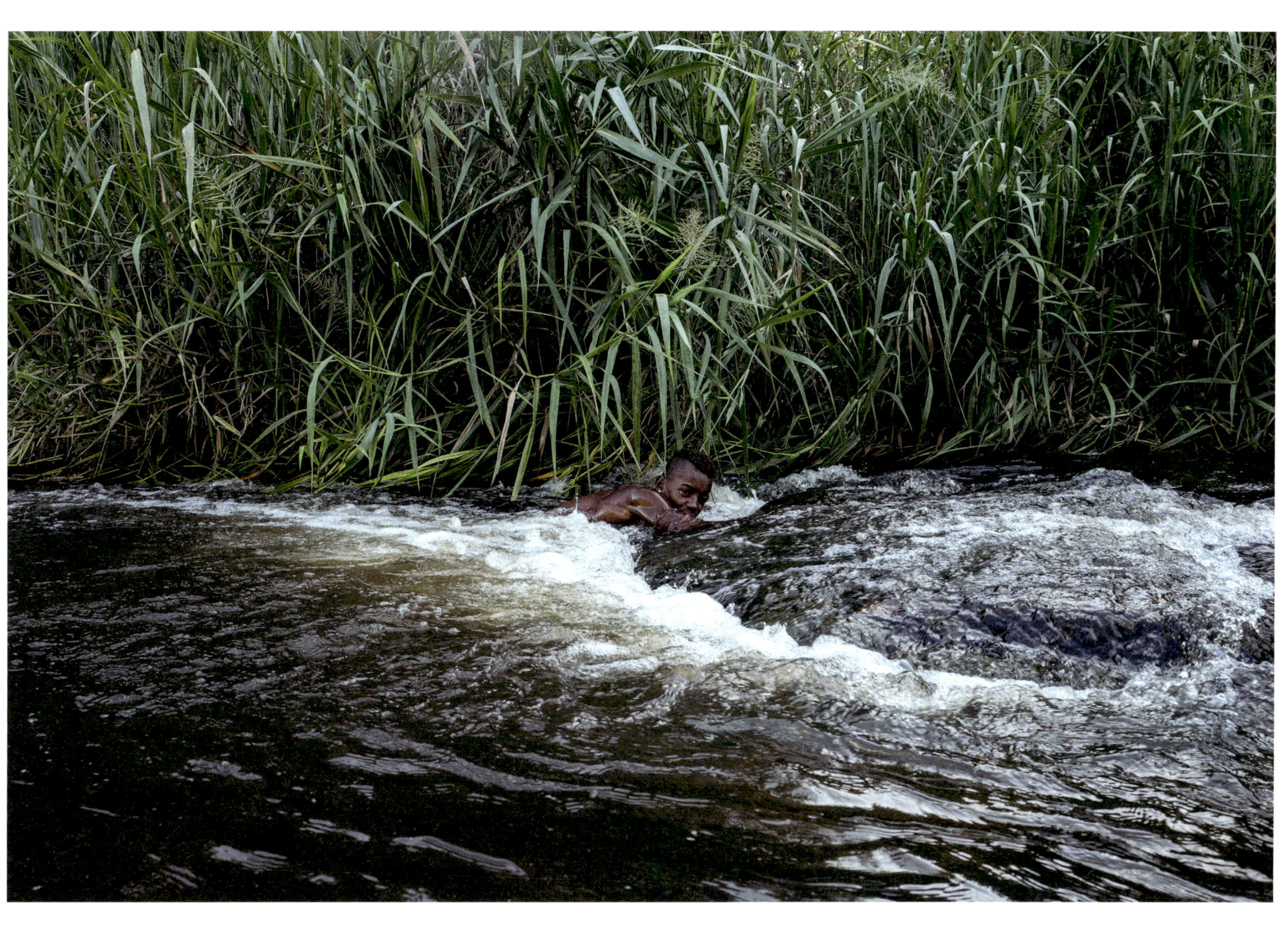

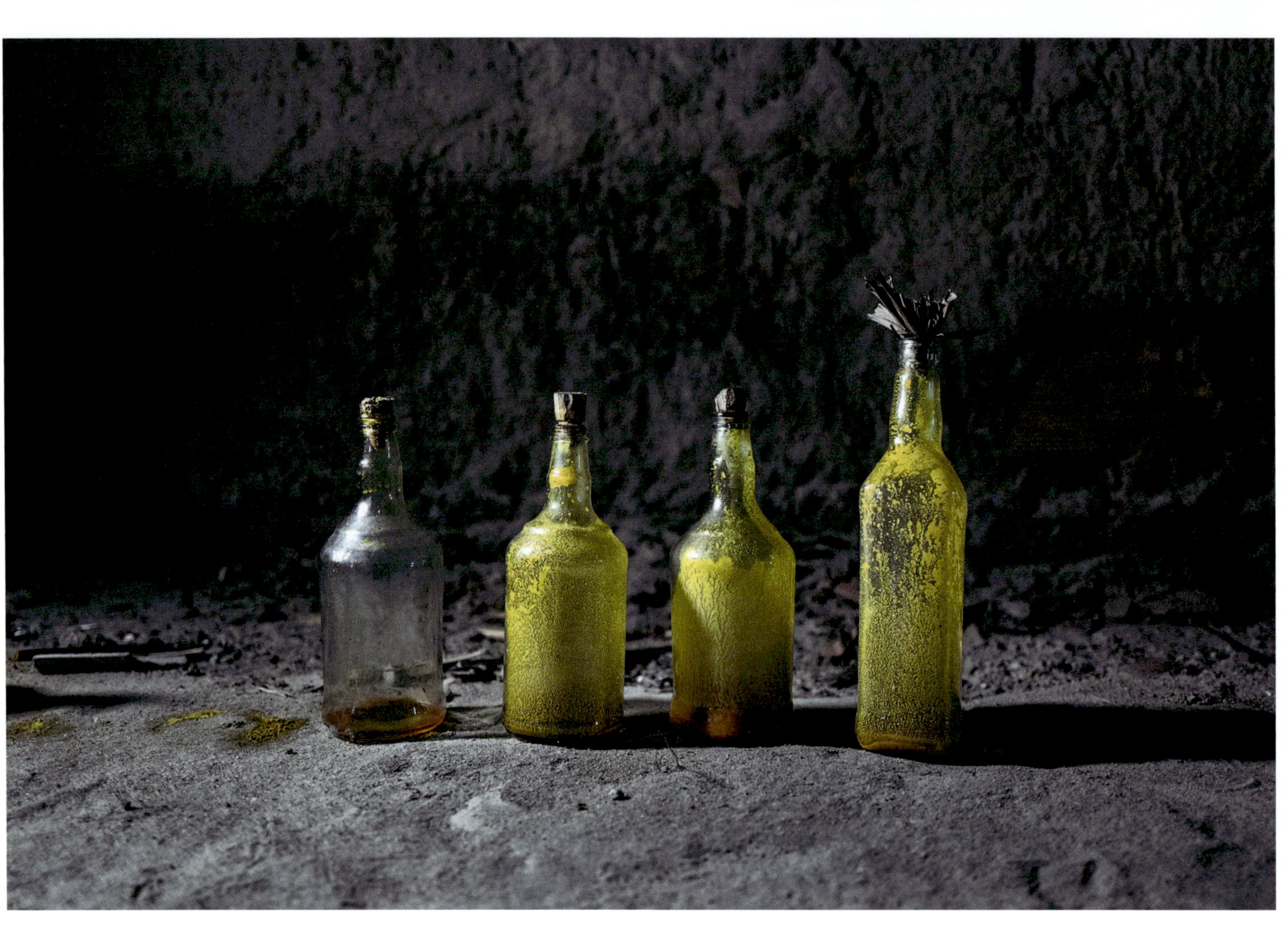

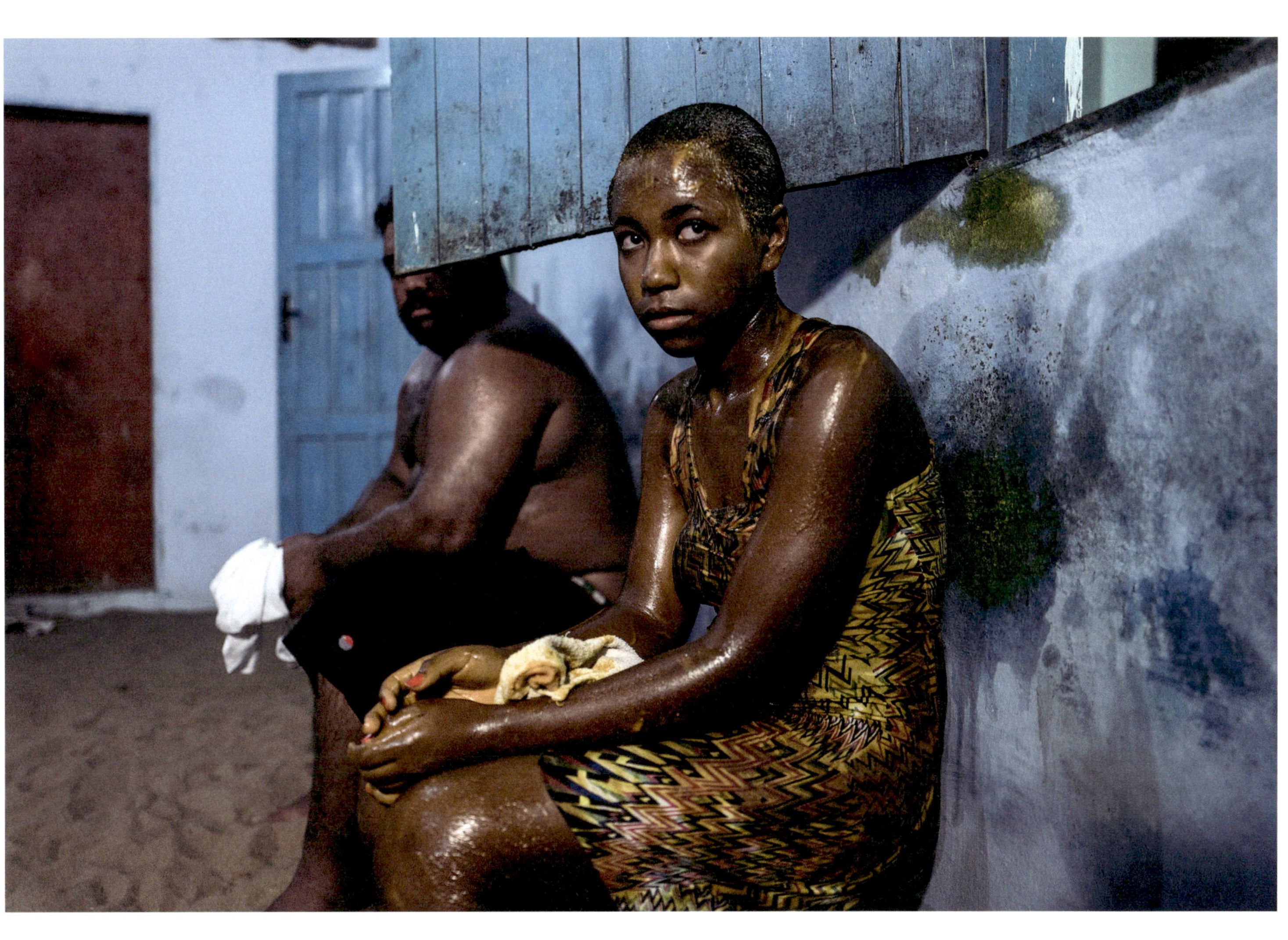

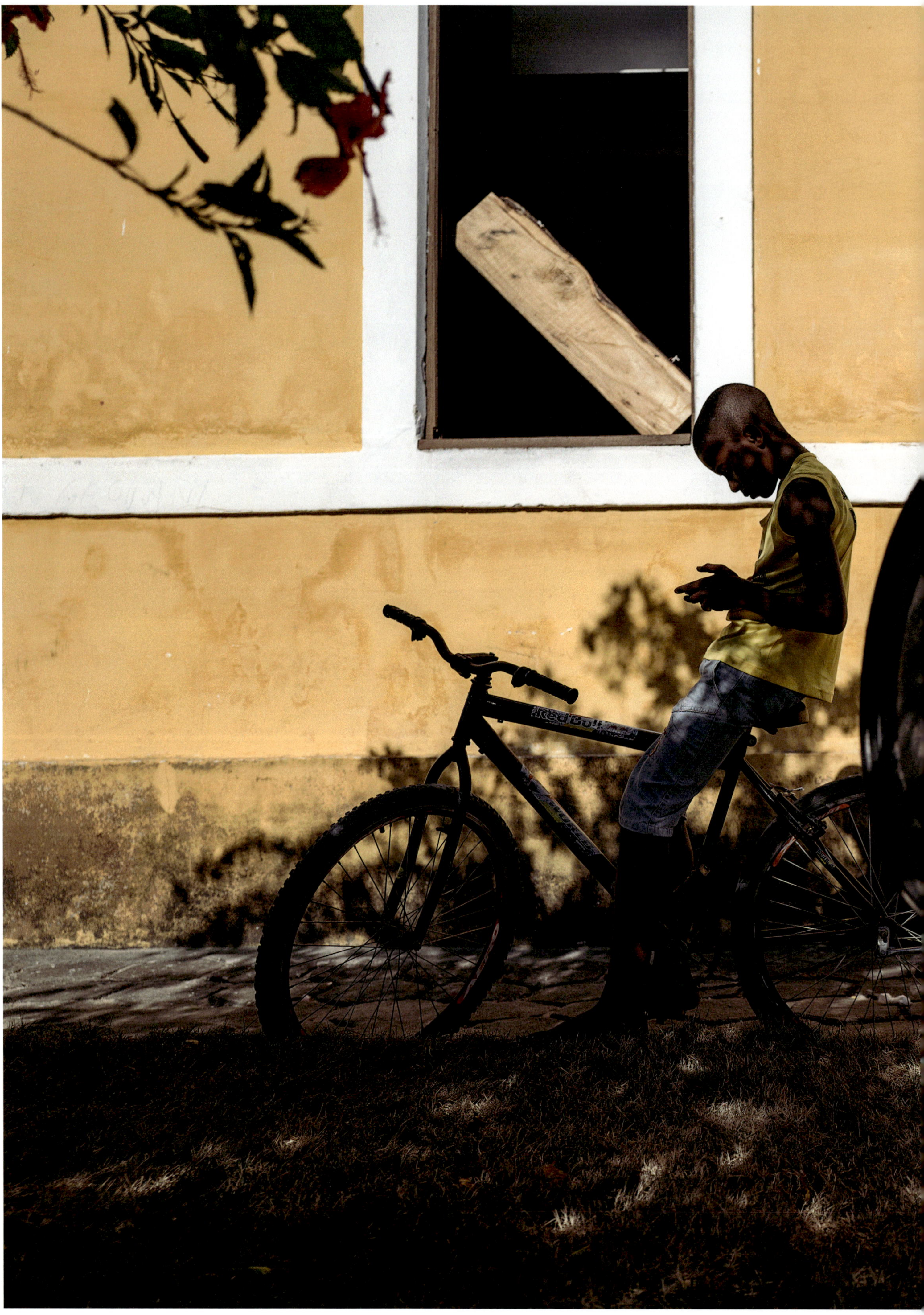

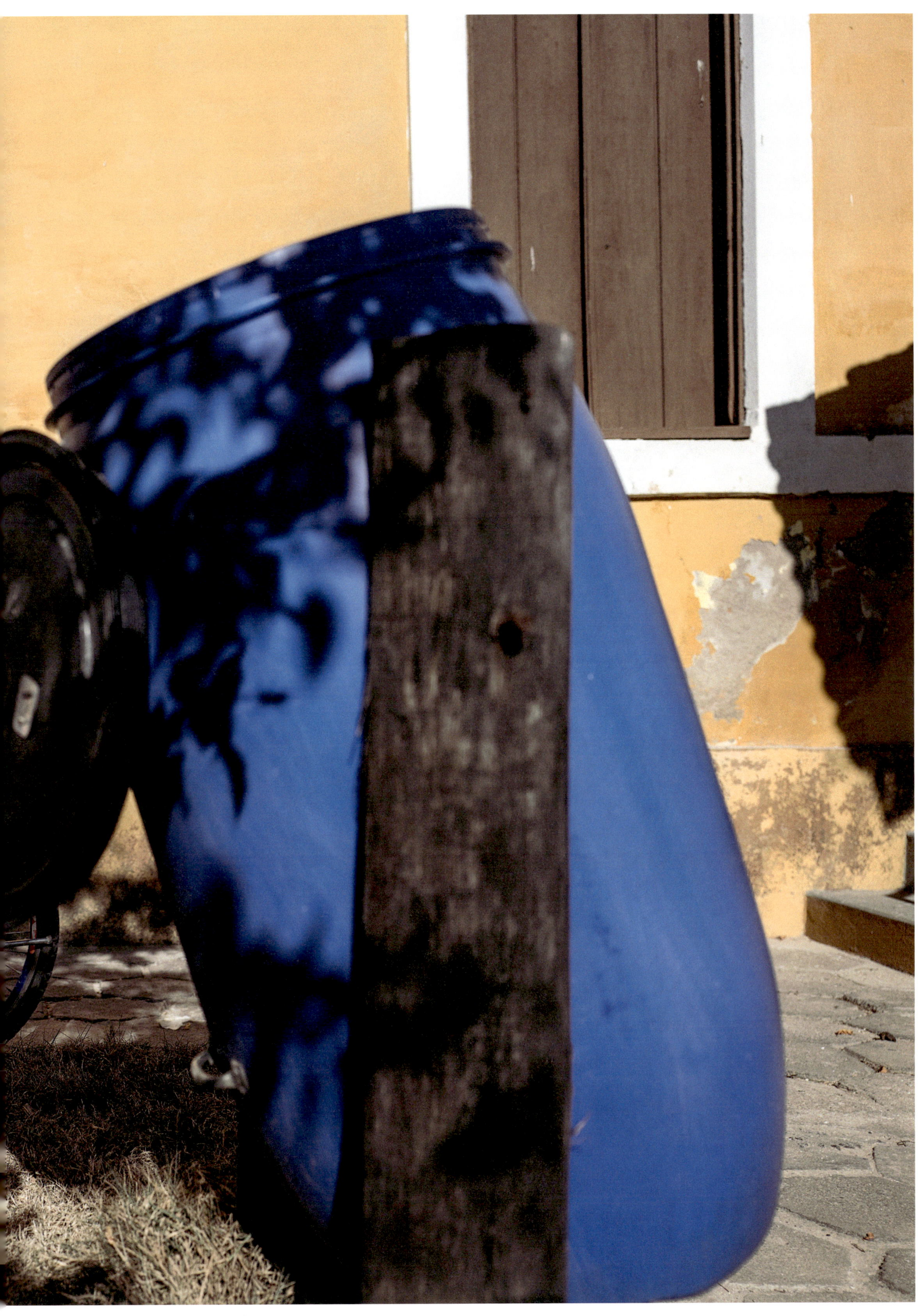

Umbanda is the root, the mother of all *orixás*.

The saints are the same as in the Catholic Church: Saint Sebastian is Oxossi; Saint George, Ogum; the Virgin Mary, Oxum; Saint Cosmas and Damian, sailors; the Pretos-Velhos ["Old Blacks"], Angola, Gegi, and Nagô. With *umbanda*, these saints support us in our work and do good deeds.

I'm very happy with this religion because it harms nobody. People are only against it because they don't understand or know anything about it. Because once they find out more, they no longer criticize it. *Umbanda* comes from Africa. Because Africa is the source of everything. I've worked with *umbanda* here in Helvécia for twenty-eight years.

Many people follow *umbanda* but in secret. They're prejudiced. *Umbanda* followers, evangelists, Catholics, they're all [prejudiced]. Because no one can choose what they like and what they want. They criticize others. I don't, because it's not worth it. But people like to gossip.

The evangelists criticize the Catholics, and *umbanda*. But there are also priests who say that it is about the Holy Spirit, who aren't against *umbanda*, and who sometimes have family who are [from the *umbanda* tradition]. And then there are others who criticize it, aren't there? Evangelism always causes the trouble, whoever's doing the talking. They say that we're deviants, that Catholics are devil worshippers. They find an image of a saint, and they want to destroy it because they say it doesn't exist. No one likes that.

I attend a Catholic church, I'm baptized, confirmed, and devoted. I'm very faithful. My children are all baptized. I attend Mass, I do my pilgrimage to Bom Jesus da Lapa. I am a faithful, practicing Catholic. And I look after my *orixás*. Mainly I'm faithful to God, to the *orixás*, and to the Catholic saints.

The evangelists who come here, they hide. They don't want to speak, but they still come. About three months ago, we had contact with two evangelists. We received them with open arms when they came. We opened our doors to them. They came here full of pain, worn out, defeated. Each body has its own type of work. And that work they do, preparing people's bodies, is about cleaning, a positive *ebo*. If there's an evil spirit, the bodies will come to take it, wherever you are. If you give your address, they'll come to look for the spirit at your home.

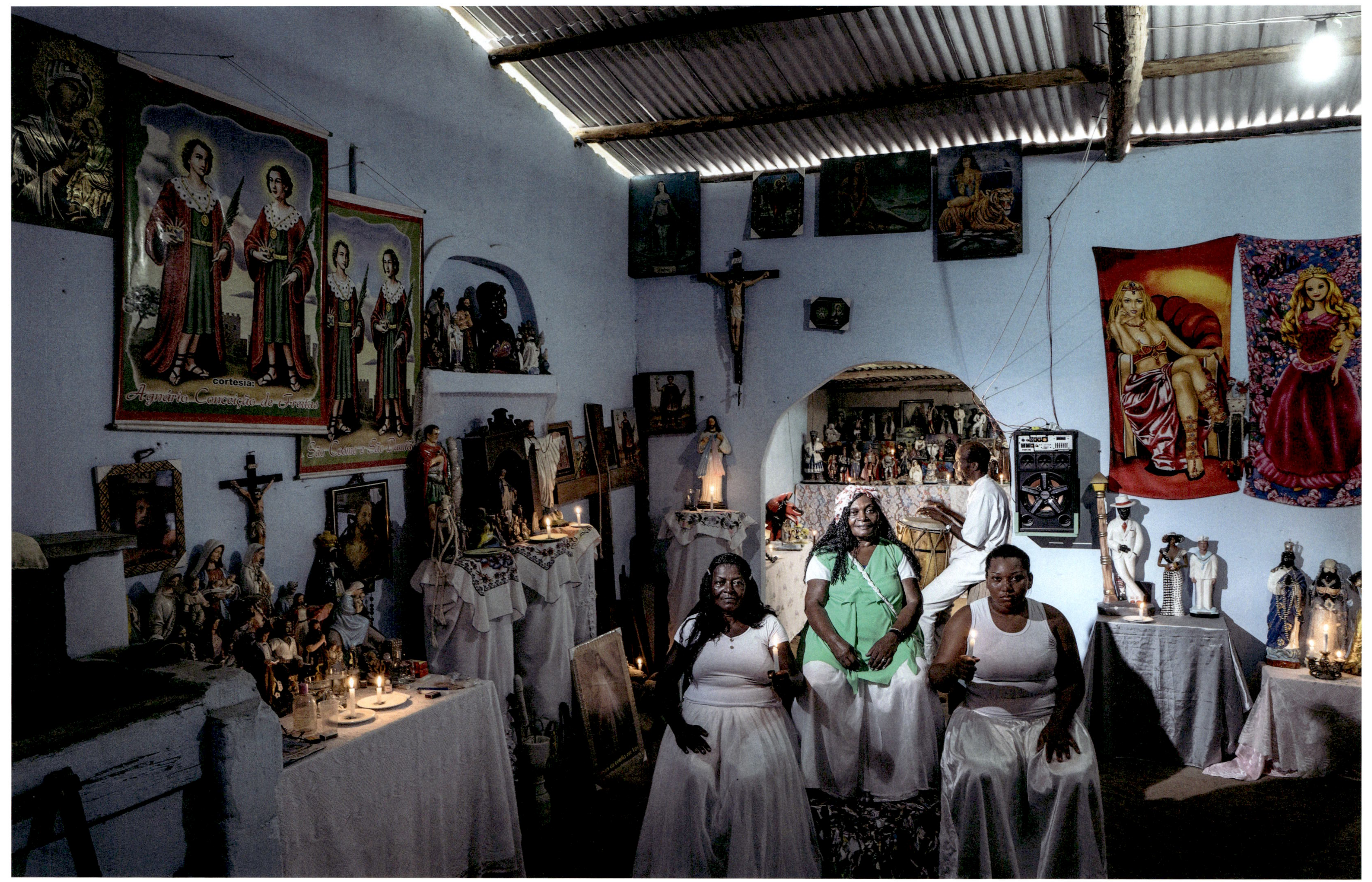

cortesia:
Aquário Conceição de Freitas
São Cosme e São Damião

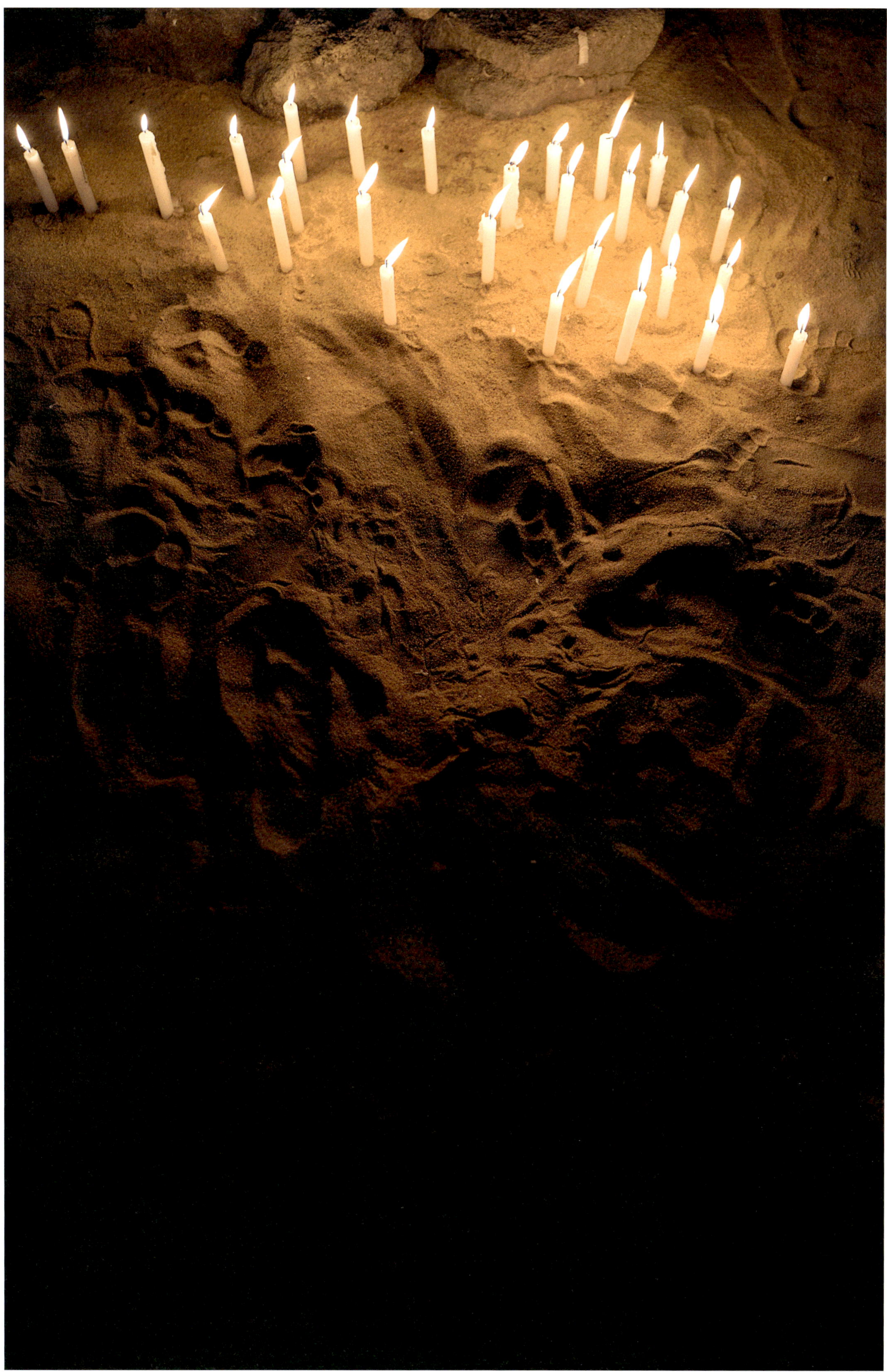

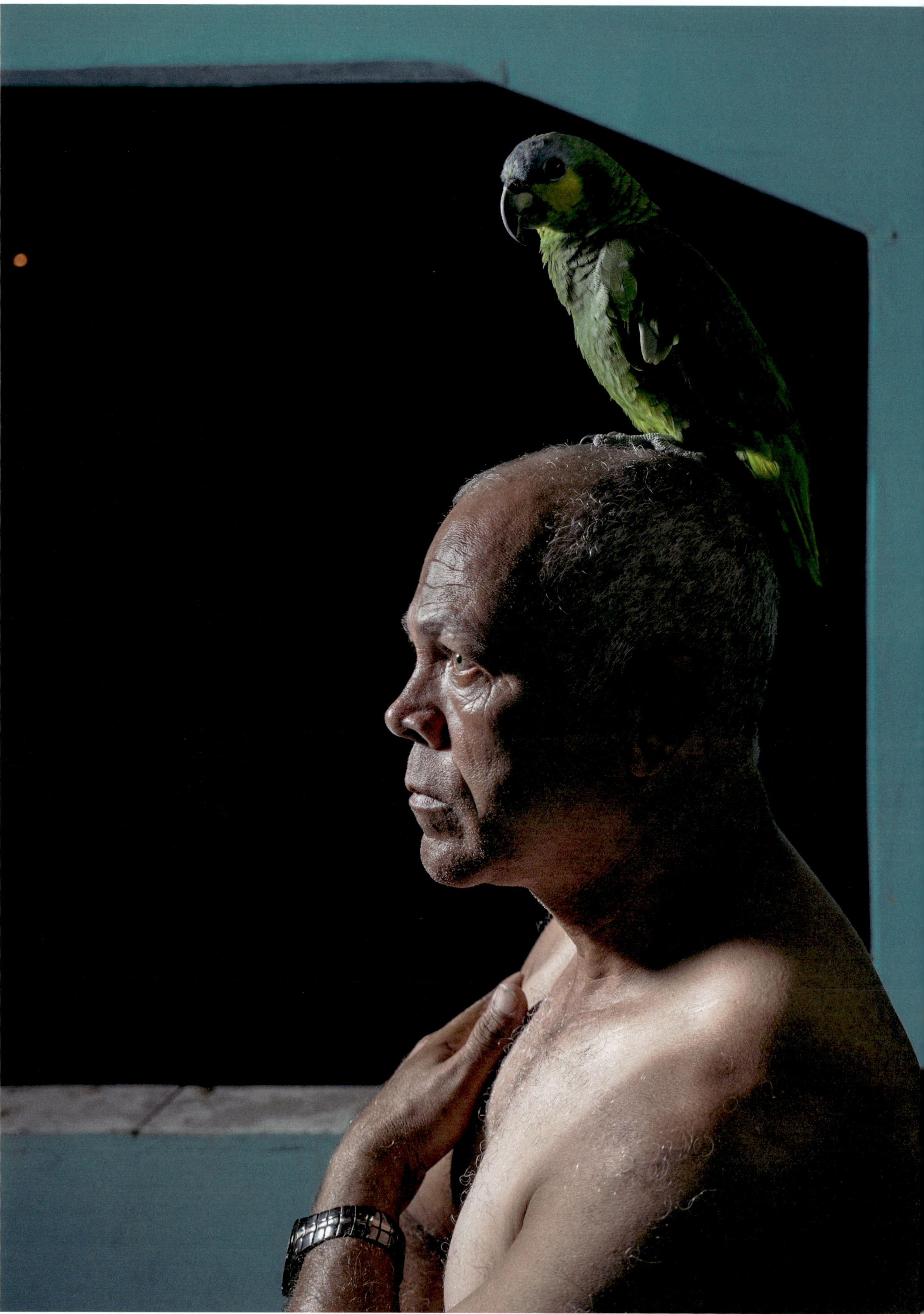

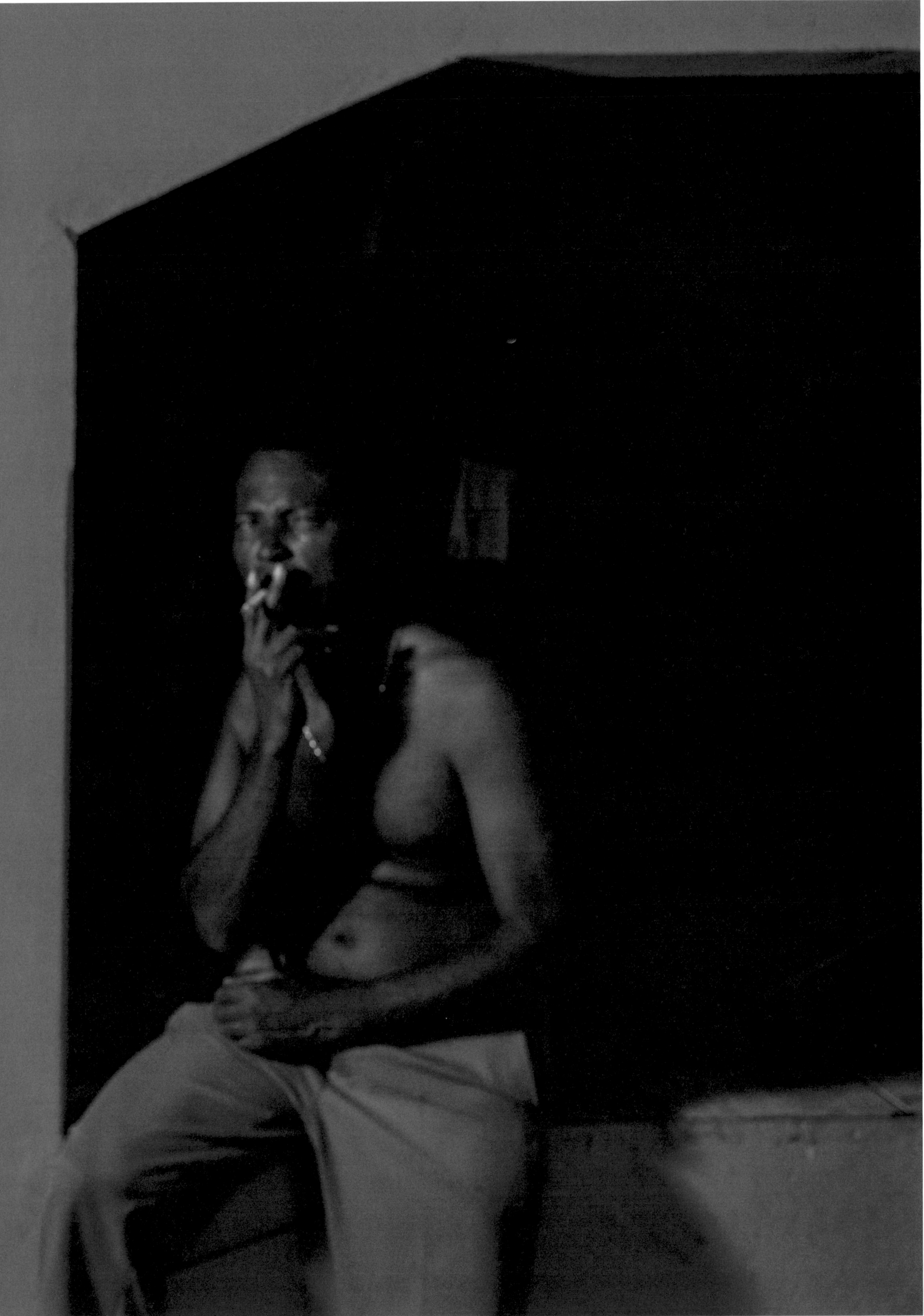

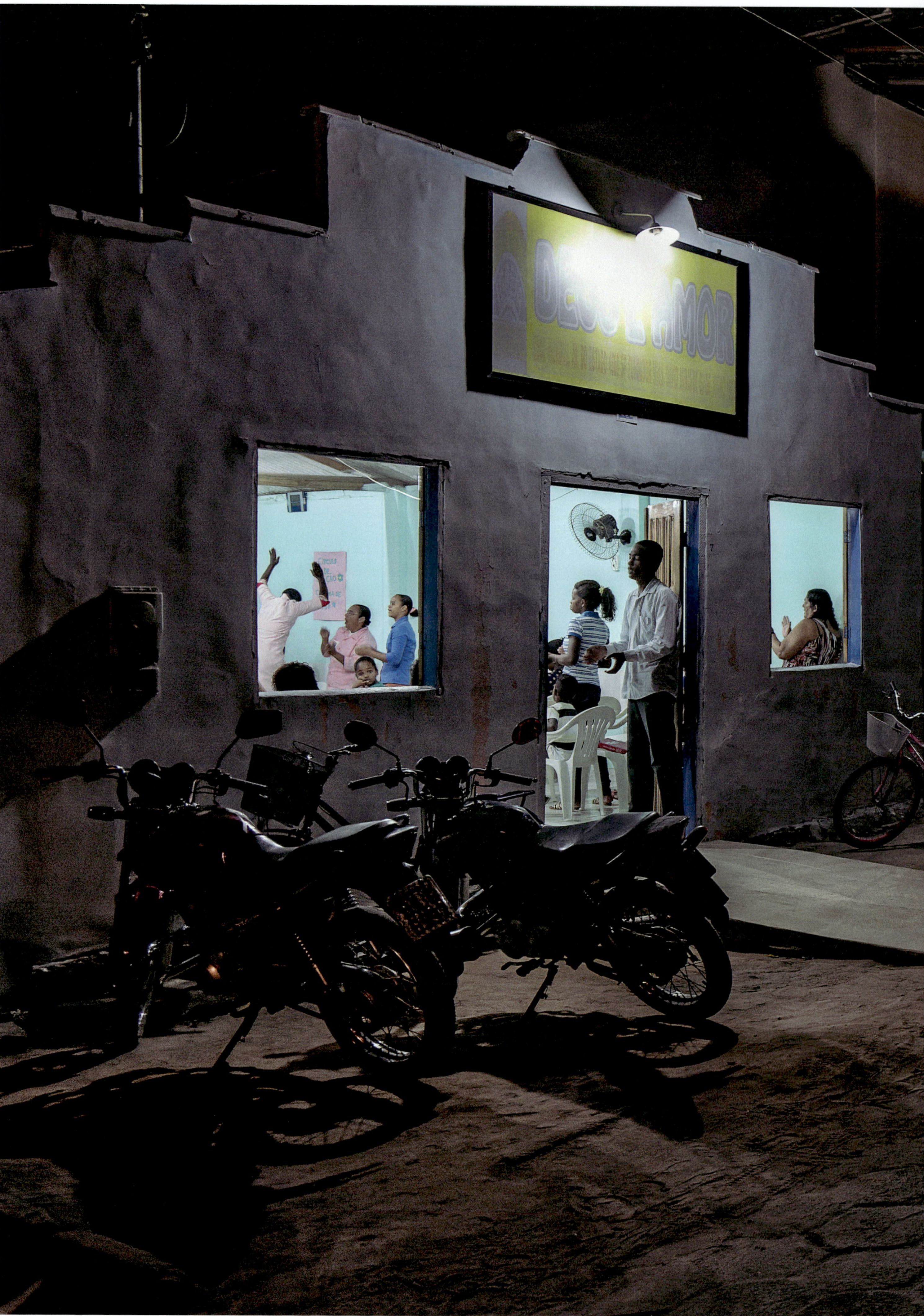

DEUS É AMOR

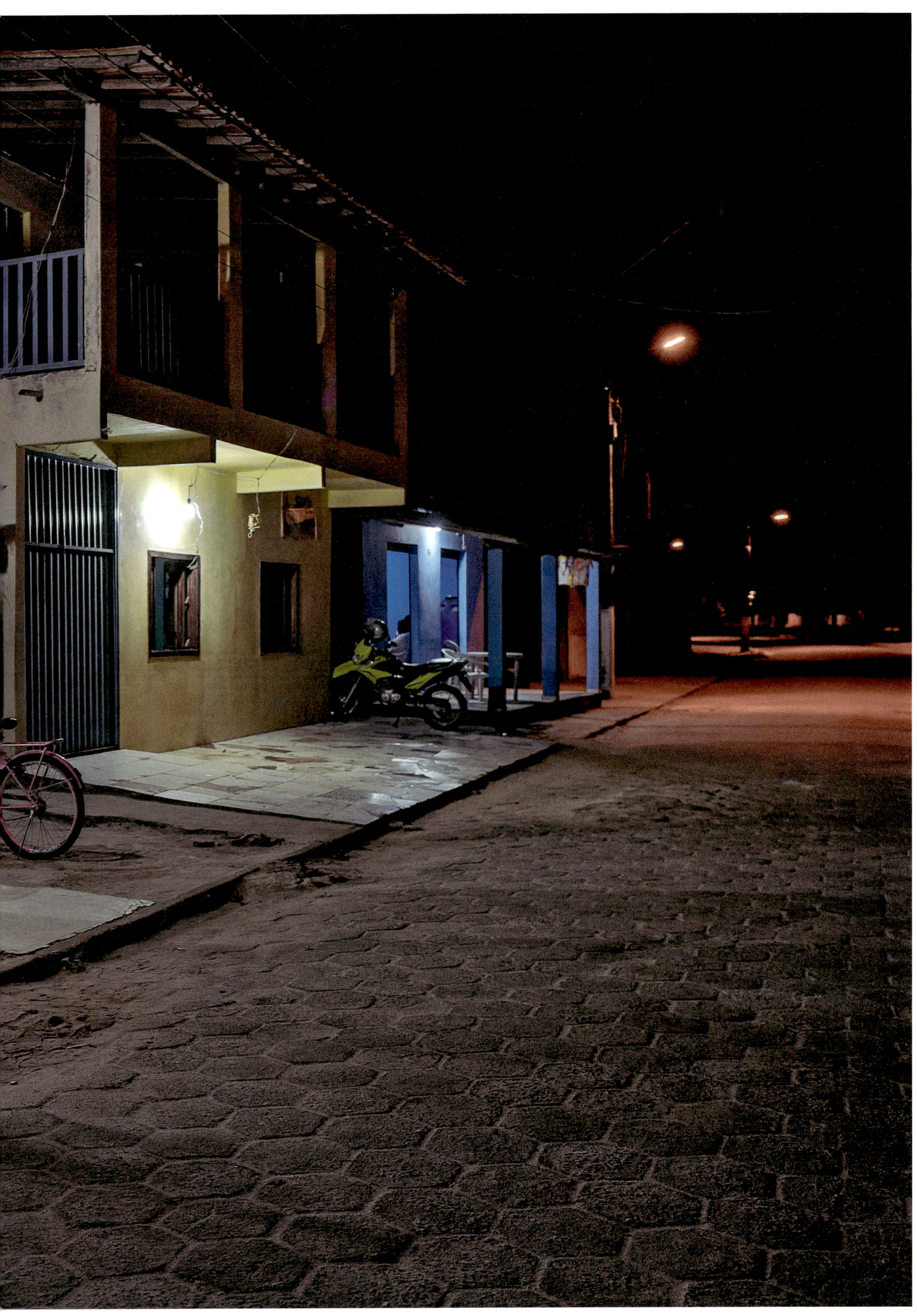

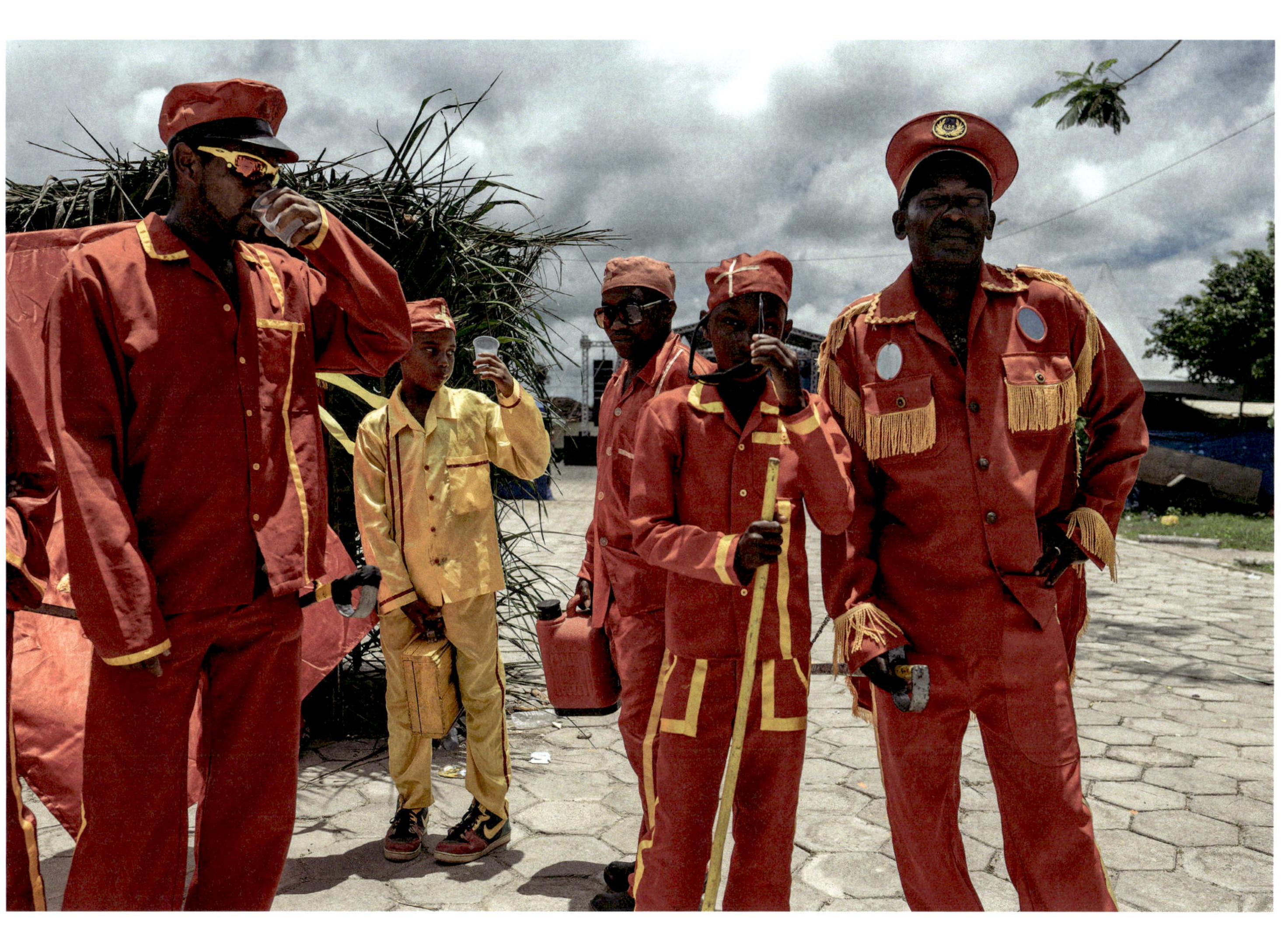

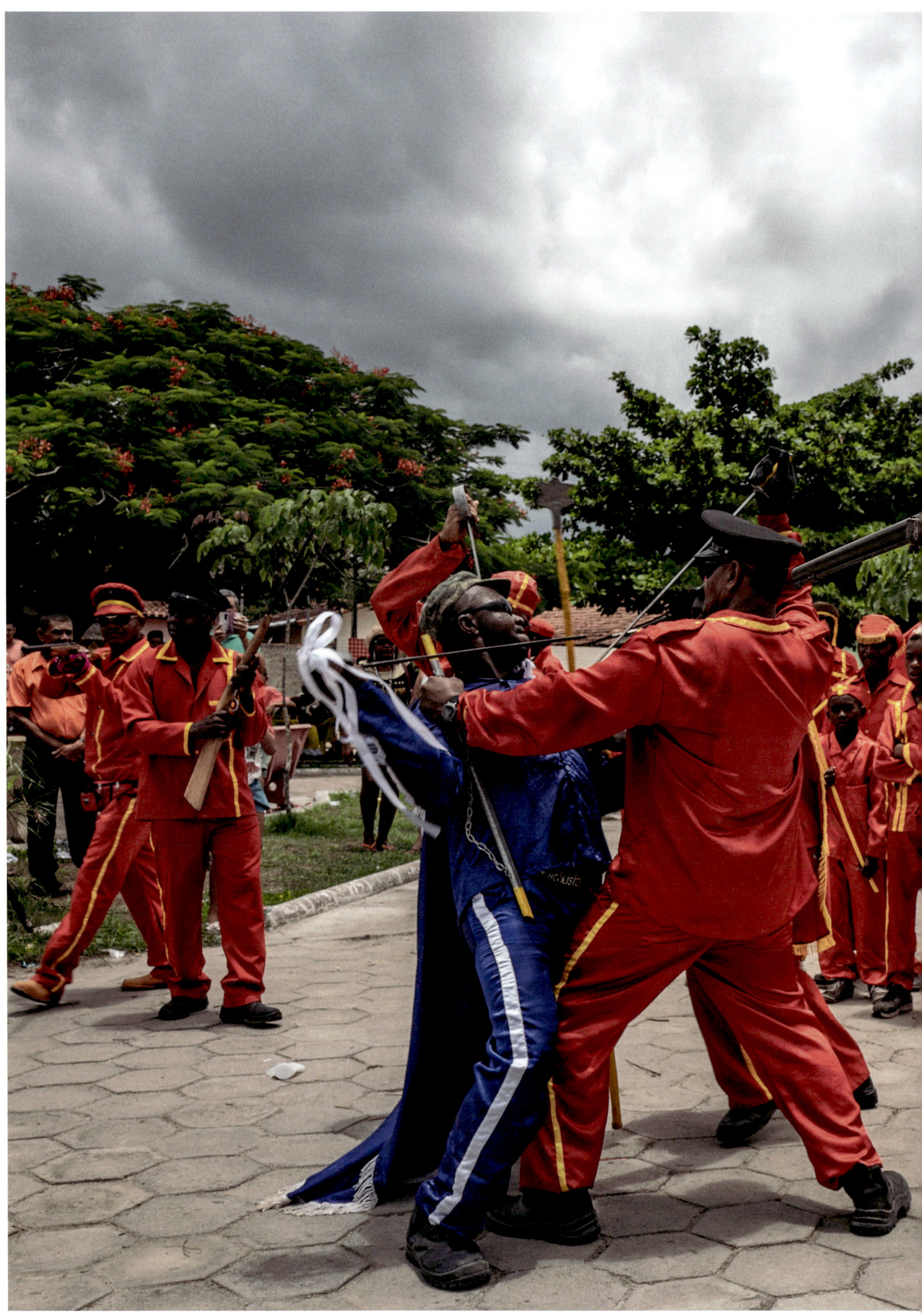

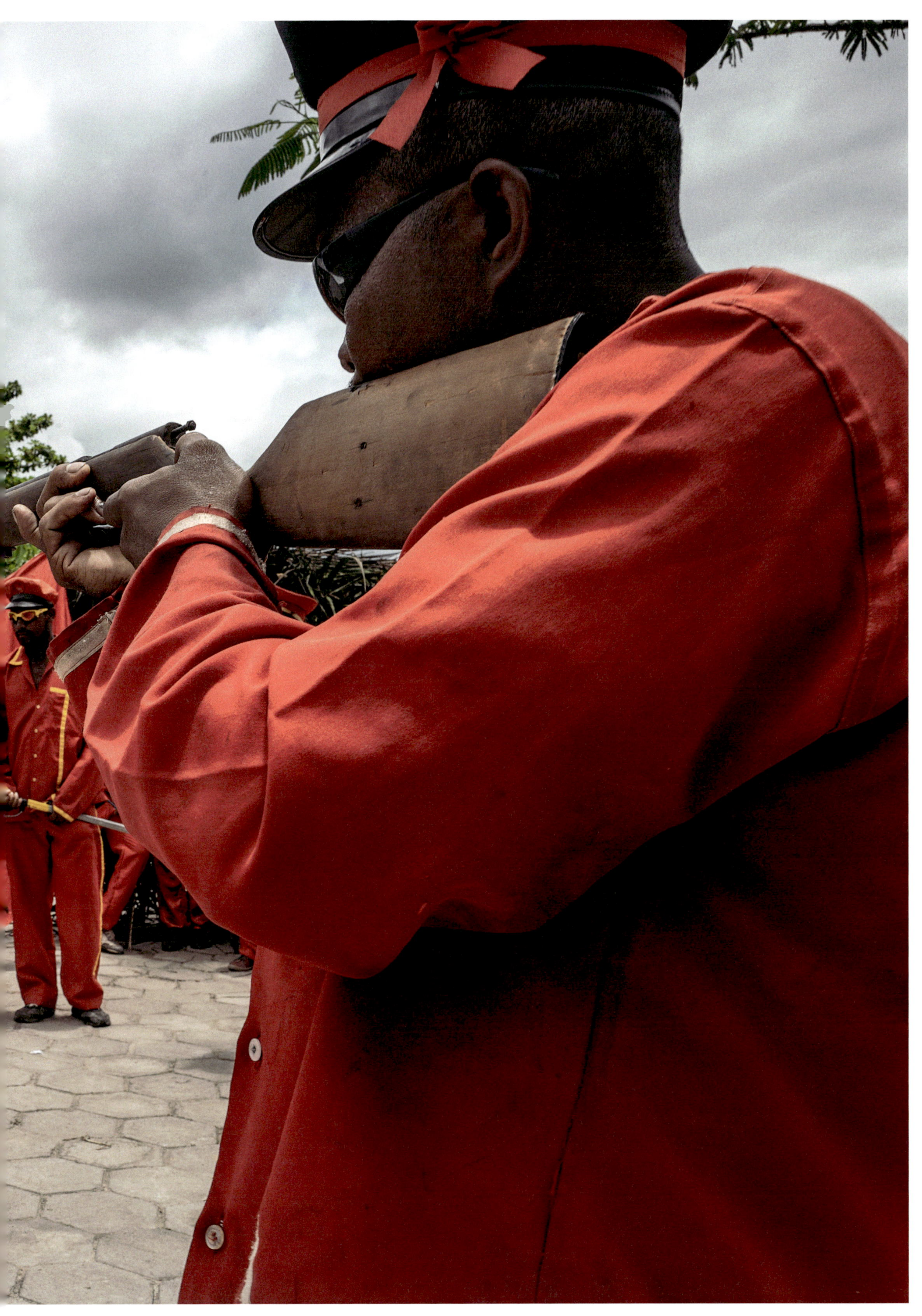

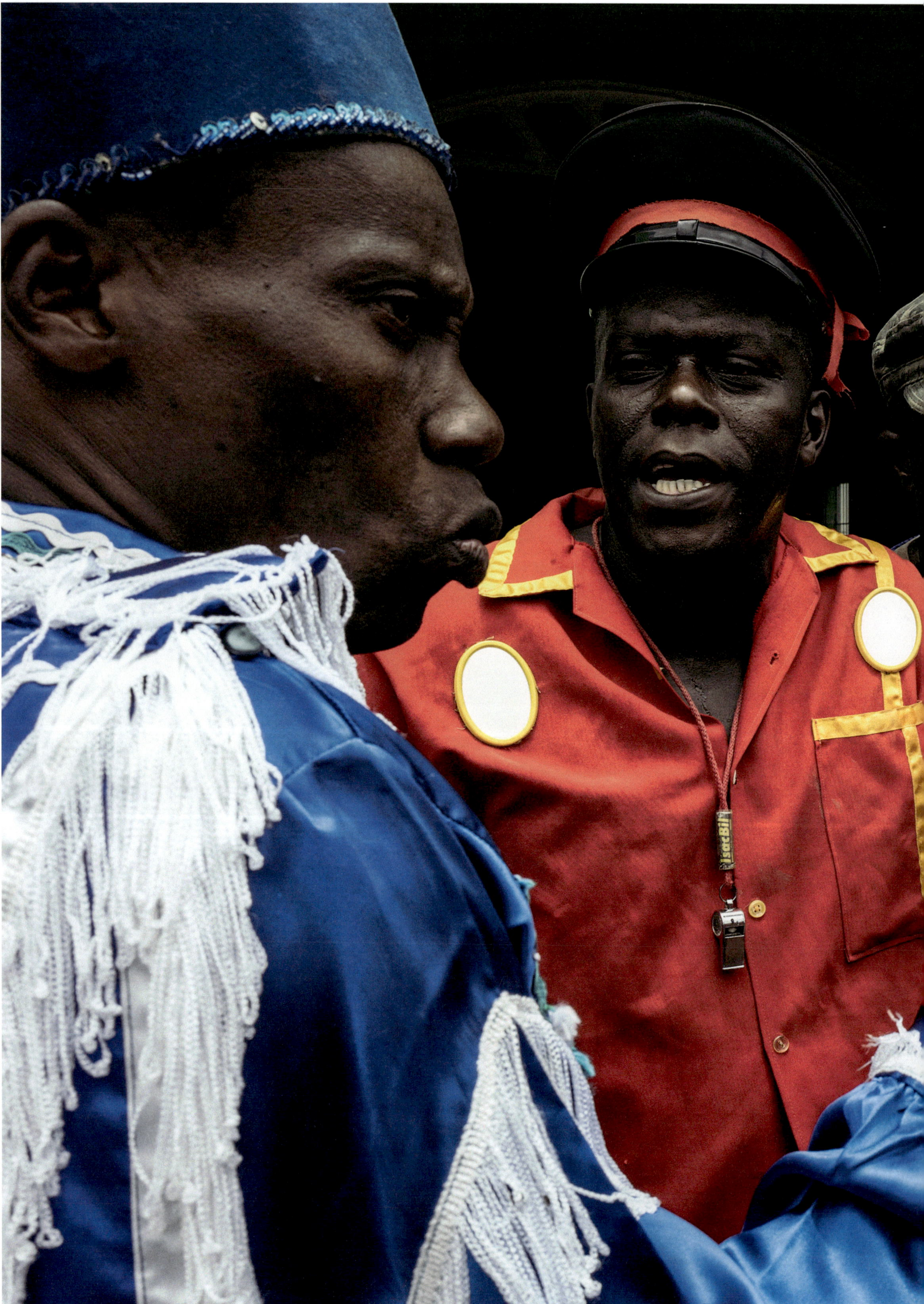

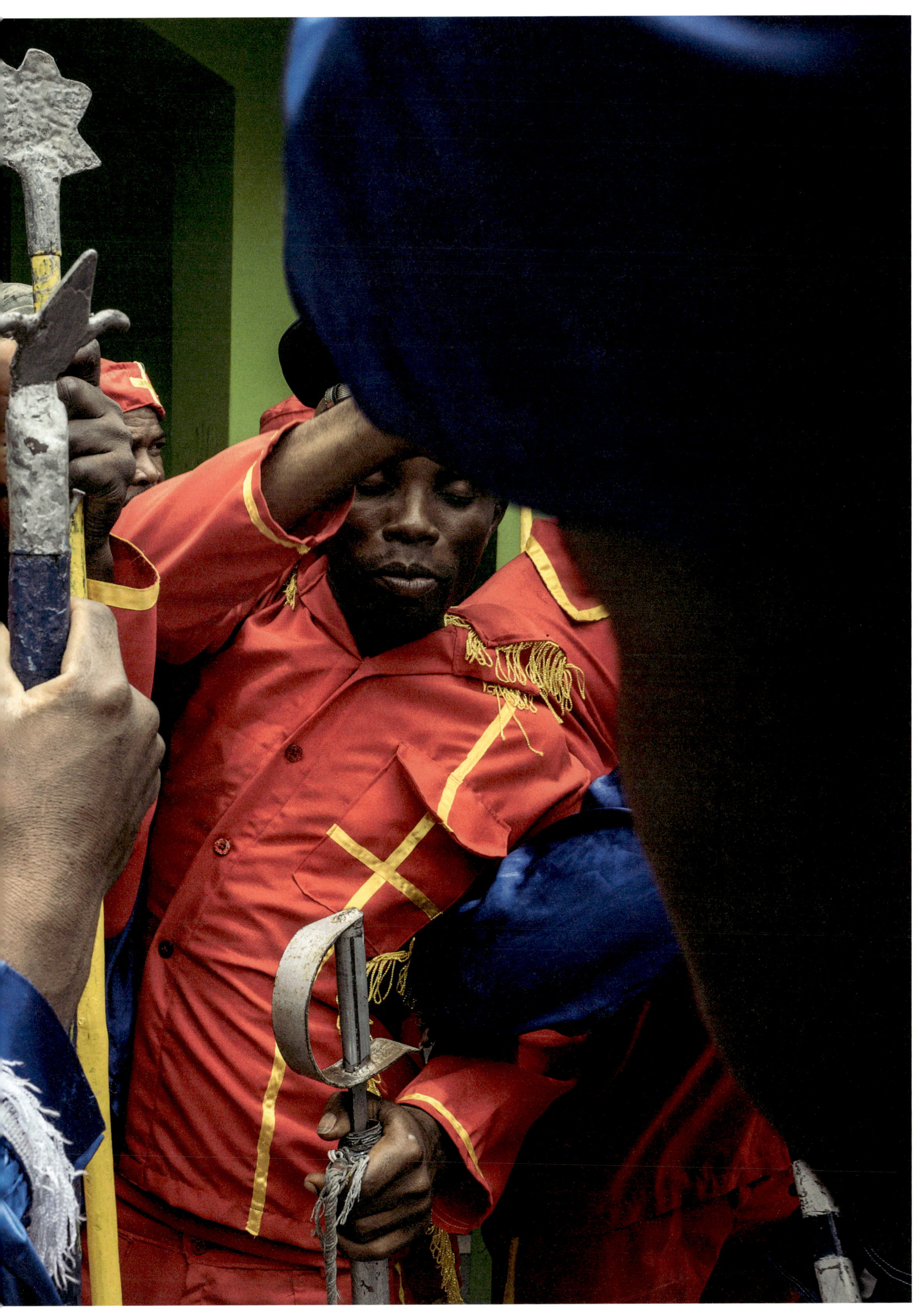

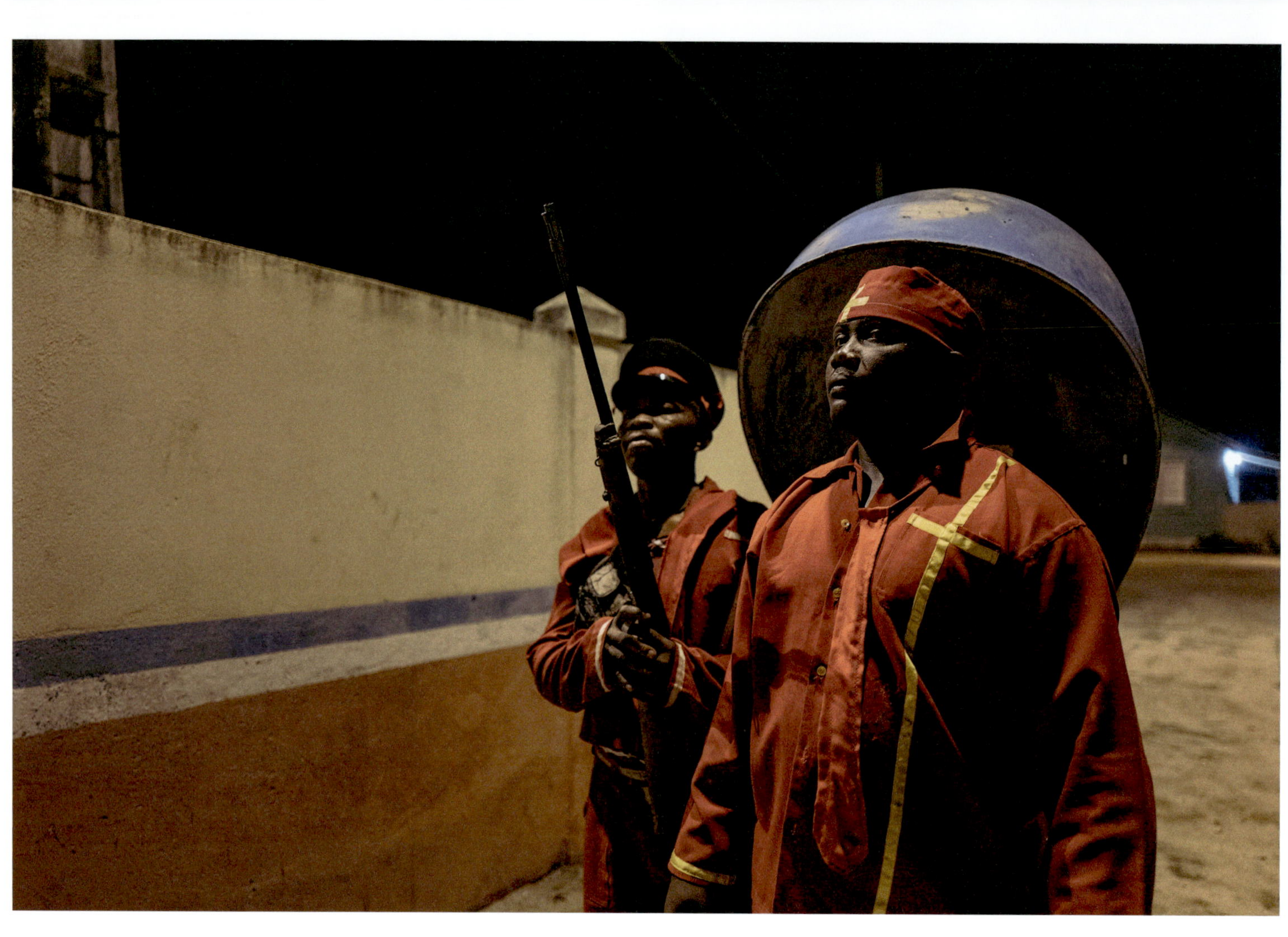

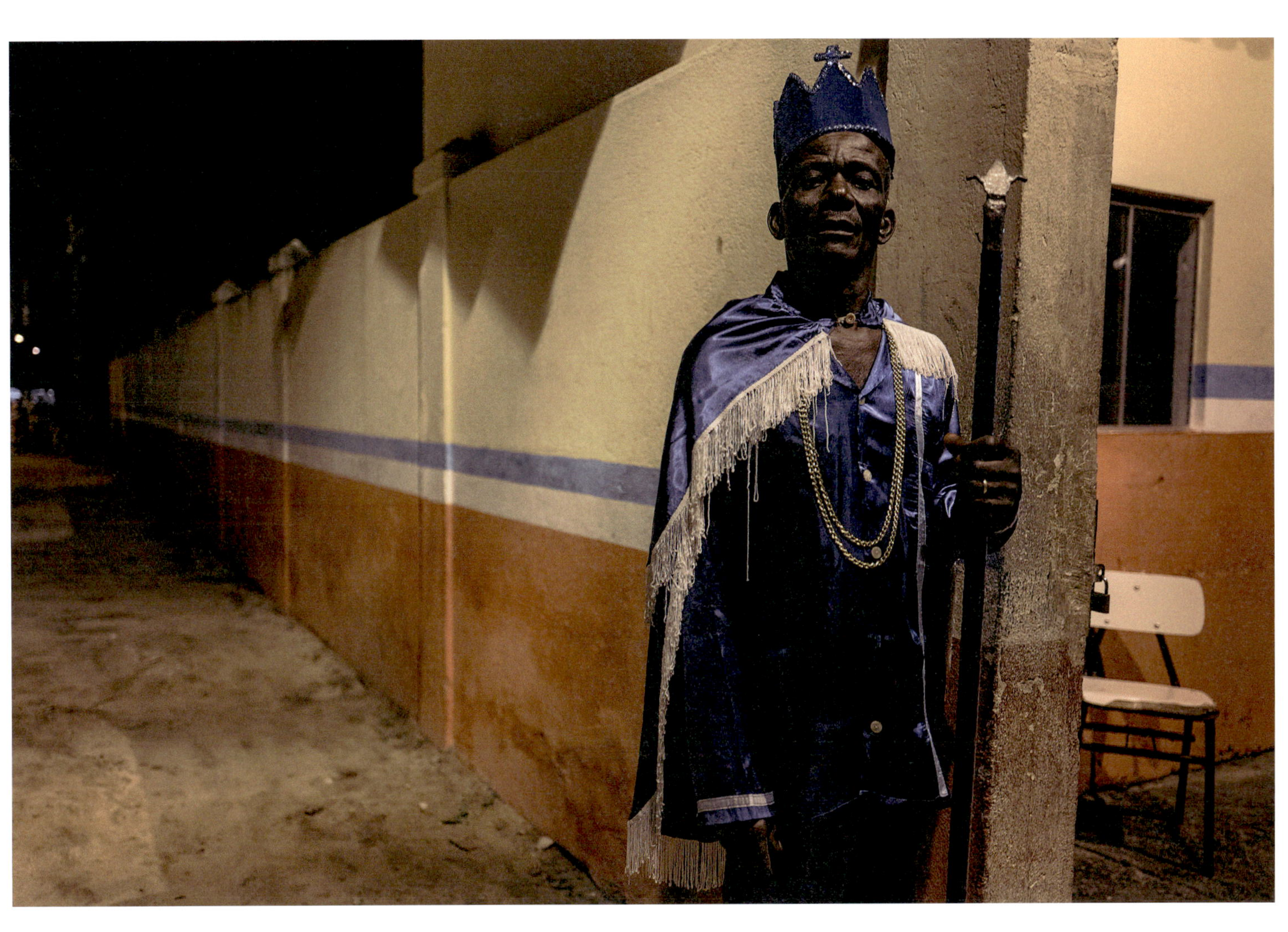

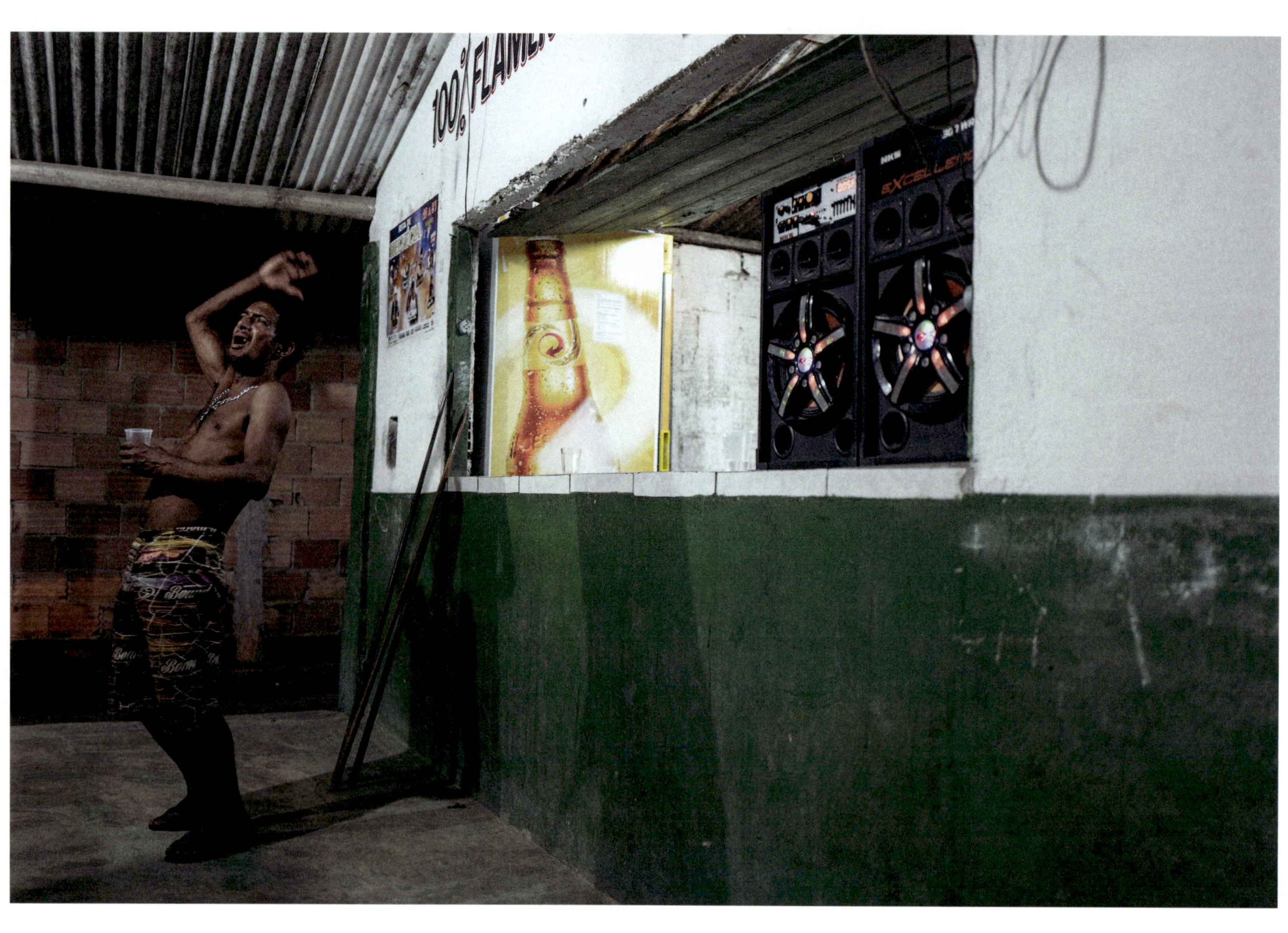

100% FLAME
EXCELLEN

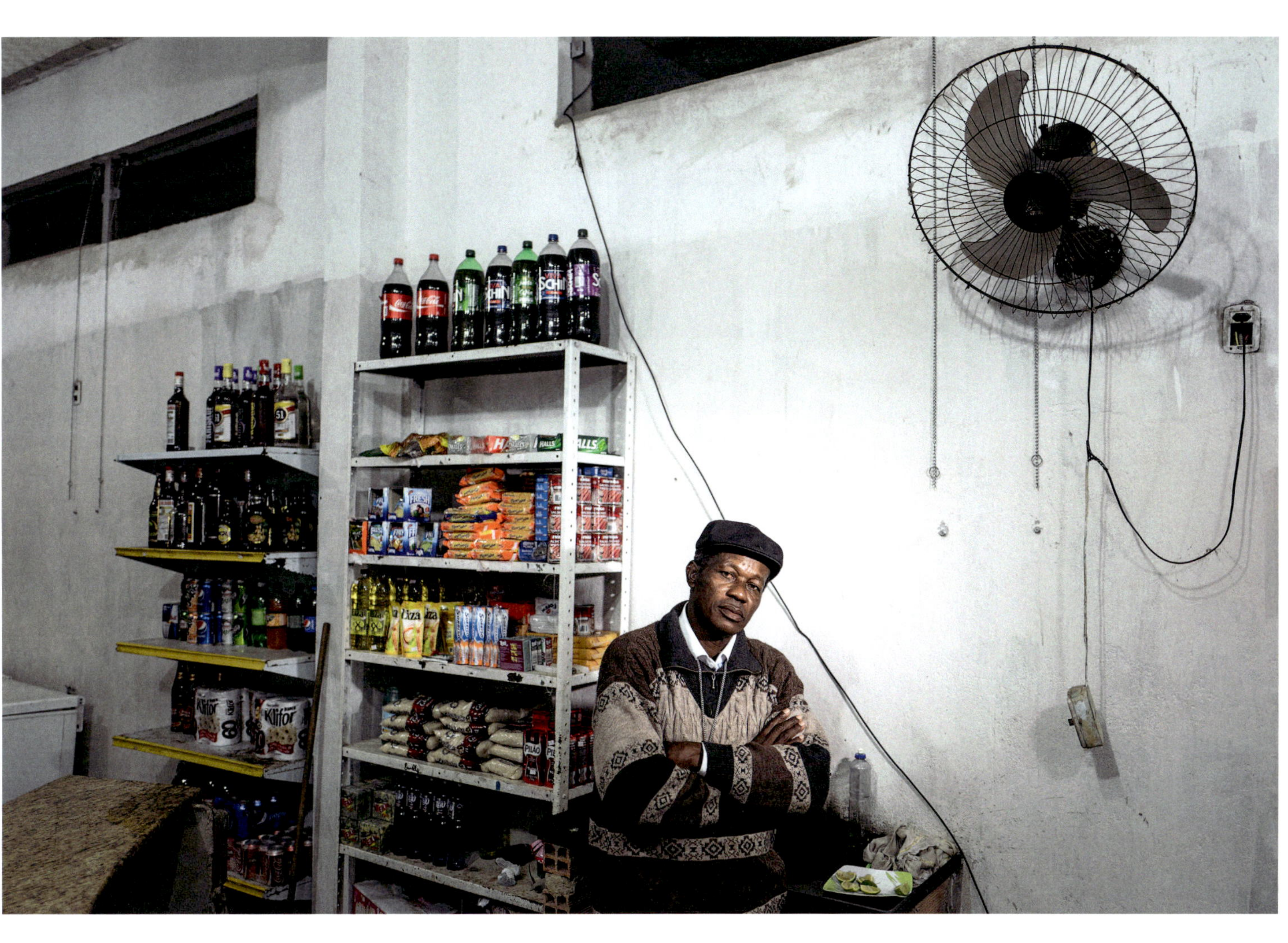

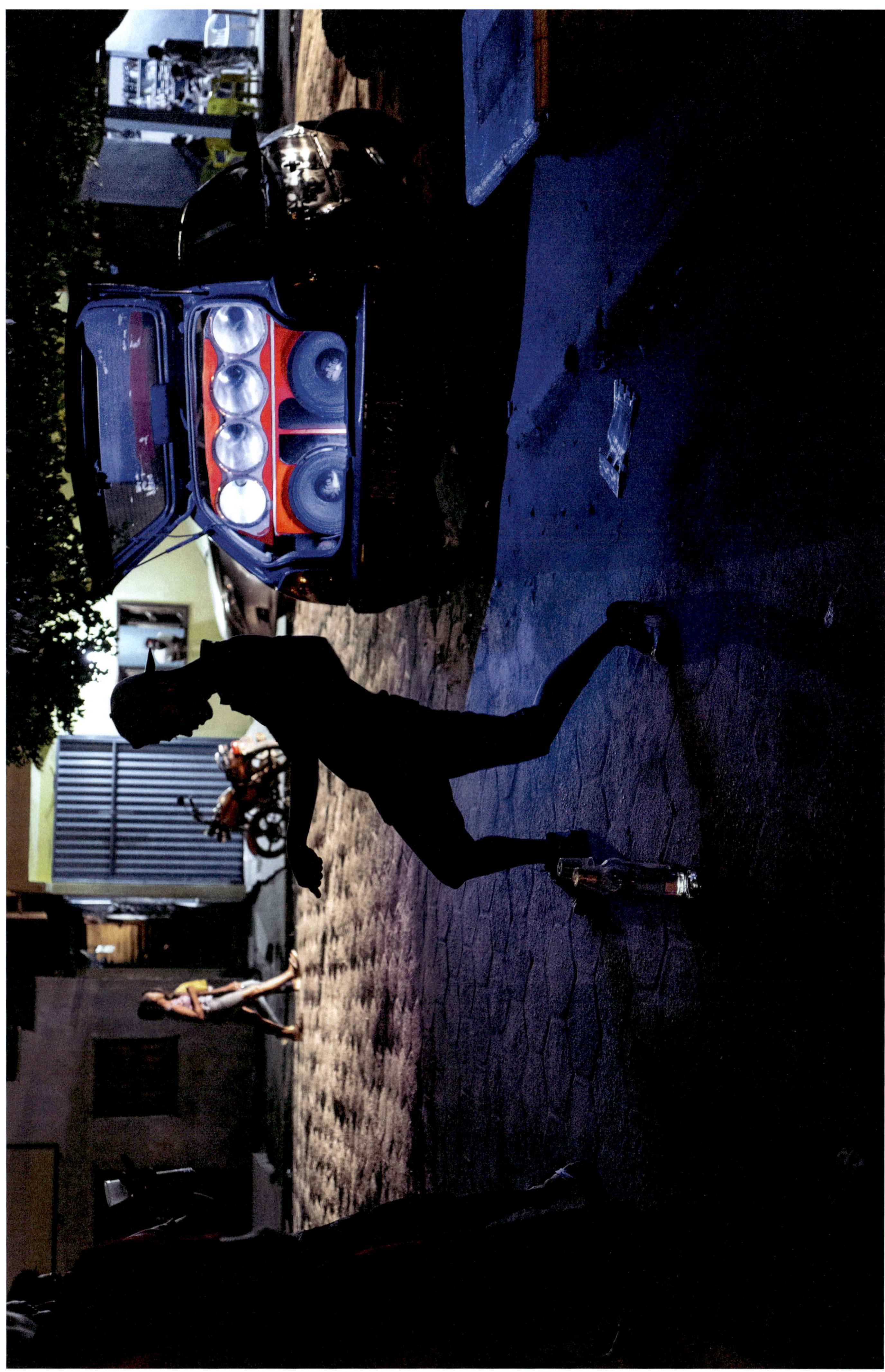

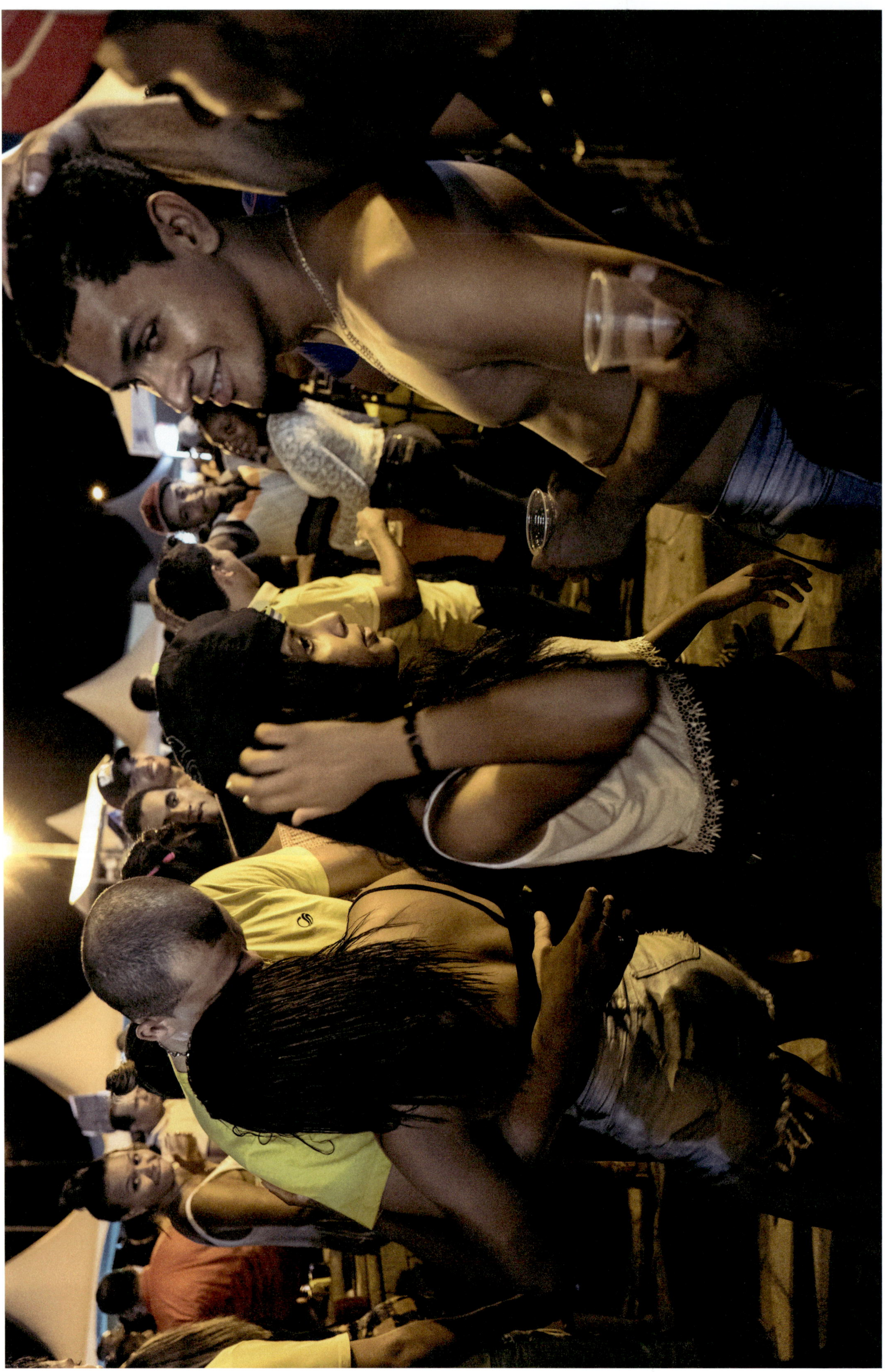

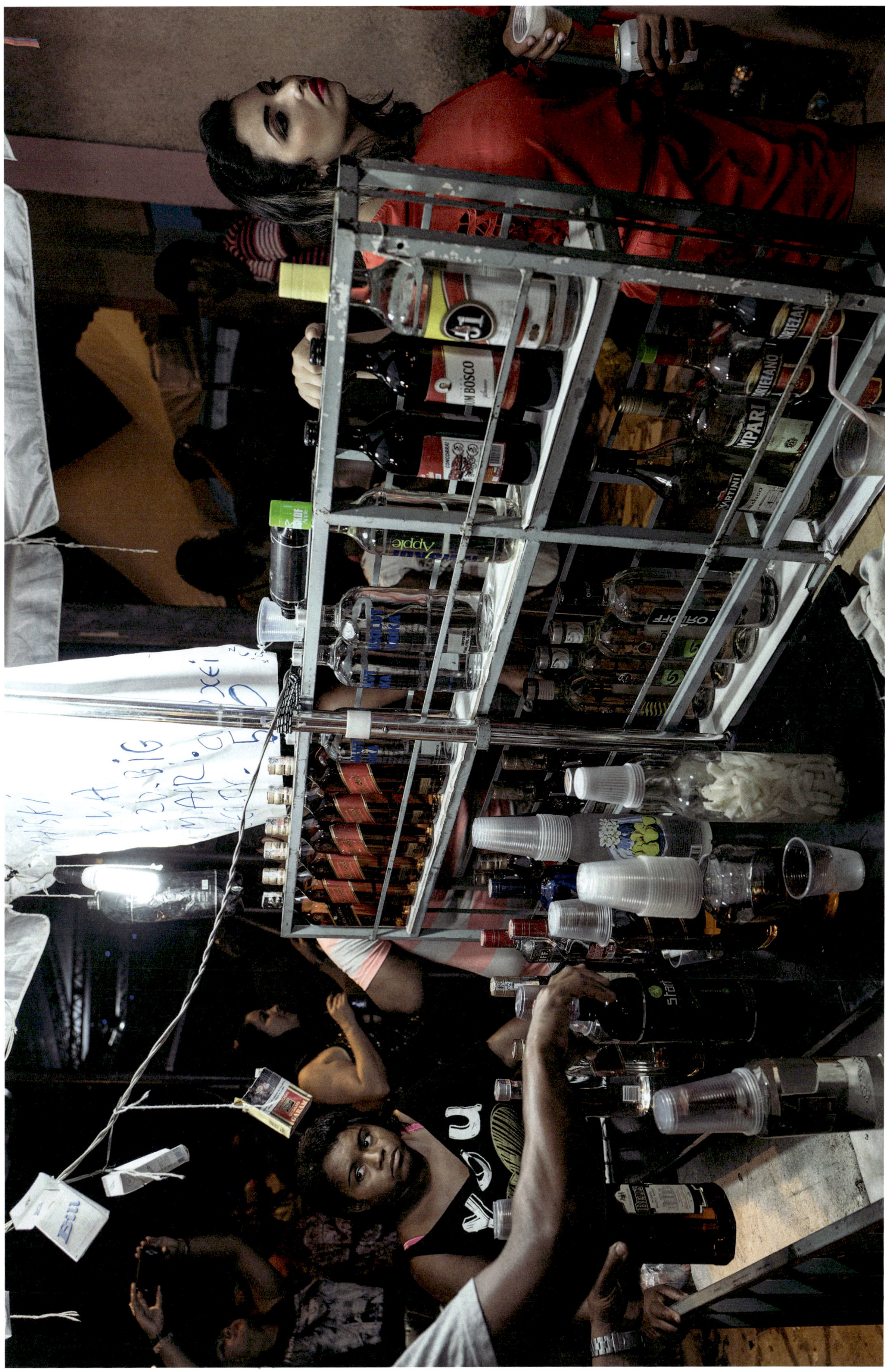

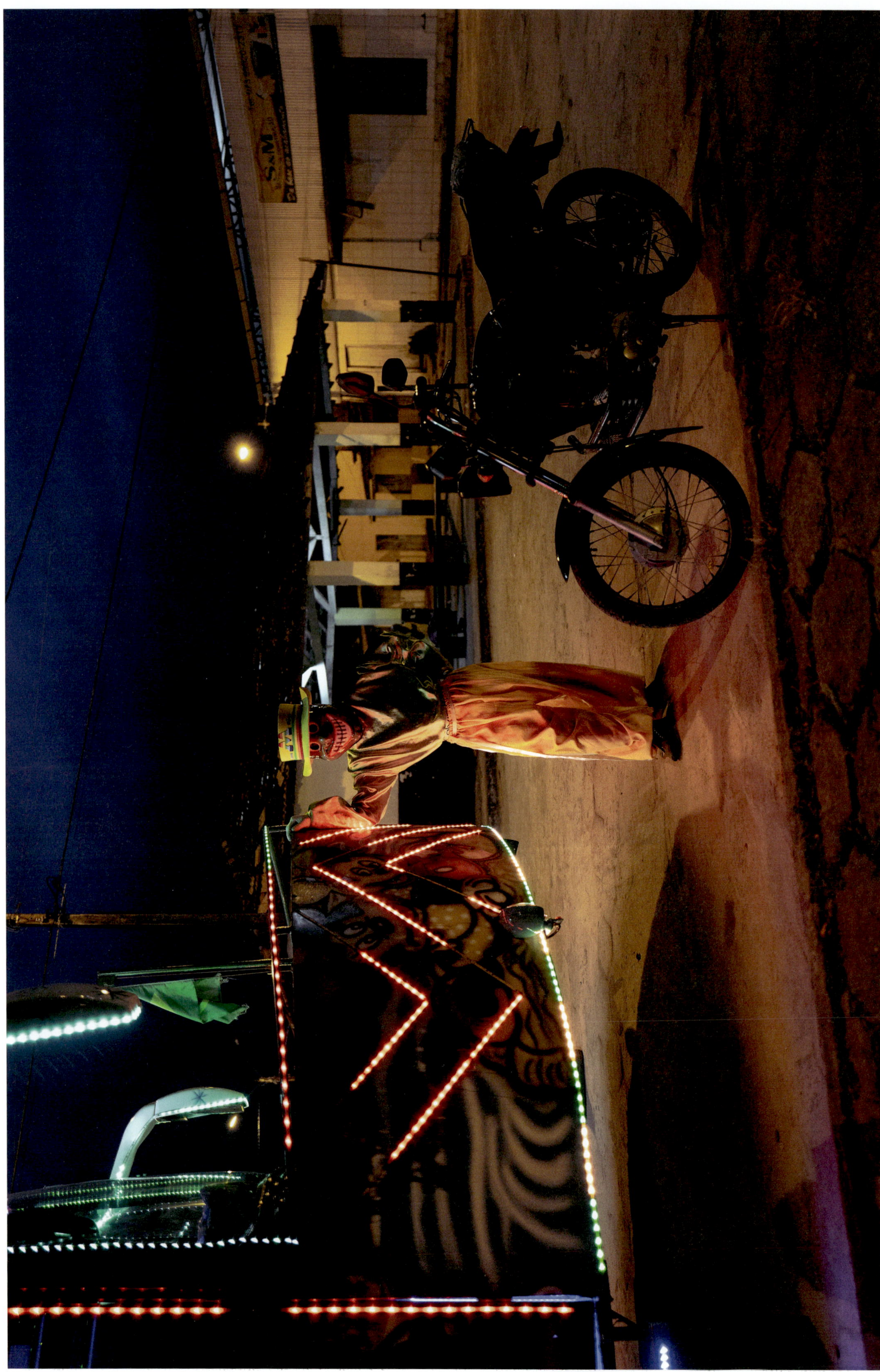

As far as I know, Helvécia had slavery for many years. Even after abolition with the Golden Law, slavery continued in Helvécia. It was only a few years later that the slaves here learned that they were free. A priest came to celebrate mass and saw that there was still slavery. The plantation owners took fright and, unlike the Blacks, the settlers fled and the Blacks remained.

We've felt that need to study our history in more depth and to set up a *quilombo*. We aren't the ones who fled; it was the settlers who fled and we kept hold of the land. We wrote a letter to the Fundação Zumbi dos Palmares,[1] signed by many community members. With this historical background, the Foundation realized that Helvécia needed to be recognized as a *quilombo*. Because a *quilombo* is a place for fugitive slaves, and Helvécia didn't have that status.

In the beginning, when Helvécia was recognized as a *quilombo*, it was tricky because the community wasn't sure what this meant. Even I didn't really understand. But since I have the same blood and share the same genes of this race, I picked up the courage to go with the flow and say: "I'm a part of this!" If it helps out my community, then I'm all in. The community itself was terrified, thinking that slavery was coming back to Helvécia. Some people wanted to sign a petition to reject the association. Tensions ran so high that we even received a death threat. Since I was young, I could still hide in the folds of the women's dresses. But over time, the community have come to understand that it wasn't like that at all and saw the benefits: young people getting into college, enrolling at federal universities that had previously been out of their reach, and receiving study grants.

The museum had a large collection of objects. Some old objects like a wolf trap, known as a trap for slaves. Slaves who ran away through the jungle were caught in the trap, breaking their legs. The trap has disappeared. We don't know where it is. The same with the old rifles, a phonograph, and other antique items that disappeared after the building's renovation.

One day I saw a Black African preacher, who was giving sermons in Helvécia against the whole Black movement. He preached so rudely, in the village square. He said that the Blacks were a curse on Brazil because they had brought over *macumba*,[2] sorcery… I looked at him and thought, my god, a Black man, from Africa, has come to a *quilombo* community in Brazil, to say this in the middle of the square. I let him have his say and finish his sermon. But as soon as I picked up the microphone – because we were about to conduct an Afro mass – I repeated what he had been preaching and told him that the next time he came to Helvécia's town square

to talk about that, I, as the association's chairman, would sue him for showing such disrespect toward us. Brazil, and the entire world, would be much better off if there was respect between religions.

The Saint Sebastian festivities represent the struggle between Moors and Christians. The Moors are dressed in red, the Christians in blue. In that era, the Christians persecuted Saint Sebastian, who was a Moor but later converted to Christianity. After the celebrations, all the Moors make their way to the Church door and become converted. They kneel down before the image of Christ, of the Virgin Mary, and of Saint Sebastian, to be converted. These festivities for Saint Sebastian help us stay strong in our faith and in our daily struggles.

We set up a council with Fibria[3] and we are working on a project to rescue lost cultures, working with the young to teach them. The council organized a gathering for the community once per month in order to avoid losing our culture. Because we know that there is no such thing as a community without an identity. It exists, but… no one will come to visit it if there's nothing to say about it.

The old cemetery had a gravestone for one of Helvécia's founders, a certain "John Flachs." I don't know if it was really just a memorial or if he was really buried there, because there's no proof. It is written somewhere that it is his tomb. One day a truck came and stole almost everything from the cemetery: the marble gravestones, the crosses. No one knows where the loot all ended up.

Sometimes Helvécia's history contradicts itself and becomes lost in the passing of time. We're left to wonder about the real history.

1　Fundação Palmares is the federal body in charge of issuing certifications to give legal recognition to communities and their lands that are linked to former *quilombos*. This certificate gives the community the benefit of receiving direct social aid, and also guarantees definitive ownership of their lands.

2　Originally, *macumba* designated the location where Black people celebrated their rituals. Today, it has become a generic term to describe all kinds of African-Brazilian religions, and for some people it has perjorative connotations.

3　Fibria is a multinational corporation and leading global producer of cellulose, with a strong local presence.

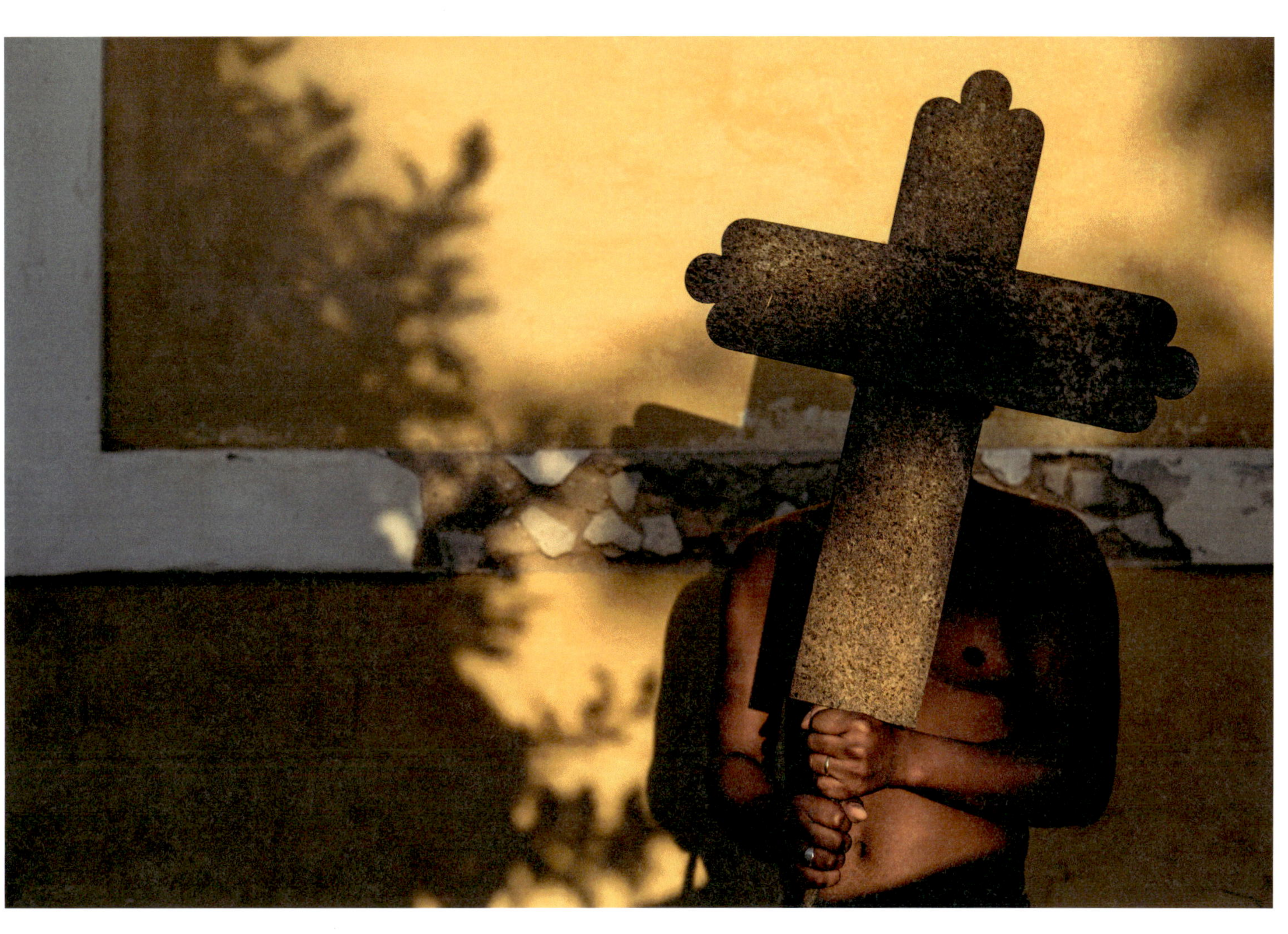

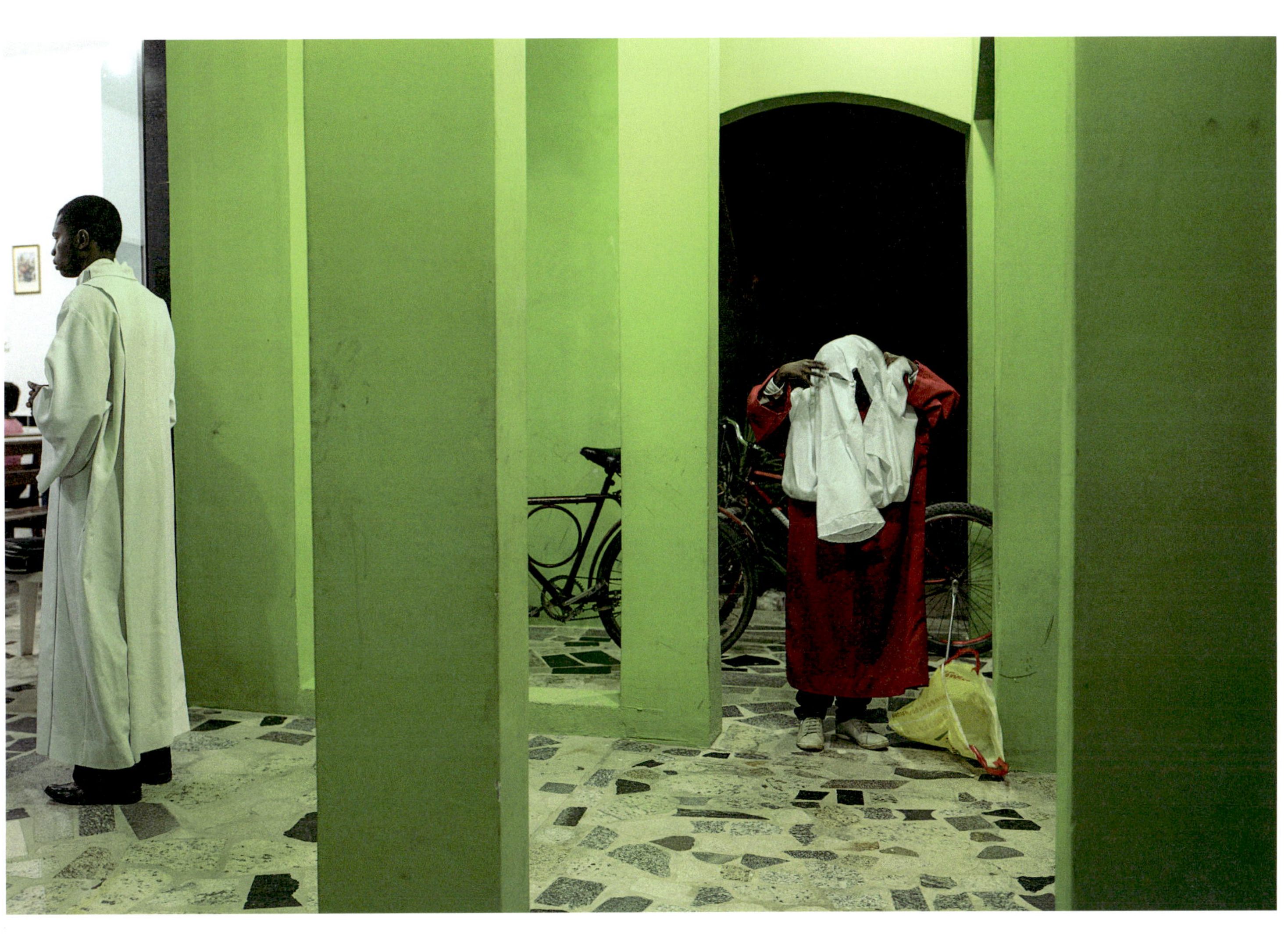

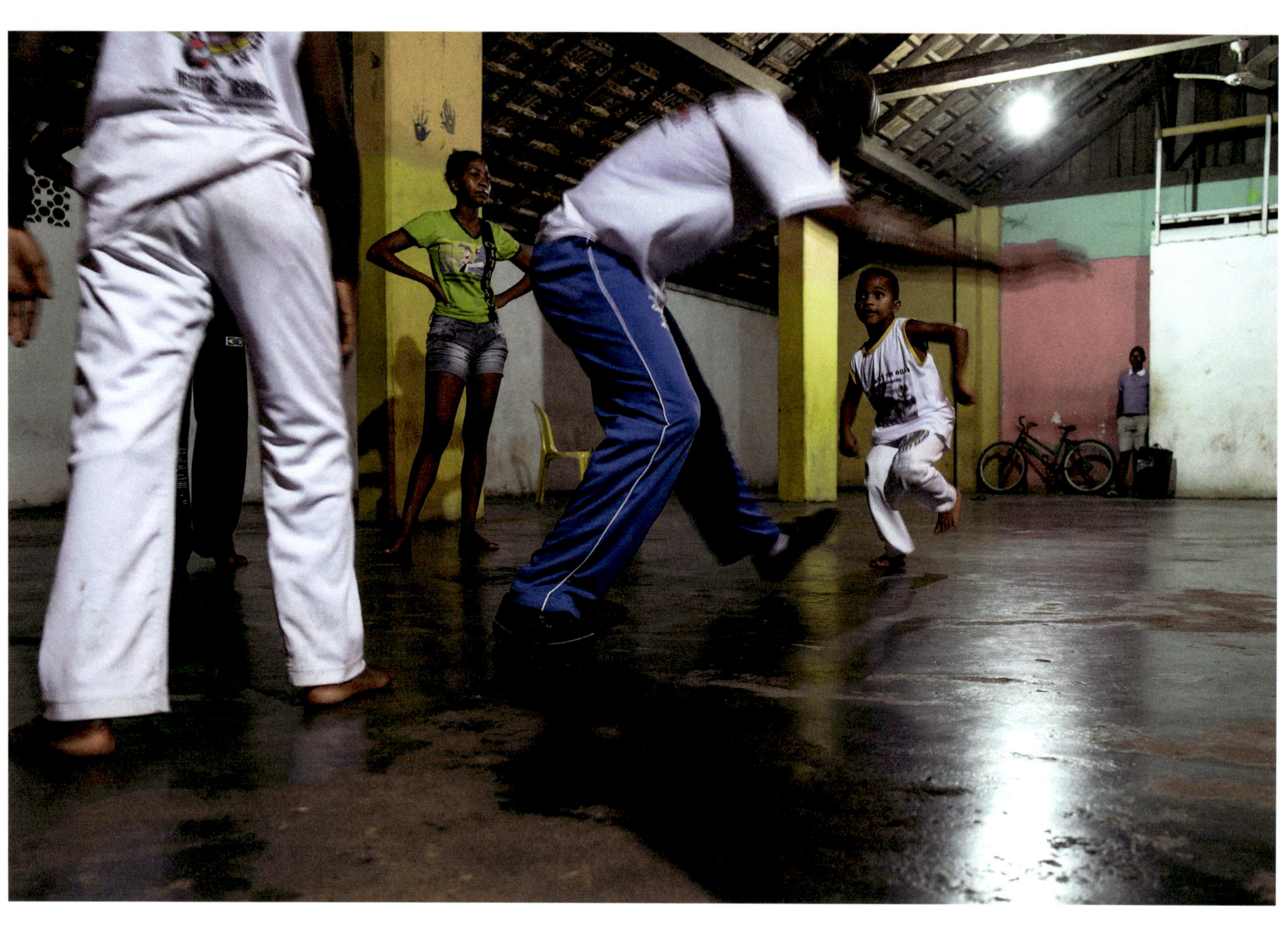

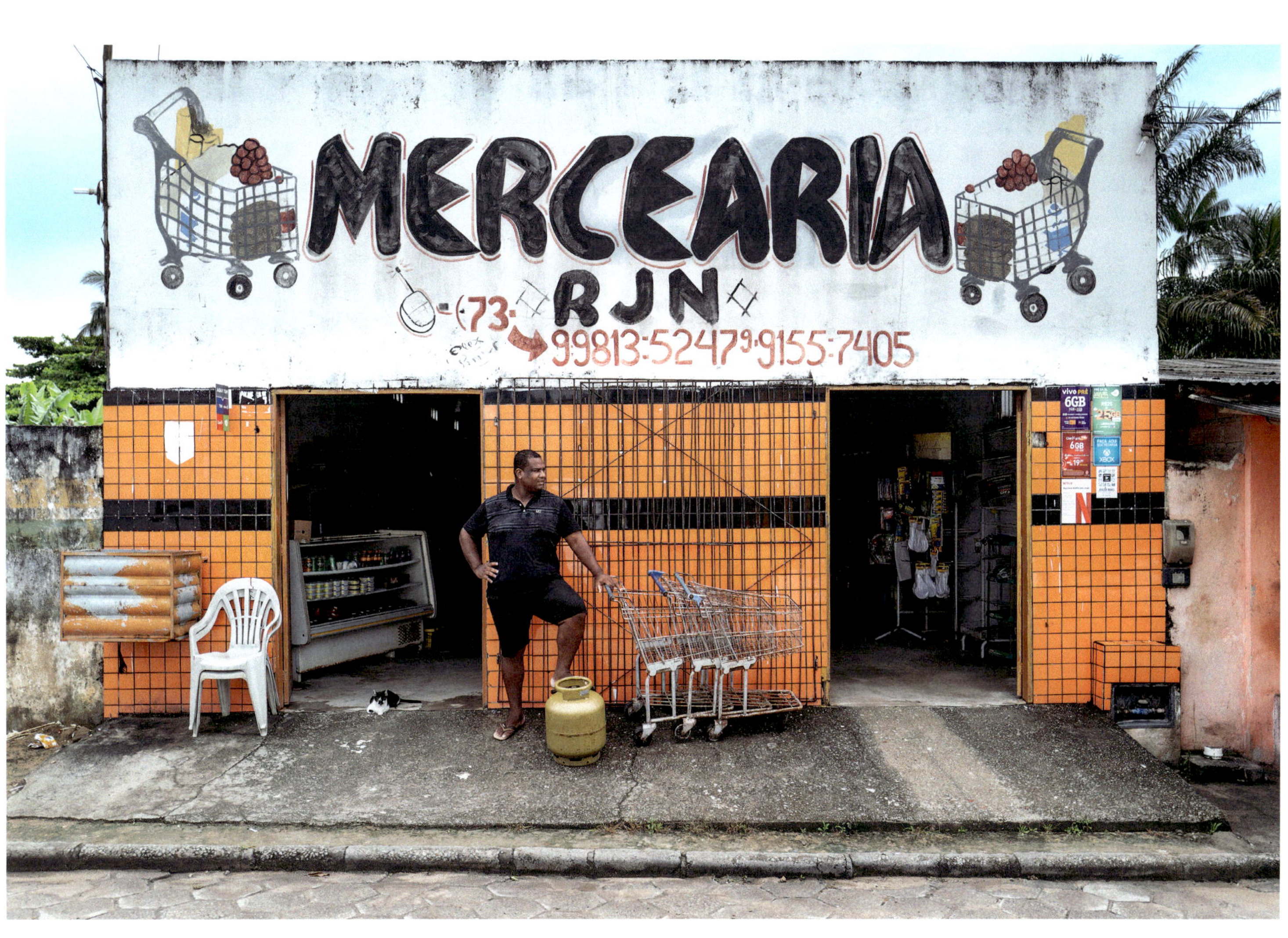

MERCEARIA
RJN
(73-99813-5247 9155-7405

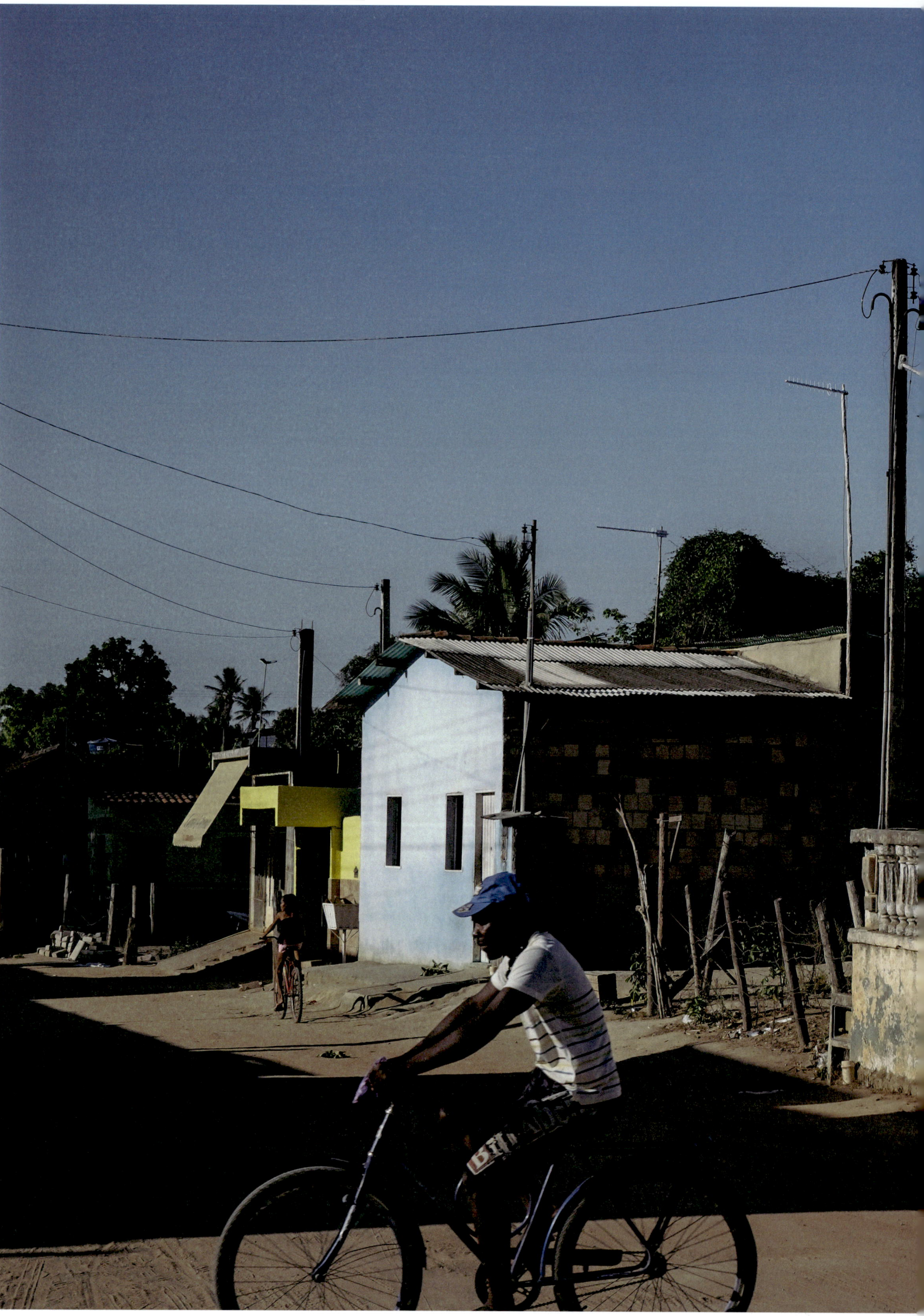

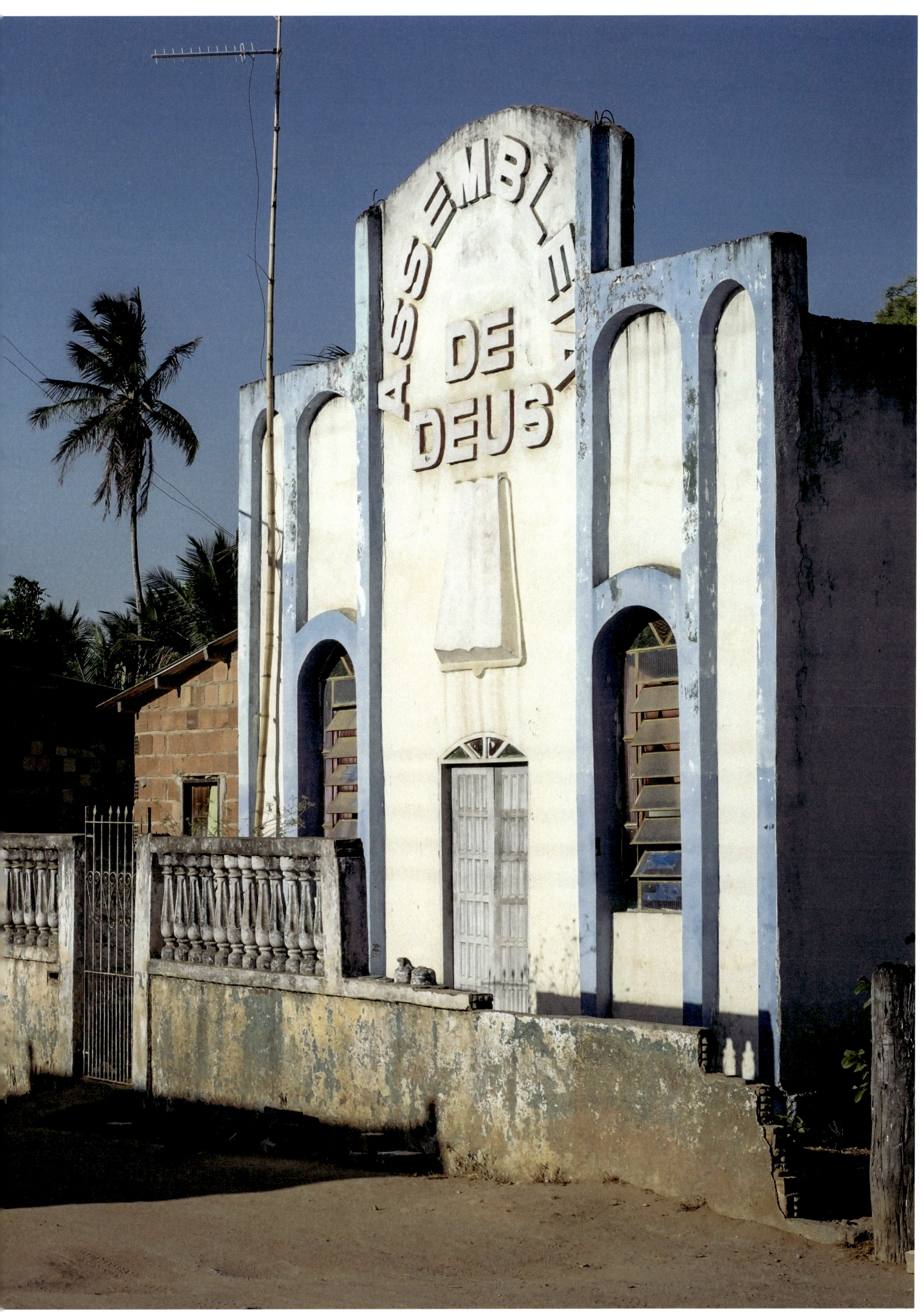

ASSEMBLEIA
DE
DEUS

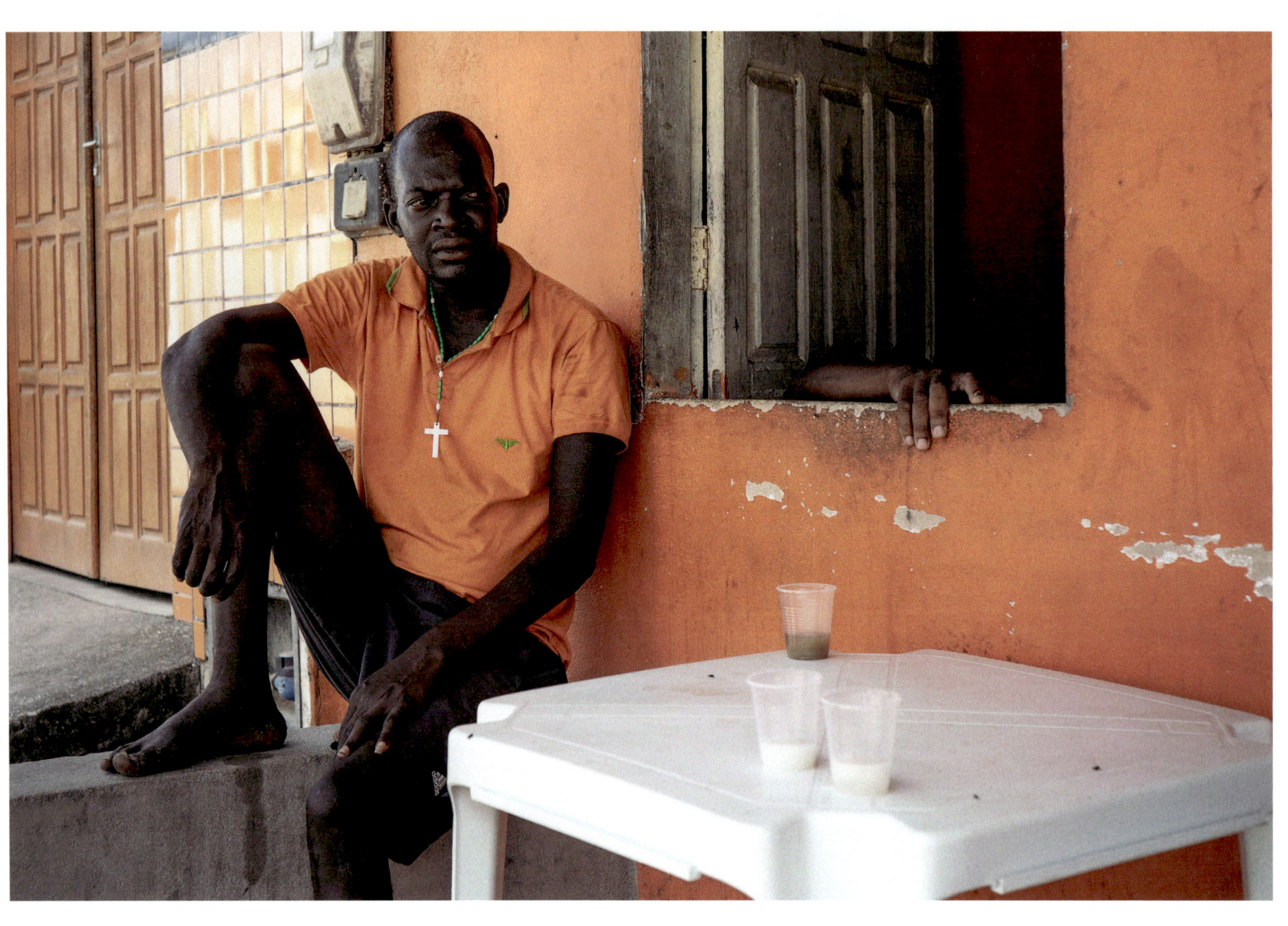

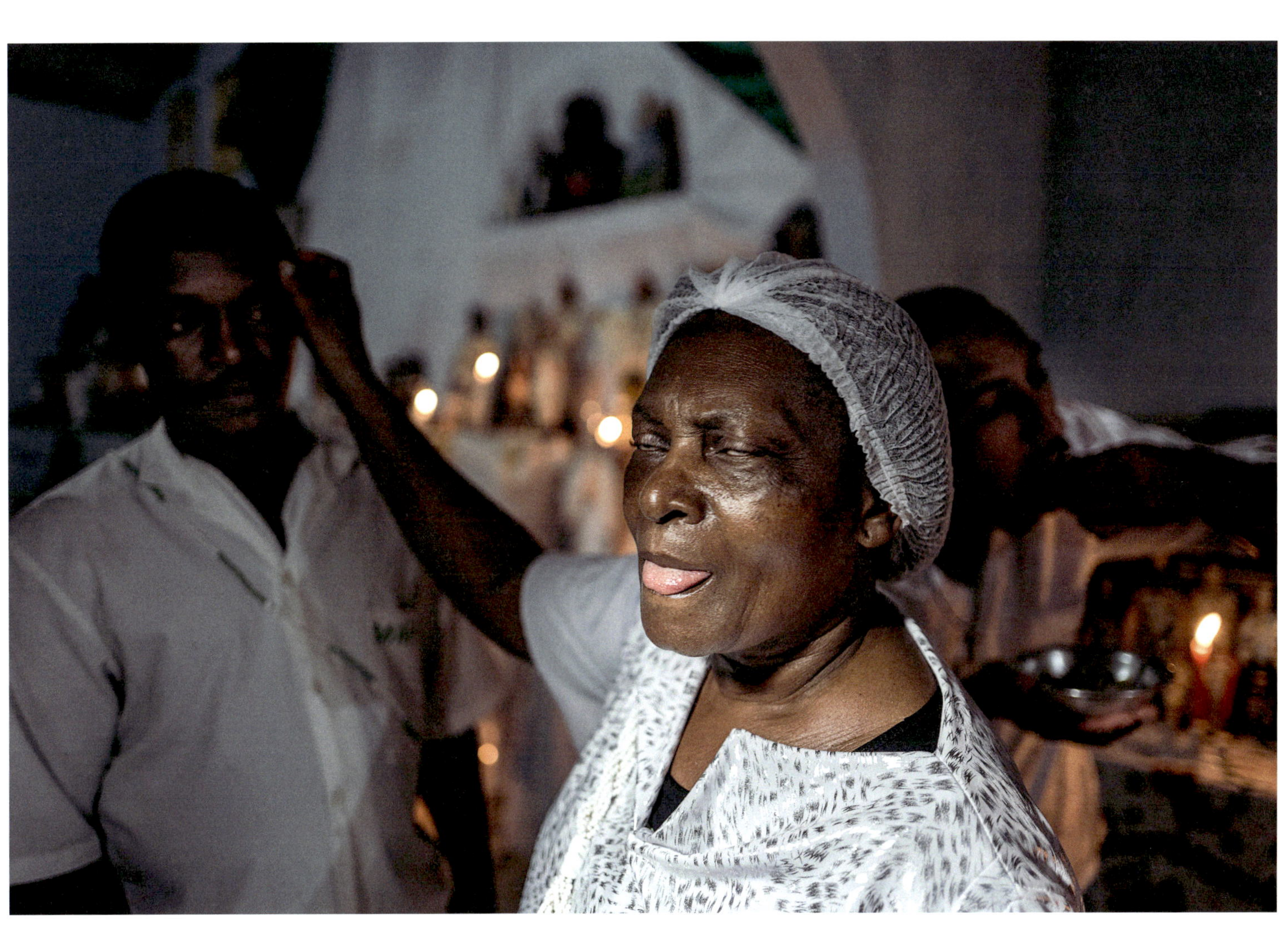

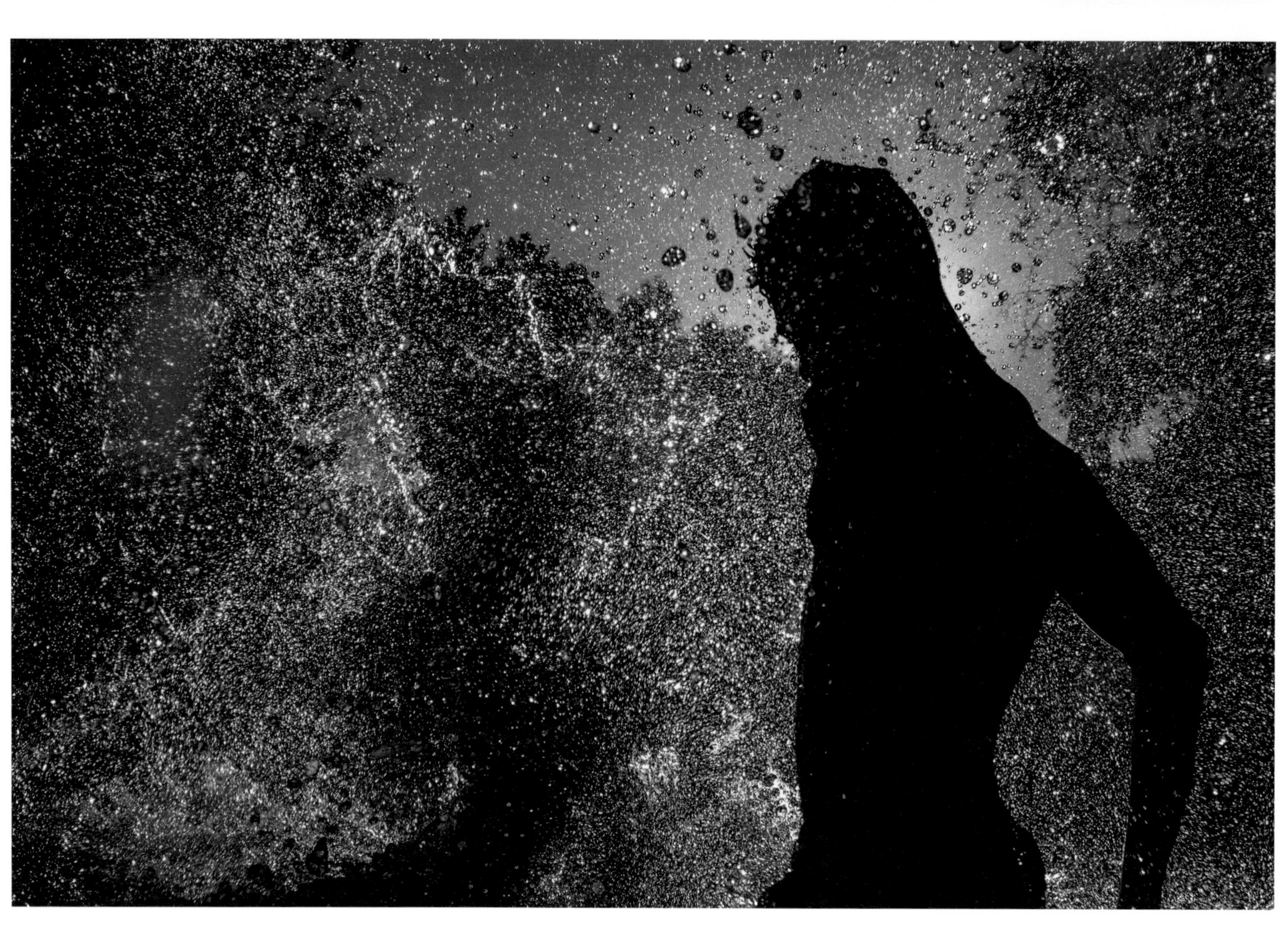

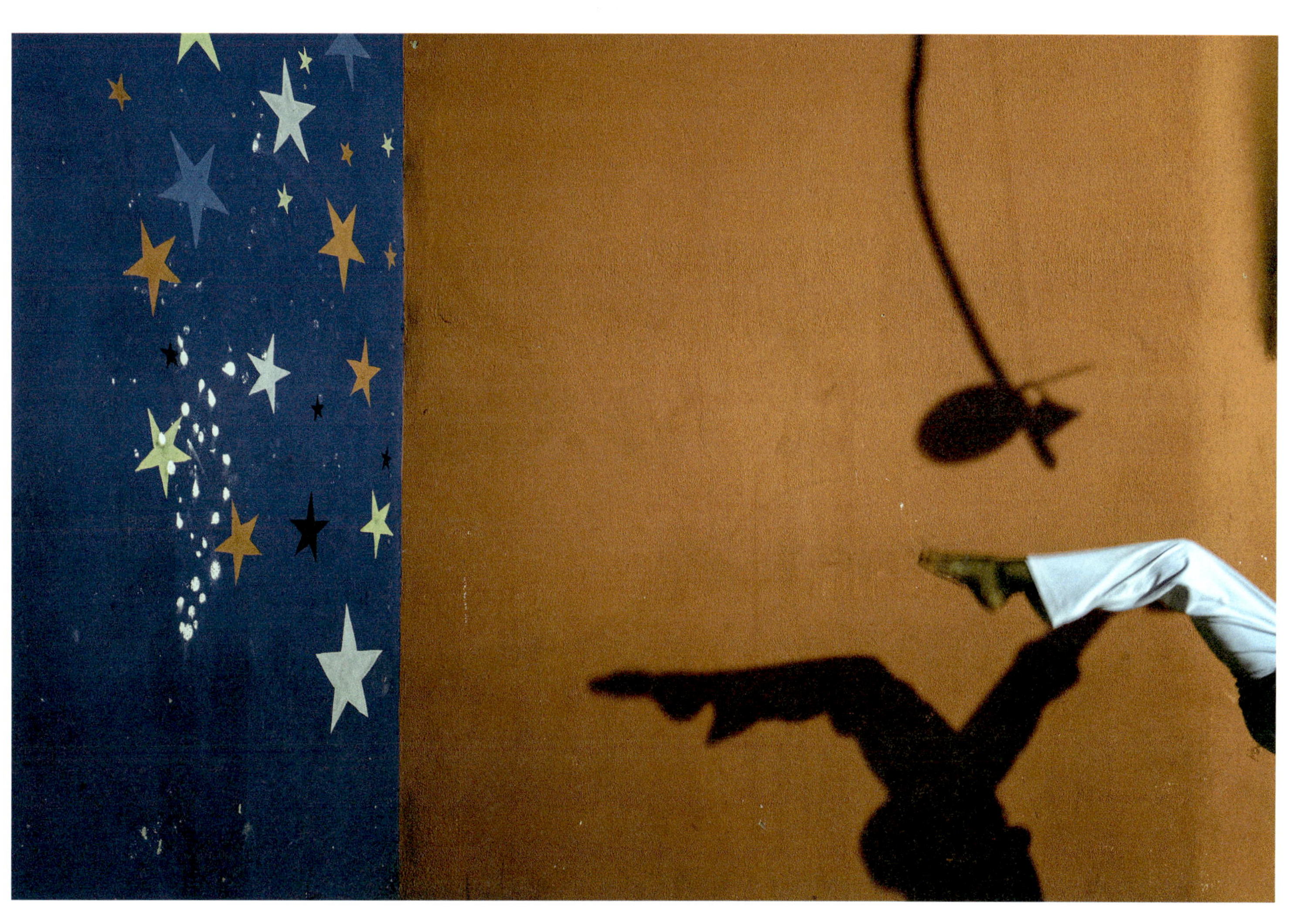

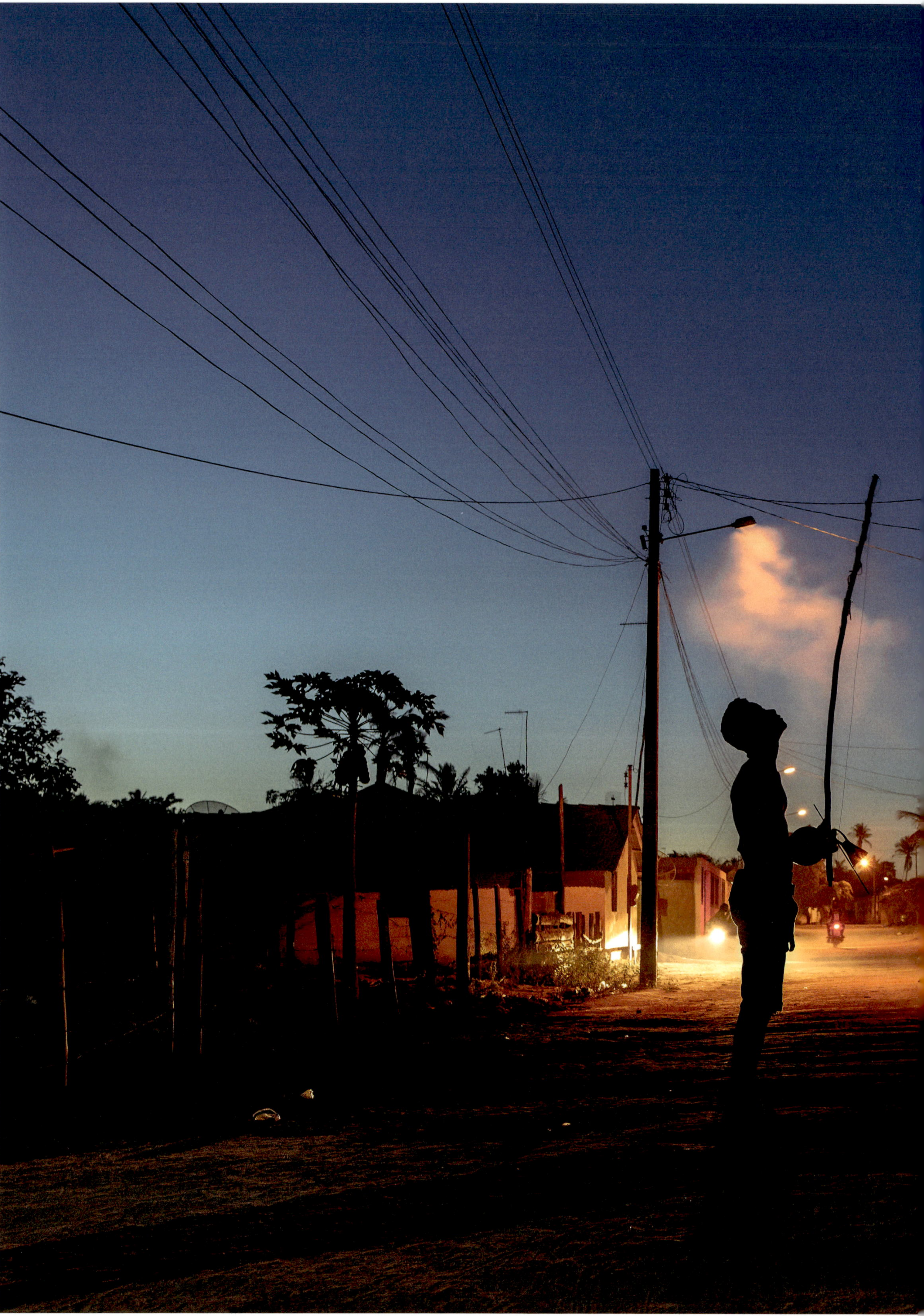

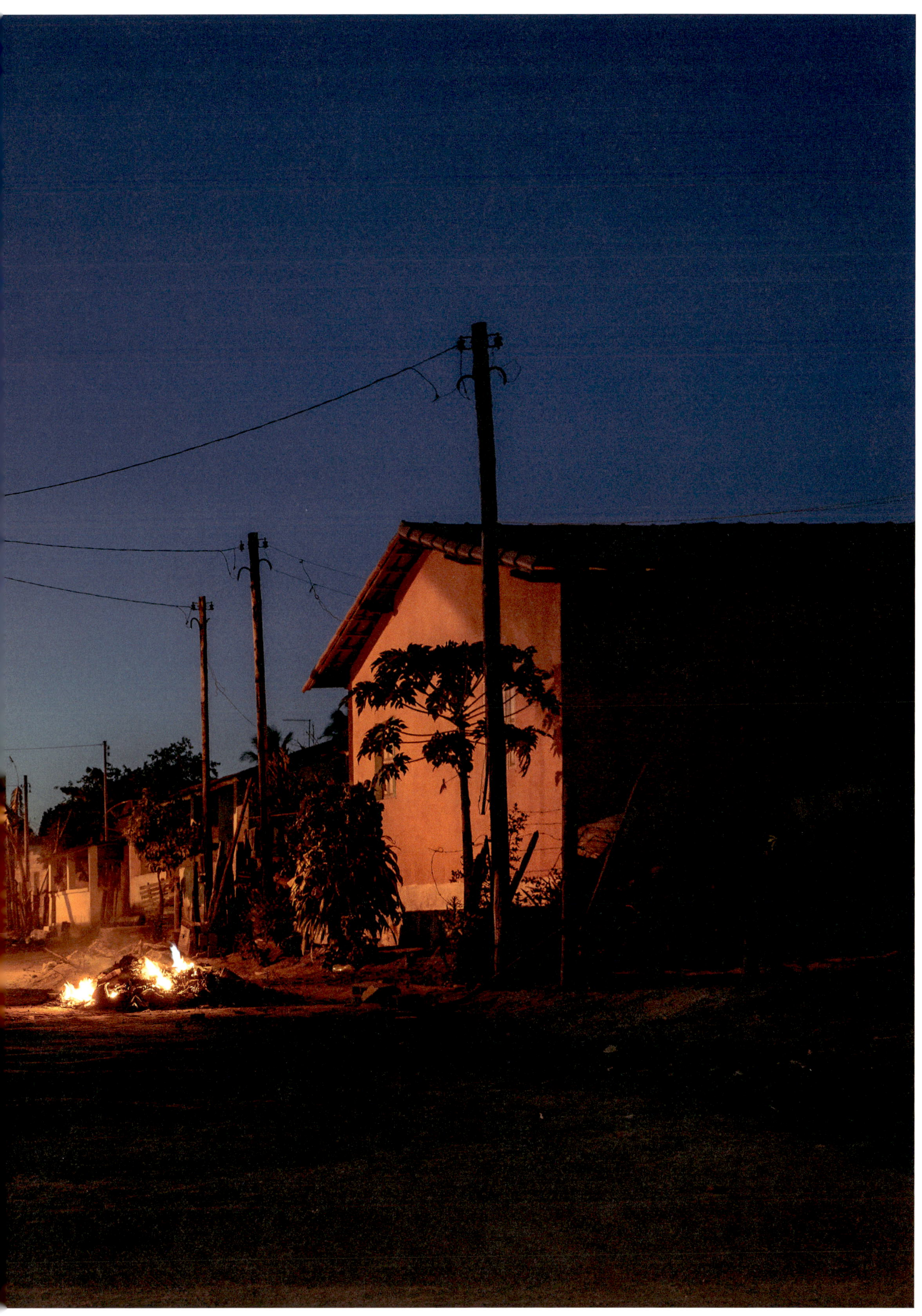

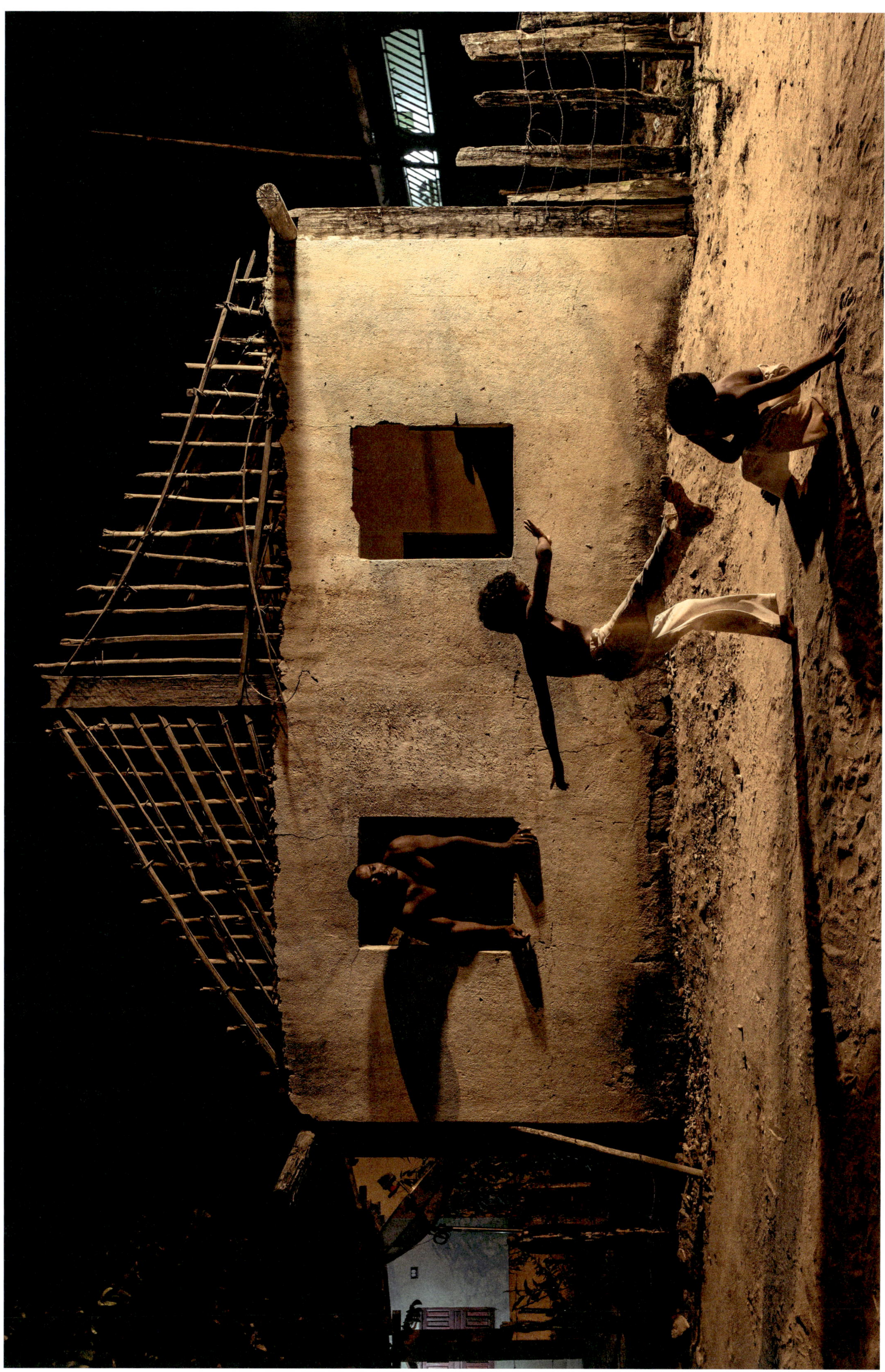

My name is Faustina Zacharias Carvalho. I'm a domestic worker but what I love doing is dancing the *bate-barriga*, the samba de viola, the *dança do Nagô*. Those dances passed down by my ancestors, my great-grandparents. They taught my grandparents, who taught my parents, and I, together with my parents, began to learn a little about the old culture.

I think that, in the same way I learned as a child, today's young people can also learn. To keep the traditions alive. Because this is a *quilombo* city where this culture exists. People have to keep on going, because my grandparents have gone, my parents too, but I'm still here. Soon, I can leave this world too. I'll have to leave my nephews, grandchildren, godchildren.

I learned these dances from my parents, who always went to the end-of-year celebrations called "the Christmas drum," celebrated in the home of someone helped by others. It wasn't organized by one person but by everyone. I'd go with my family, with everyone contributing something for the party with a community spirit. They still have an association like in the old days. Except it wasn't necessary to have your name in a book to be a member. Before it was something passed down from one generation to the next, from the elders to the young, even to the children.

All of this has been forgotten, and in particular I have been the one to remember it. I'm now sixty-five years old, and I learned at the age of ten. We have now formed a group of women and now the children enjoy themselves around us too.

Before we lived on the farm, there were places where there was nothing, not even electricity. We only had candles. So we didn't have to go to sleep so early at night, I formed a circle with children and adolescents to tell our story. My mother and grandmother also told their story. How things used to be, how they lived. They suffered abuse, torture. They had masters. And these masters grabbed their maids to take them to work. While their own wives rested they "used" these maids to produce more workers. The maids' children then became slaves. There were many slaves at that time.

Everything started out because of slavery. They were all slaves, they lived in the *senzalas*,[1] and were cruelly treated. When they were freed, they were overwhelmed with joy. When they jumped, they did somersaults. The women bumped their bellies into each other, singing, shouting; others banged on boxes. Then they began looking for names to give to these dances. The men's somersaults became known as *capoeira*, and when the women bumped their bellies into each other, it was called *bate-barriga* or *batuque*.

And why was the end of the year chosen for the celebrations? To commemorate the birth of Jesus. Today people prepare a big meal, but in those days they would dance *capoeira* or *bate-barriga*.

I've heard it said that the prejudices have changed. Now when people make the presentation in other cities, the reaction is different, the joy is different to here. Here the people don't feel completely overjoyed, perhaps because they are more used to it. I prefer to do the presentations in other towns. Here I do it more out of a sense of duty. Elsewhere people seem to appreciate them more.

I think many people in the community are prejudiced because they hide behind the Bible. They preach the word of God, but they don't put it into practice. And if they come to see us dance, showing our culture, they say: "Look at that, it's macumba!" But they're totally wrong. In a macumba people are possessed and sometimes don't even know what they're doing. But when people are dancing, everyone is having fun and knows what they're doing. Here the people mix up the two things. I've come across this here, but not outside the community. In other places, you get lots and lots of praise. We receive lots of invitations, though sometimes there's no money to pay us. You do it for free, but there has to be some kind of appreciation, right?

It would be great if there were more people giving encouragement, talking, preaching, shouting, and fighting for culture. But there's not enough support for these things we are doing. They could help, but they prefer criticizing you behind your back.

1   The name given to the shacks where slaves slept.

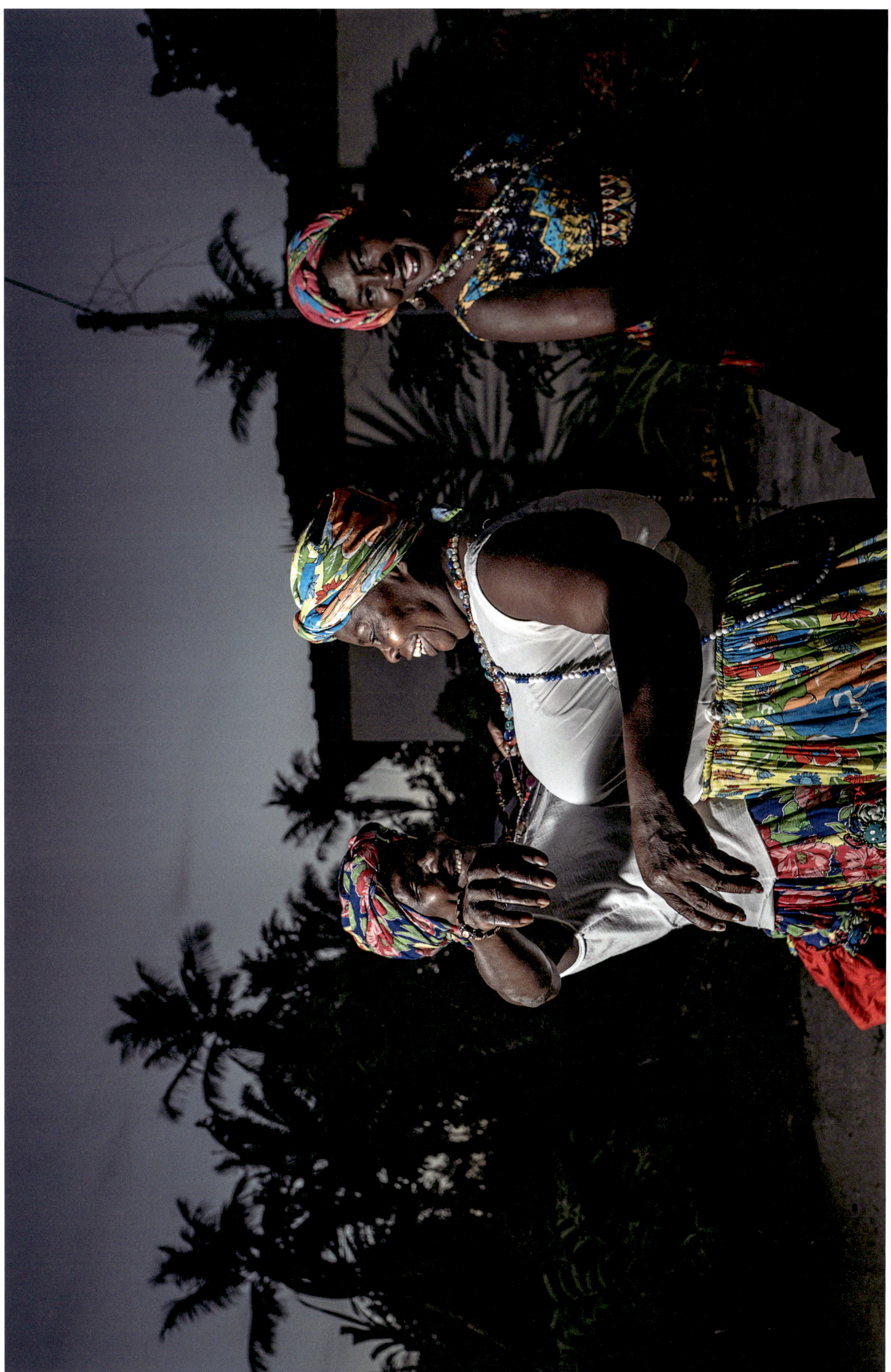

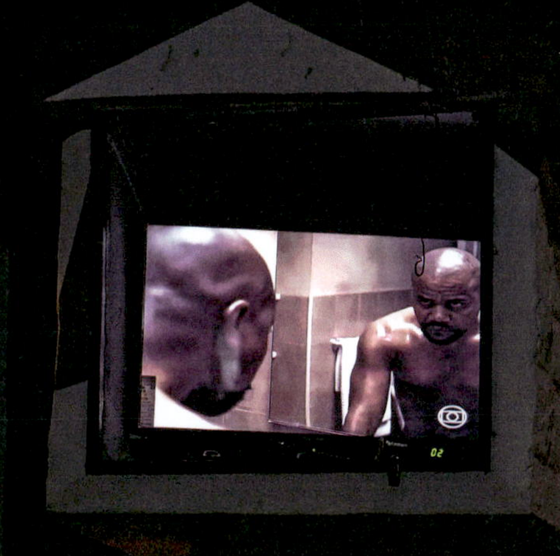

1897
HELVECIA

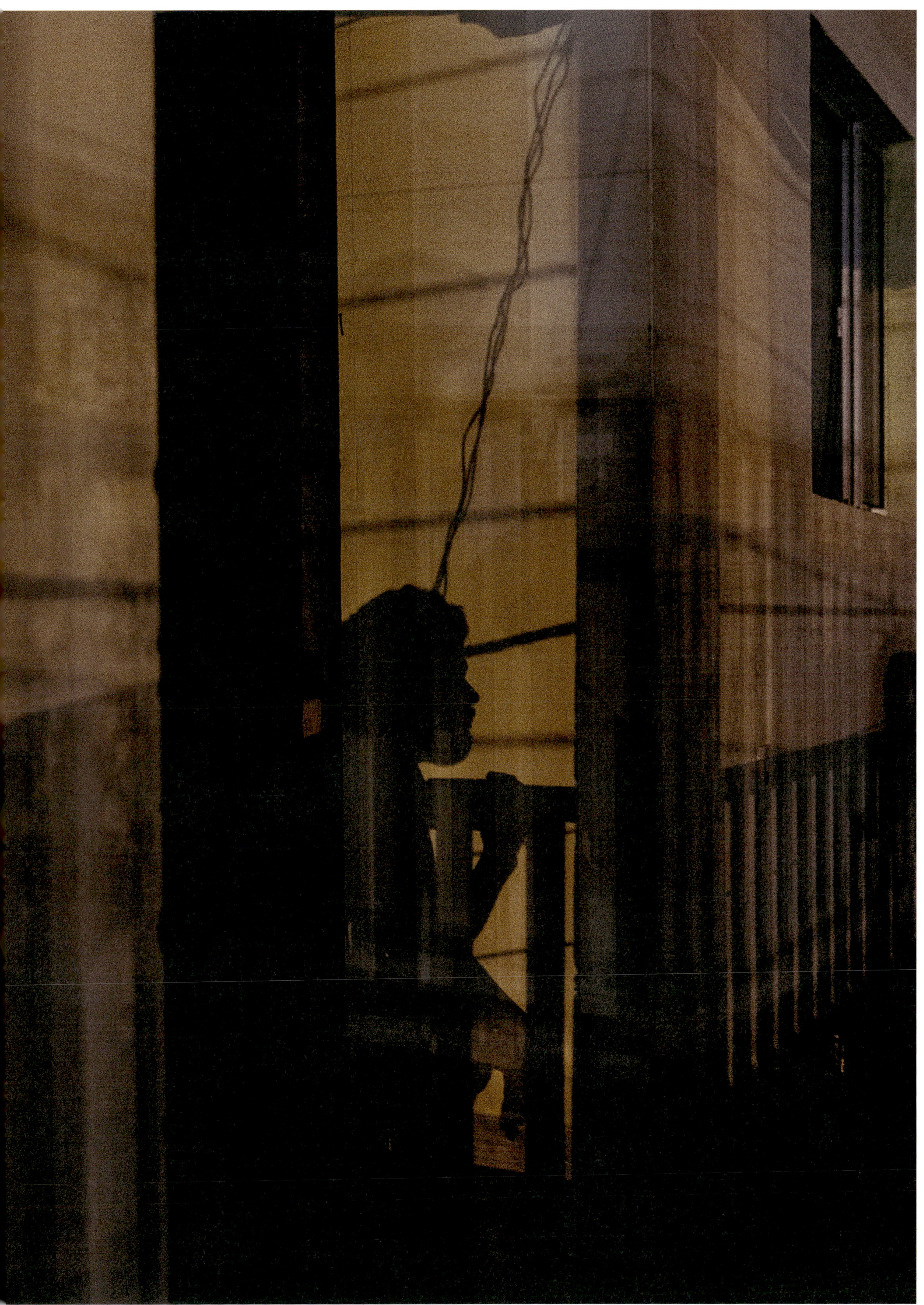

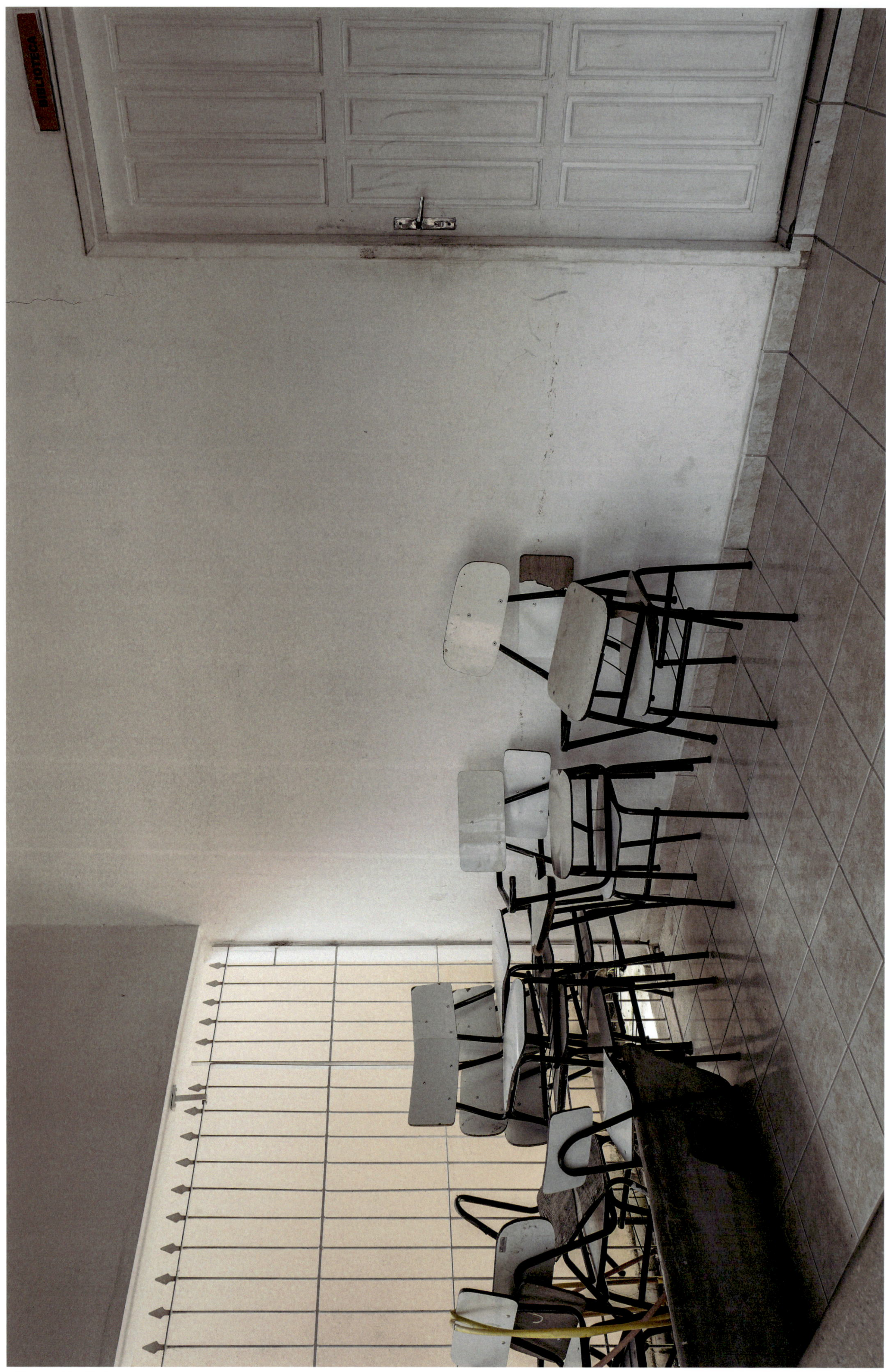

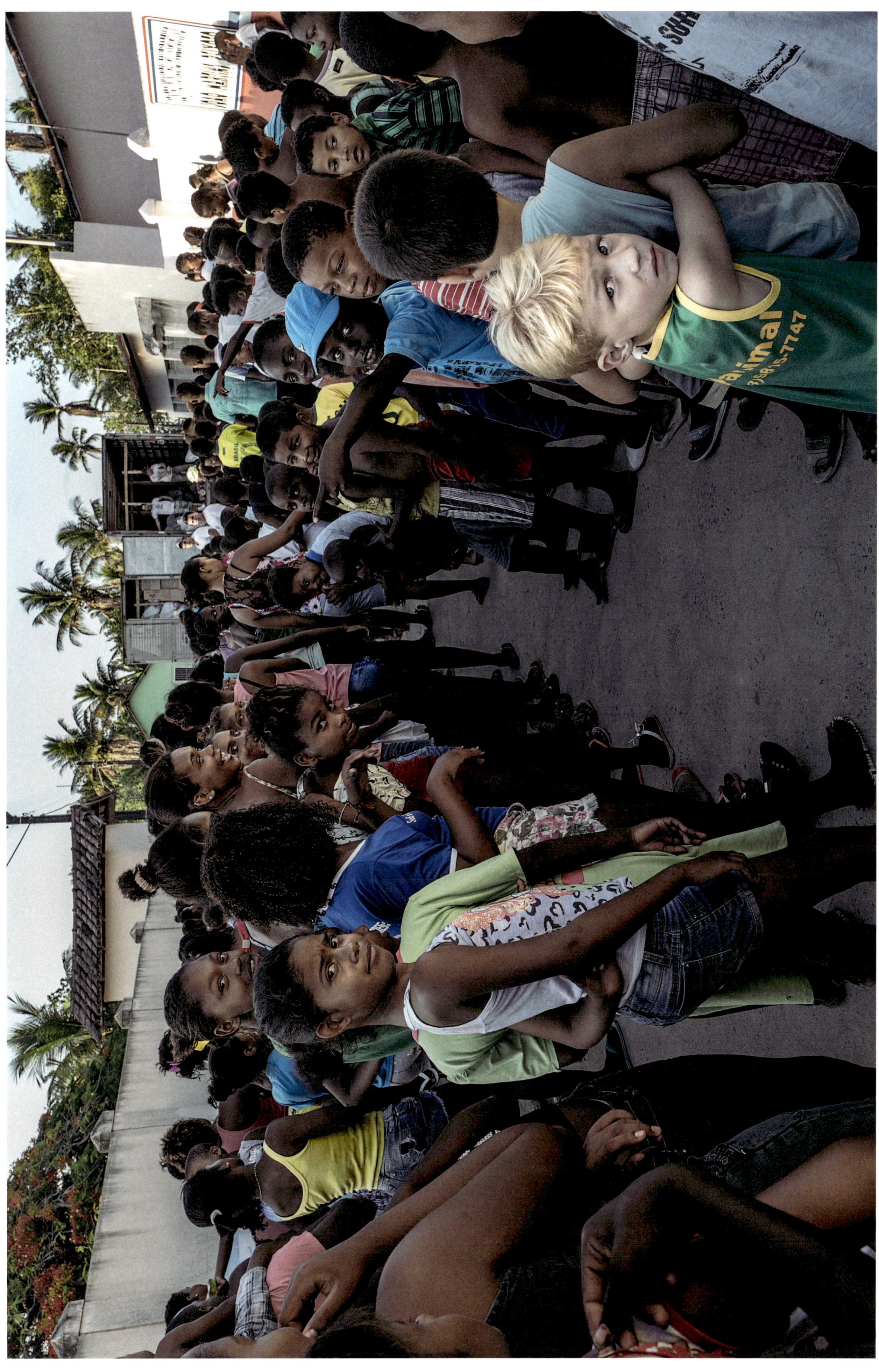

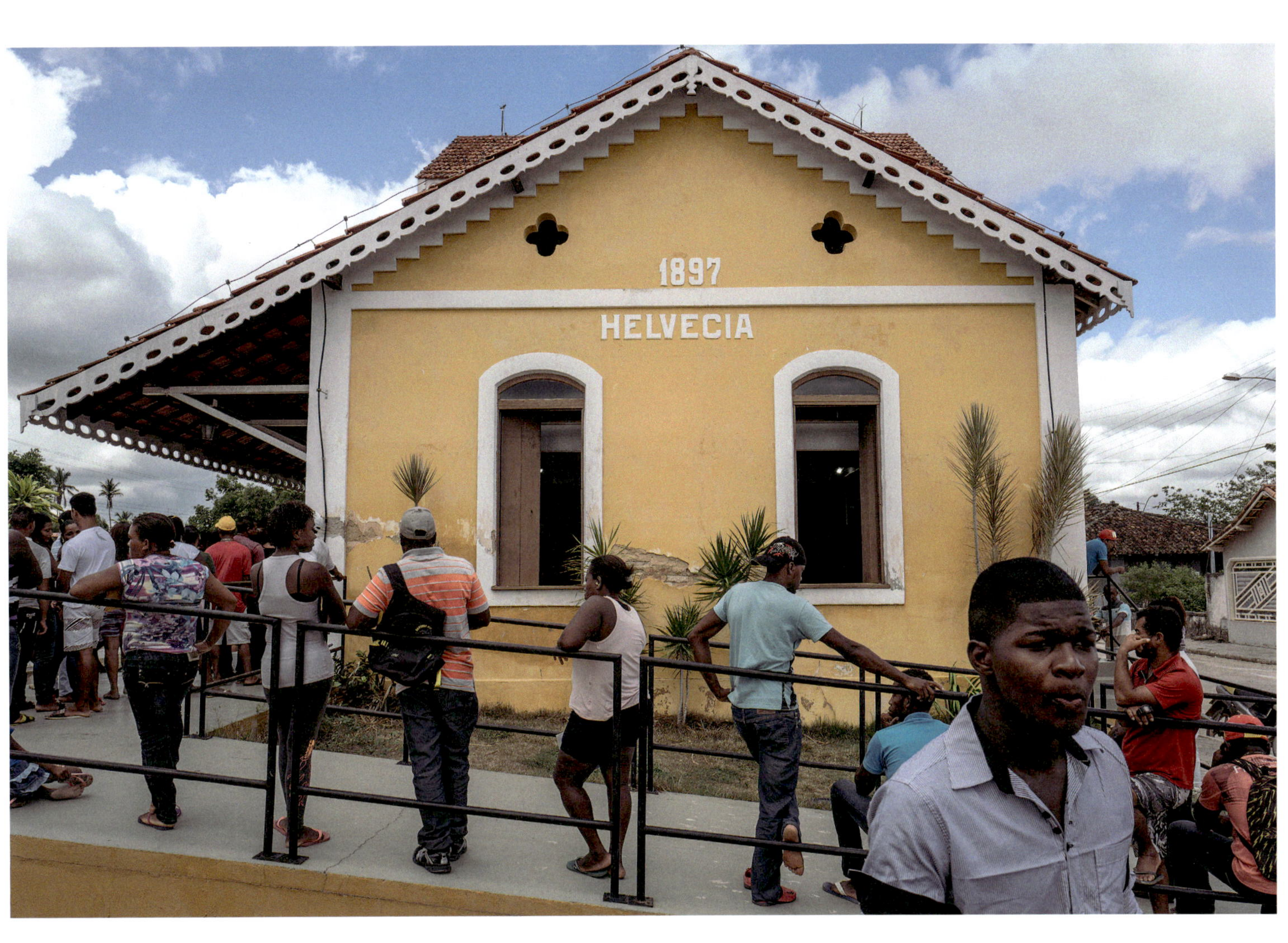

1897
HELVECIA

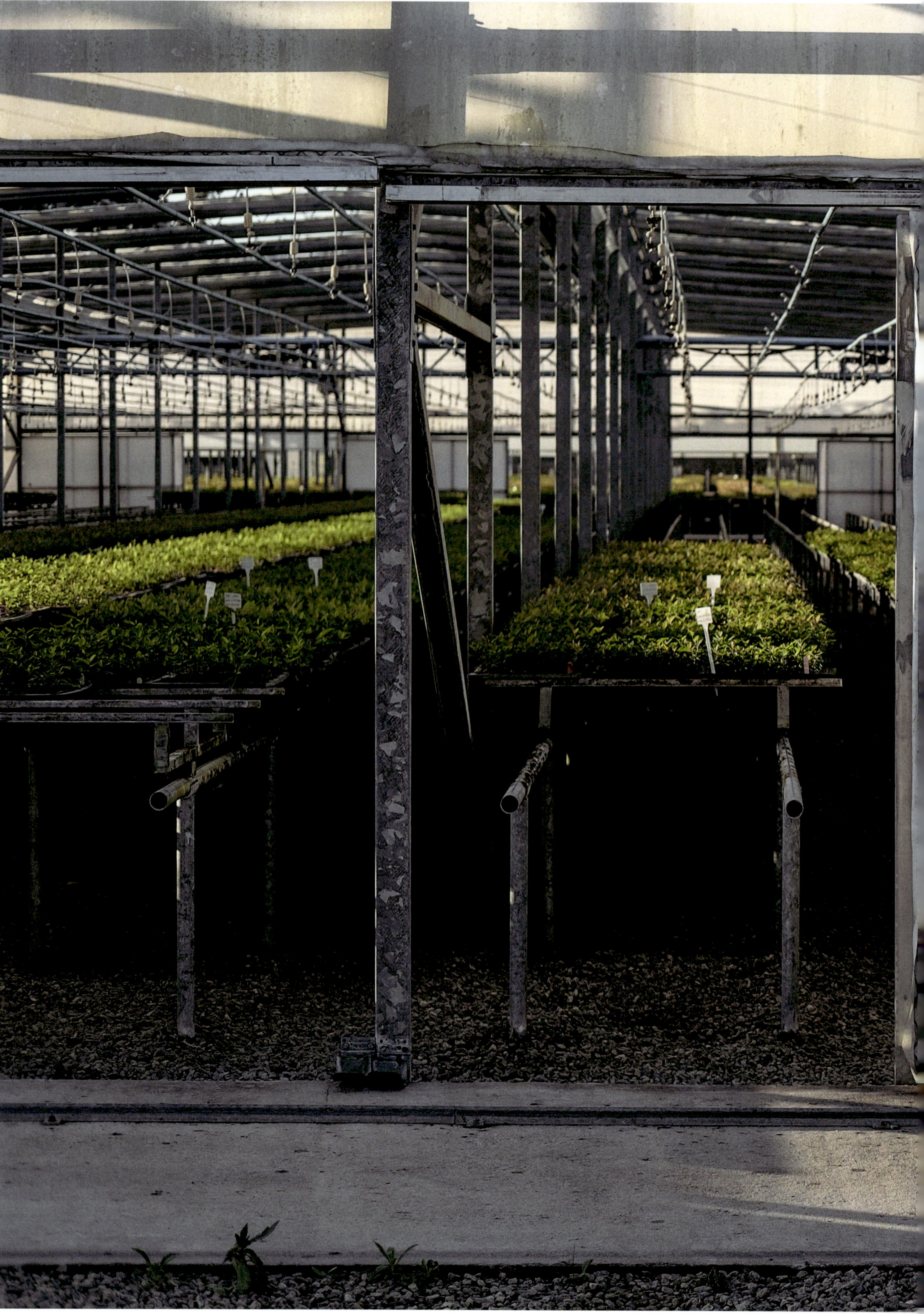

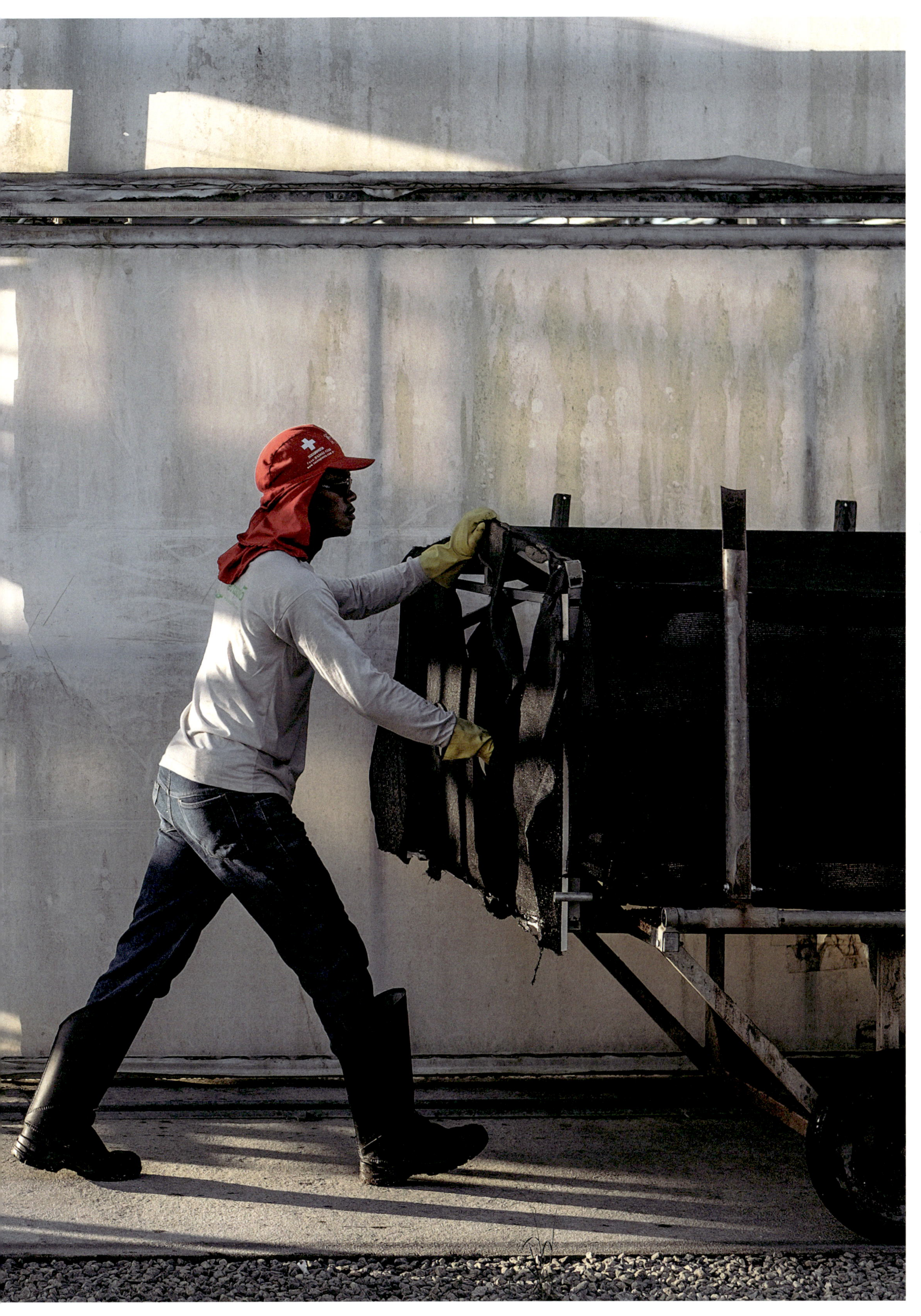

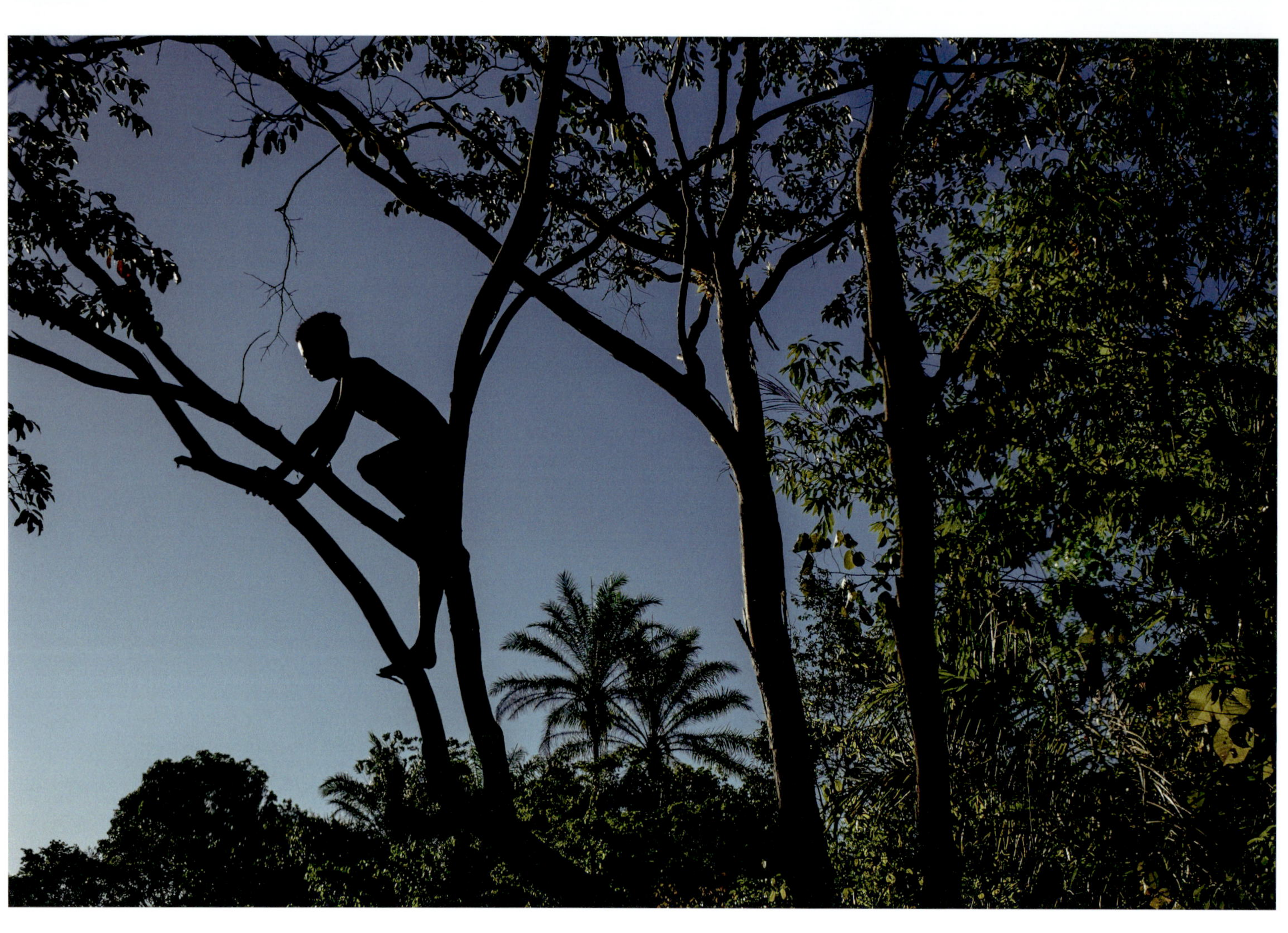

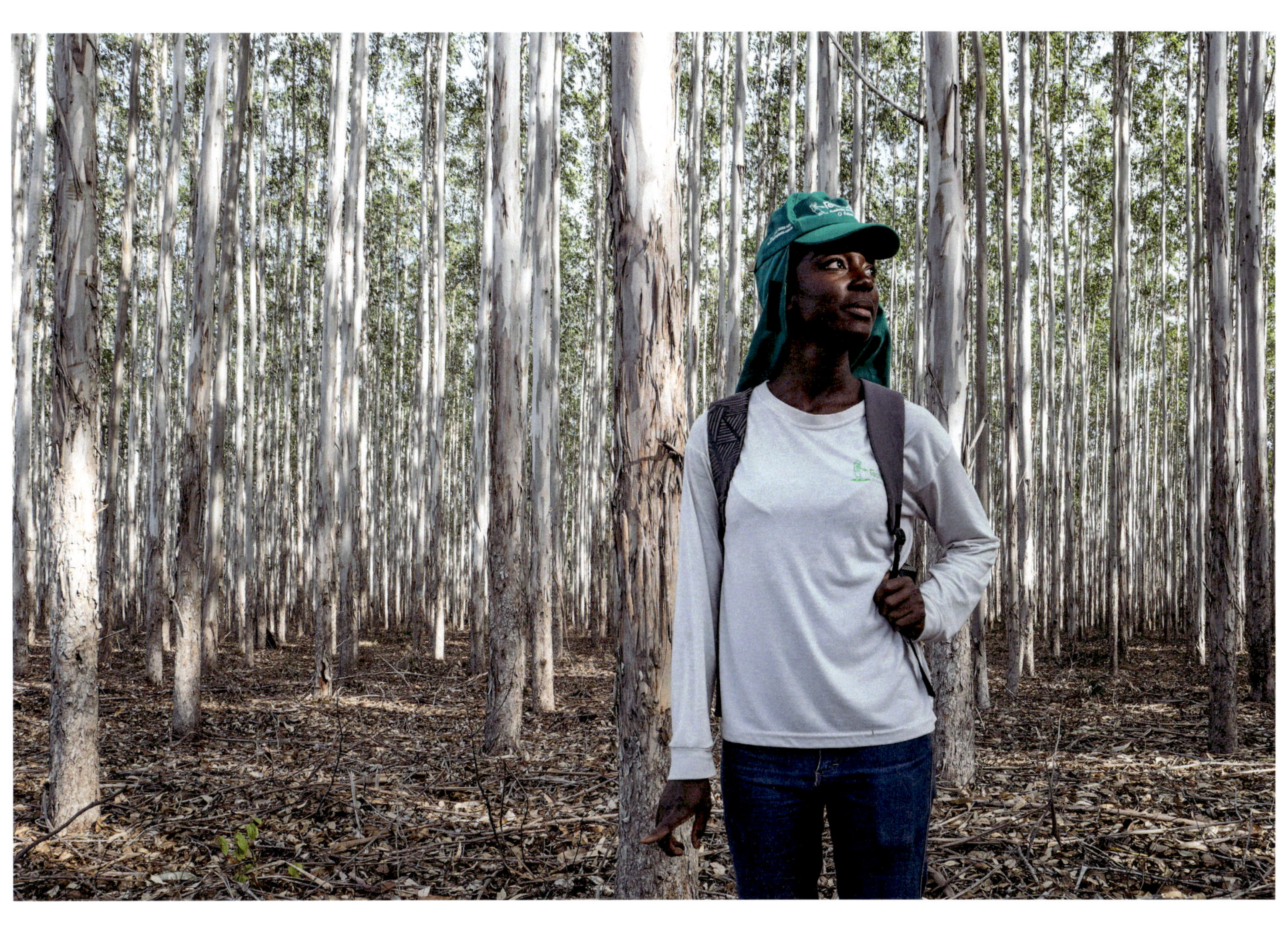

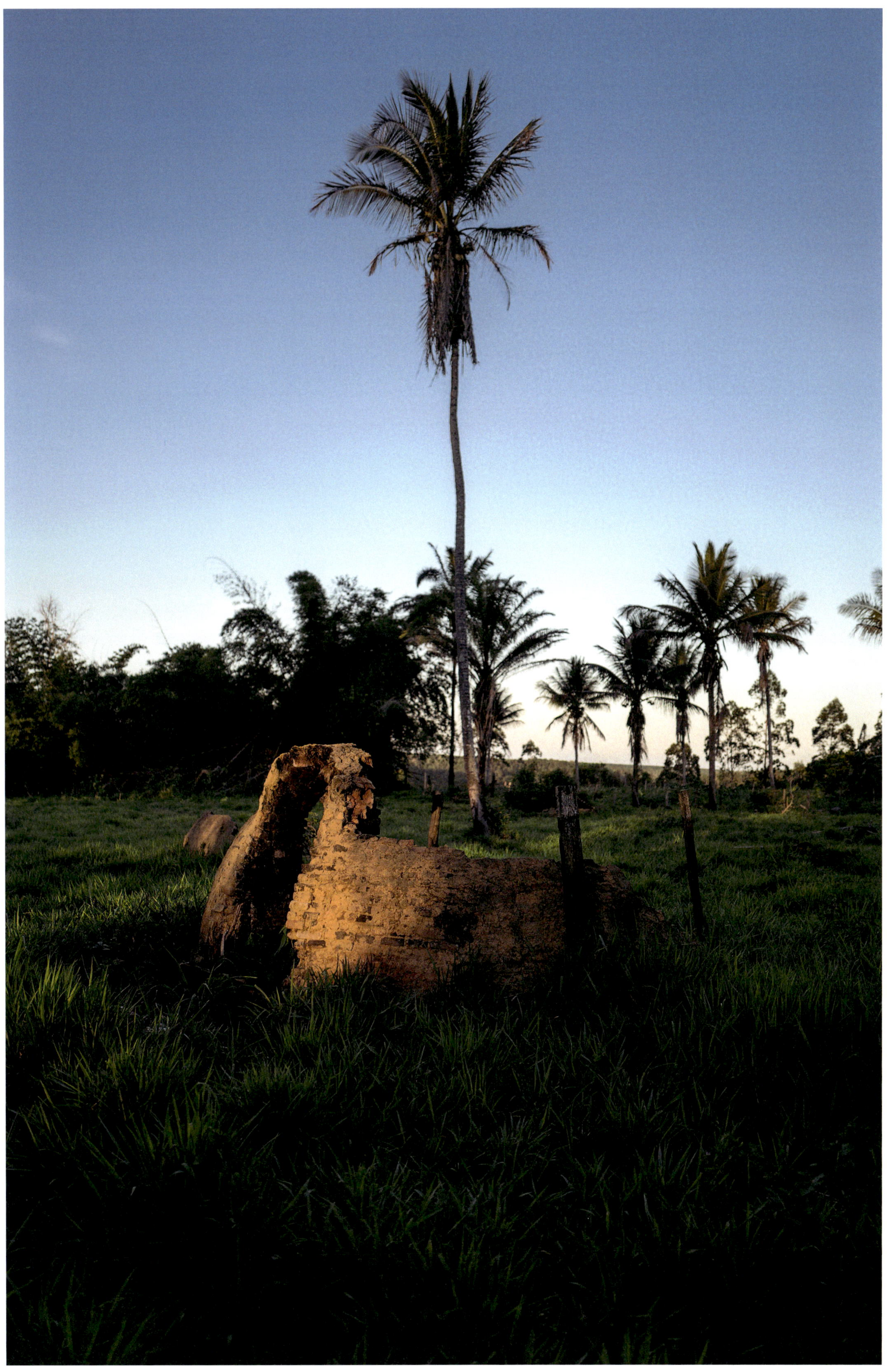

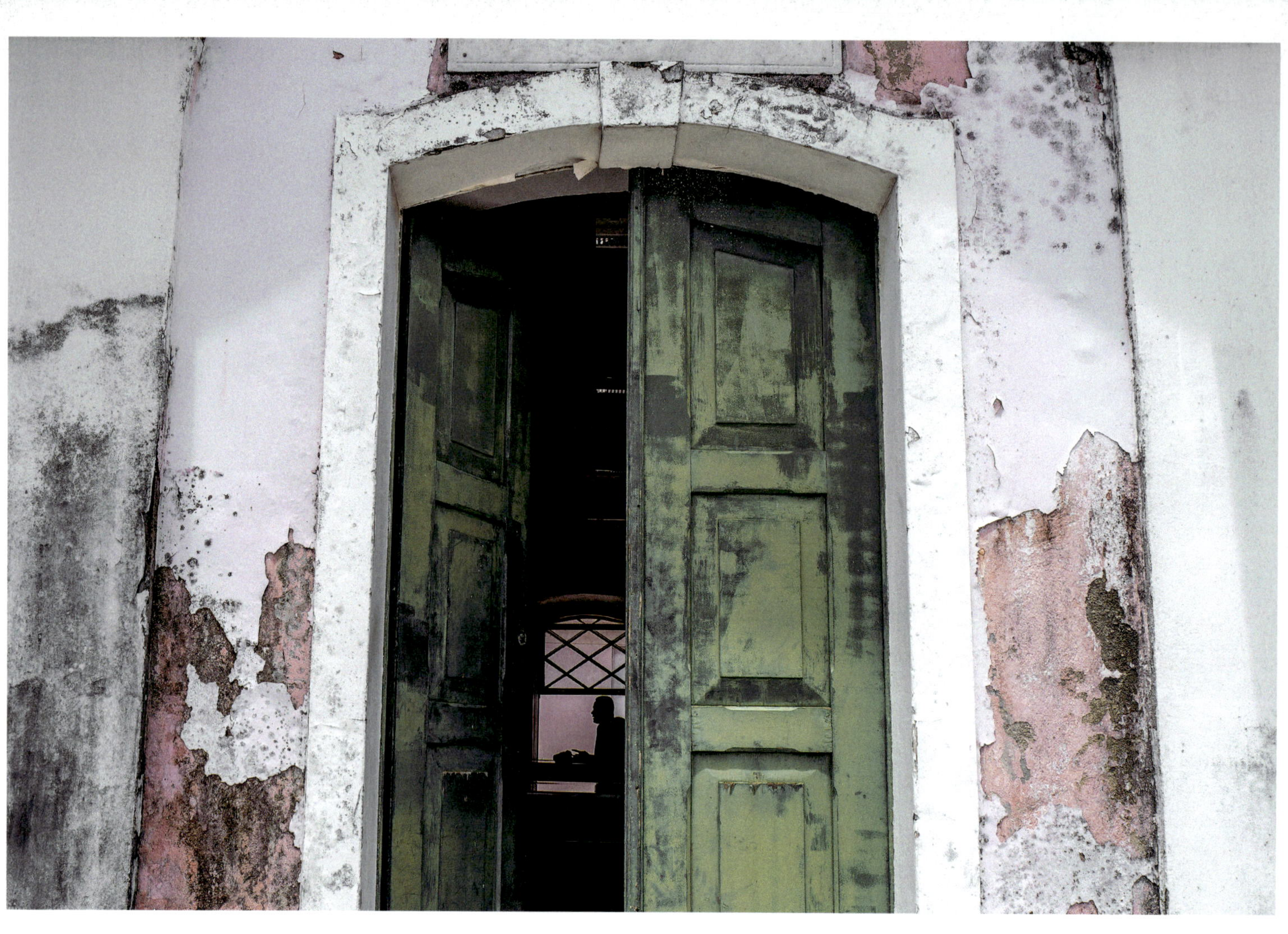

Milena Machado Neves

When Dom raised the possibility of a connection between Helvécia and Switzerland, my first reaction was denial. Impossible! I grew up in the region and knew the village was largely made up of people of African descent, yet I had never heard of the presence of Swiss colonists in the area. So when I began to research the subject, my intention was to verify these facts above all.

Immediately, though, I was quite captivated by the story. I found out that Helvécia had its roots in the former colony of Leopoldina, and its Swiss and German colonists used the labor of enslaved people to produce and export coffee to Europe. That was the start of six years of research: making contacts, conducting interviews and traveling in Brazil and Switzerland.

During my first trip to Helvécia, the village history professor, Gilsineth Santos Silva, introduced me to the work of the historian Carlos H. Oberacker Jr., which was the starting point for my own research. Then, in 2017, we met the Swiss journalist Christian Doninelli, who had just published a piece on Helvécia on the Swissinfo.ch website. We shared what we had each learned and cowrote a long article for the Swiss newspaper *Neue Zürcher Zeitung*. The following year, for the museums MK&G in Hamburg and Johann Jacobs in Zurich, I conducted research in the archives of the State of Bahia in Salvador. It was there that I found the first original documents on the colony. In Switzerland, Christian carried out his own tireless research in various public archives, where he unearthed other documents that capped the information found in the present book.

To research the history of Helvécia was to delve into the past of my native corner of Brazil. It was a chance to better understand the particularities of a place I've always been close to but didn't really know before beginning this project. It was an opportunity to learn and build with Dom an understanding of a history that is unusual but also common.

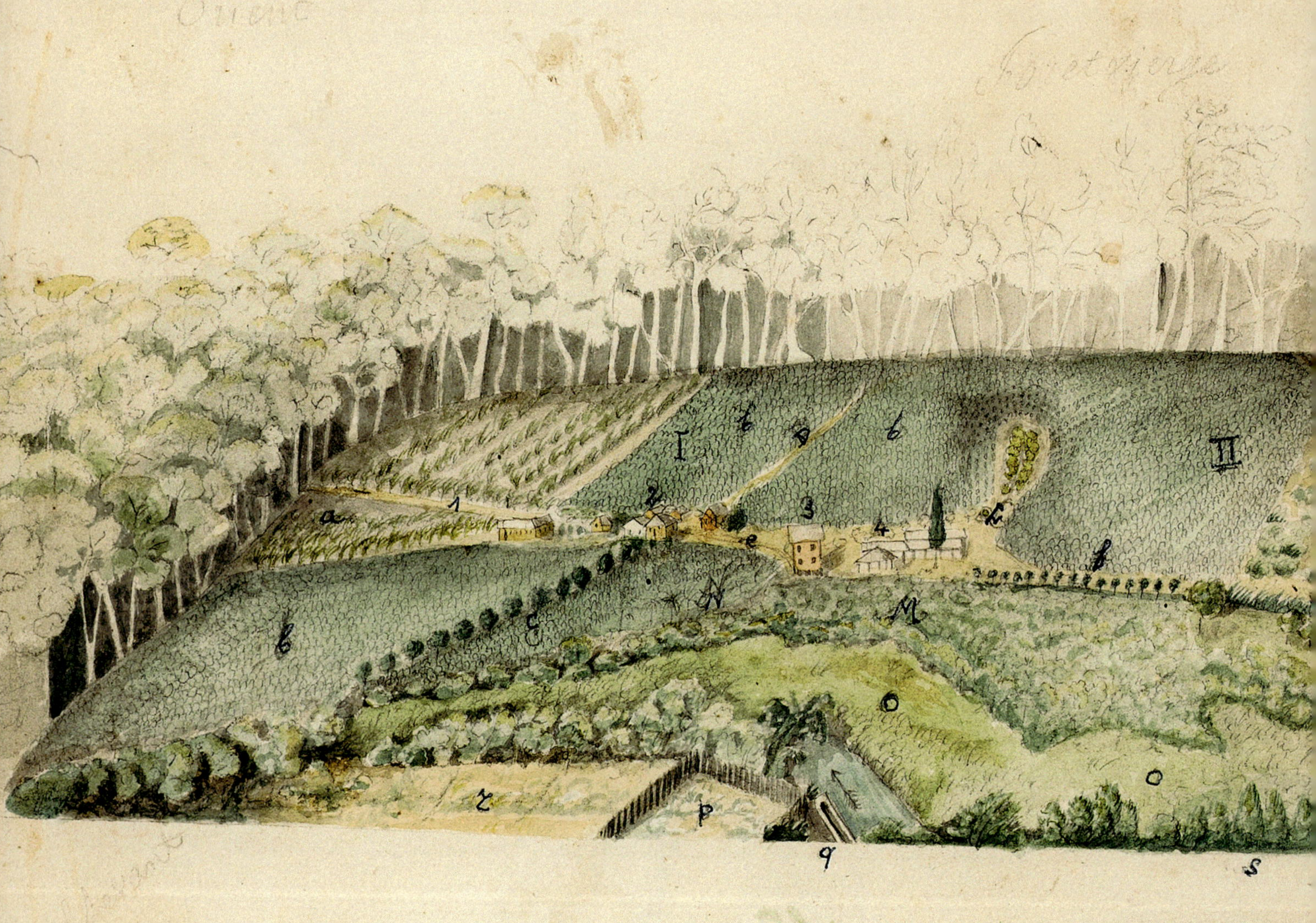

Pombal =

Plantation de café d'une co[...]

Nᵒ.1. chemin conduisant chez Mr. de Coffane à Alta Riva), la maison en dessous, en celle de
Nᵒ.5. Cuisine à préparer la Manioc, Nᵒ 6 Ecurie pour Chevaux & Vaches, 7 Maison des Flo[...]
(a) Plantation des Bananiers en dessous du chemin conduisant à Haute Rive, au dessu[...]
(c) Chemin bordé d'orangers, conduisant au Port; (d) chemin conduisant dans la fo[...]
paturage, bordé d'orangers (g) haye d'aloès, (giavata) fermant le paturage et condui[...]
gros bois tombés pêle mêle, et charbonés par le feu; (L) petit ration cultivé en ca[...]
(N) ligne de cocotiers depuis la maison Nᵒ3 jusqu'au marais. (O) Terrein pour[...]
porcs, de Mr. Wasserfallrivère (q) Port à canot au même, (r) ancienne rivière (...
la forêt vierge bordant la plantation est un peu trop haute, les arbres trop gros, p[...]
Voyez les gravures du Voyage Wied Neuwied) d'une couleur gris clair, l'espace entre
les Cacaotiers d'un vert moins vif, la cime d'un brun presque rouge, les bananiers
brunes; le terrein grisâtre plus ou moins jaunâtre suivant la pente, les chemins
plus foncé et presque noir pendant les premiers six mois; les toits des maisons qui bordent
jaune ou gris suivant le sable; la manioc d'un vert bleuâtre et clair... vu de loin cher[...]
foncés que le tapis, les gd généralement plus foncés quels expetits, beaucoup sont couve[...]

lombier)

neuchâteloise au Brésil.

...3; Maisons cuisine &c de Pombal 17.º 2) Magasin à Passé 17.º 3, Pile & séchoirs 17.º 4.
...r. Huguenin, 8 habitation du même; 9 Maison de Mes. Eugène & Guill. Borrel.
chemin se trouve le terrein dans Noirs limité par des bananiers; (b) Caffeyers —
) chemin conduisant à la maison 17.º 3 du magasin (f.) chemin conduisant au
...au 3 Sot (h) manioc; petit ralon où coule un ruisseau (K) colline couverte de
...ies choux & légumes, (M) terrein marécageux parsemé de buissons
...sous l'eau et couvert d'un gramen, (cap) herbe d'un verd pâle, (O) enclos à
...issons ou petits arbres bordant la rivière & en empêchant l'arriée
...viegnent pas ainsi r'aprochés, d'un verd foncé, les trunes généralement droits
...ne tronc très foncé; les caffiers sont plantés en ligne, ils sont d'un verd foncé
...verd clair, les nouvelles feuilles presque j'année & les vieilles piquées de tâches
...entes rapides en terres remuées d'un jaune d'ocre, le terrein nouvellem.t défriché
...en chaume diffèrent peu l'un de l'autre en gris clair brillant au soleil, les murs
...be achol à de petits buissons; les buissons M. au dessous de la plantation sont plus
...iennes formant un bosquet impénetrable

1818	The German naturalist Georg Wilhelm Freyreiss (1789–1825) is awarded lands in the State of Bahia by John VI. To found the colony of Leopoldina, Freyreiss invites the Swiss A. and L. Langhans and D. Pache, as well as a German, Baron W.F. von dem Busche, to join him there.

1819 — The colonists of Leopoldina engage, for the first time, in slavery, a practice that is in fact outlawed by the terms of the document granting the status of colony to the area.

1820–1824 — Arrival of new Swiss and German colonists, who enter into a partnership with the founders. They are the Swiss P.H. Béguin, P. Huguenin, and E. Borrel; and the Germans P. Peycke, the Consul of Hamburg, as well as J.G. Philipp, N. Kroos, J. Graban and C.G. Mohrhardt.

1850 — The Law of September 4, 1850, officially abolishes the slave trade in Brazil, but despite the law's enactment, slavery will continue to be practiced illegally in the country.

In the late 1850s, the economy of the colony reaches its highest level of activity and wealth. The region of Leopoldina accounts for around 90 percent of coffee production in the State of Bahia. The colony comprises about two hundred whites for 2,000 enslaved persons divided among some forty farms.

1860 — The growing importance of the Leopoldina colony induces Switzerland to create a vice-consulate in neighboring Caravelas, a port city from which local coffee is exported to Europe.

1882 — A slave revolt breaks out in the lands of Frédéric-Louis Jeanmonod, a large landowner and the vice-consul of Switzerland in Caravelas. This episode is part of the context of rebellion in Leopoldina, leading to the colony's decline.

1888 — The Golden Law (*Lei Áurea*) is promulgated on May 13, 1888, abolishing slavery in Brazil. Already weakened by both the depletion of the soil and competition, the colony is abandoned by its landowners, some choosing to return to their homelands.

1895 — Vice-consul Louis Bornand resigns. Switzerland deems it unnecessary to replace him and decides to close the vice-consulate of Caravelas for good.

1897 — The brand-new railway line begins making stops at the Helvécia train station.

2005 — Helvécia obtains the status of a *quilombola* community. *Quilombos* are former sites where enslaved people fleeing bondage found refuge; the Brazilian government officially recognizes these places for their past and distinctive qualities.

← Map of the Pombal (Dovecote) Plantation, with detailed caption:

1. The way leading from M. de Coffrane's place to Alta Riva; the house below is that of the Blacks…
2. Coffee warehouse…
7. House of M. Huguenin's Blacks…
9. Messrs. Eugène and Gustave Borrel…
b. Coffee trees…"

Jean-Frédéric Bosset de Luze (Geneva 1754-1838), between 1820 and 1838 (watercolor and pencil drawing on paper, 20.3 × 44.5 cm). Collection of the Pinacoteca of the State of São Paulo, Brazil

Balance sheet of the Pombal Plantation from the years 1826 and 1827, Leopoldina colony.

Archives of the State of Neuchâtel, Switzerland

The balance sheet of this plantation co-owned by Charles Louis Borrel, Pierre-Henri Beguin, and Philippe Huguenin, all hailing from Neuchâtel, mentions the presence of several Black slaves. Among the "objects" listed we find "9 Blacks, viz., 6 men and 3 women, at 250 thousand reis apiece, as well as a "small negress estimated at 40,000 reis."

Illmo Snr Doutor Juiz de Direito.

Nᵒ 117.

As plantações, que existem no lugar chamado Colo
nia Leopoldina e pertencem a estrangeiros, nas quaes se
cultiva o café com braços de escravos são as que enumero
abaixo:

Banda do Norte do Rio Peruípe:

Fernando Kunde, Prussiano
Gustavo e Constancio Jaccard, Suissos
Defunto Abrão Vouga, Suisso.
Henrique Borrel, Suisso.
Salomão Jaccard, Suisso.
Francisco Taté, Suisso.
Madᵐᵉ Geoffroi, Franceza.
Luiz Maulaz, Suisso.
Felippe Moers, Hanoverano.
Alexandre Coasandier, Suisso.
Felippe Roeder, Alamão.
O Doutor Blum, de Francofurto.
Ernesto & Francisco Krull, Hanoverianos
O Major Metzger, Alamão.
Carlos Hertsch, Alamão.

Banda do Sul do Rio Peruípe:

João Martinho Clach, Suisso.
Pai Borrel Suisso.
Defunto Alexis Borrel, Suisso
    „   Gustavo e Eugénio Borrel, Suisso.
Henrique Huguenin, Suisso.
Pedro Beguin, Suisso.
Defunto Augusto Coffrane, Suisso
    „   Alfredo Coffrane, Suisso.

Gourdroeuf Francez.
Carlos Augusto Toelsner, Hanoveriano
Lambert, Alamão.
Langhans, Suisso.

Fóra destas fazendas nomeadas tem varios sitios lavra-
dos por Indios, e outras pessoas com as suas proprias
familias, mas que são tão pequenos que não mere-
cem nem podem ser lembrados aqui, como o dono
muda de instante em instante, e as propriedades bra-
sileiras ja por sim não entrão nesta enumeração. —

De Va Sa mto respeituoso Crdo e Vendor

João Conrado Lang
Doutor em Philos. & Medicina

Recebico a [...] a [...] lavra-
da 18 de Março dsp. do Feve-
reiro de 1847 [...]

A. [...]

L. I.

A list of the properties in the colony of Leopoldina dating from
1848 that notes the name of each plantation, the names of their
owners, and the number of "whites" and "slaves" working each
landholding. The total amounts to 130 whites for 1267 slaves.

The document also mentions the quantity of coffee exported,
"In 1847, between 66,000 and 70,000 coffee plants, increasing
each year."

Public Archives of the State of Bahia, Salvador, Brazil

Norte do Rio Peruípe
Colonia Leopoldina.

Plantações	Proprietários	Brancos	Escravos
Pedras	Fernando Roz. de Senna	6	62
Destacamento	Major Carlos Metzner	10	14
Rosa d'Agua	Carlos Hartstein	4	12
Leopoldina	Ernesto - Francisco Krull	15	125
Sarmonet	Frederico Blum	5	8
Jacarandá	João Vicente Glz. d'Almeida	9	30
	José Antonio Ferr. Salã		6
Boa Vista	Felippe Roeder	6	10
Monte d'Alegria	Anna Jorge da Conceição	3	14
Monte Real	Os herdros de Mea. Lacerdios		62
Carlota	Felippe Moers	4	44
Sapucaeira	Luiz Blaula	5	44
Alban	Luiza Petersen		14
Patley			35
Somma		67	475

Plantações	Proprietarios	Brancos	Escravos
Luiz Geffroy	Luiz Geffroy		12
"	Marmillon		4
"	Salomon Sacard		8
"	Henrique Borel		10
Saphia	Os herd.ros do Vega		14
Helvetia	Gustavo e Const.o Sacard		18
"	Fernando Secunde		9
Colina	Bento José da Costa		64
Maturin	Carlos Augusto Poelonet		16
Hesperia	João Dias d'Azevedo		25
"	Sul do Rio		
Boa Vista	Miguel Glz. dos S.tos Santos		19
Riacho d'ouro	Abrahão Langhans		45
Saûgo	João Henrique Lambert	3	10
			272

Plantações	Proprietarios	Brancos	Escravos
Germania	Carlos Augusto Poelonet	2	9
	Gurneau	1	22
Esperança	João Baptista Bacalhao	1	24
Hacd. de Reix	Os herd.ros de Augt.o de Cofrane	5	84
Providencia	Os herd.ro de Alfredo de Cofrane	1	32
Pombal I.o	Pedro Henrique Bazin	8	44
Pombal II.o	Henrique Huguenin	4	48
Castello de Pombal	Eugenio Borel e os herd.ro de G. Borel	2	80
Constancia	Os herd.ro de Alcina Borel	2	36
Luiza	Luiz Borel	1	30
Helvetia	João Martinho Flach	4	108
Somme			512
Total		130	1267

A exportação do caffé estava no anno de 1847 entre 66,000 e 70,000 arrobas, augmentando-se annualmente.

Map of plantations in the Leopoldina colony, including the plantation called California owned by Maulaz, Jeanmonod and Giroud, dating from 1857.

Federal Archives, Bern, Switzerland

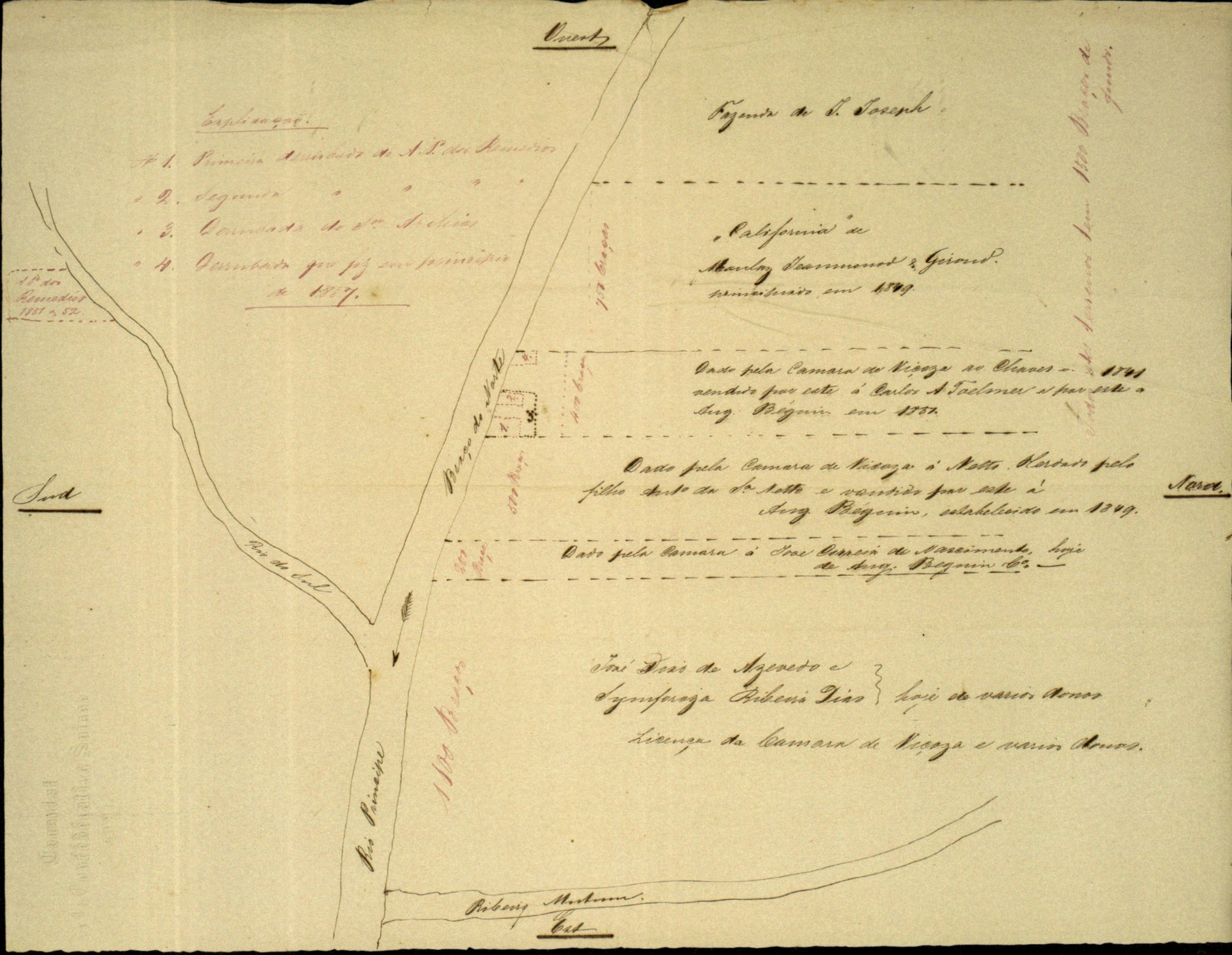

Oeste

Sud

Nord

Est

Fazenda de S. Joseph.

Explicação.
#1. Primeira derrubada de N. S. dos Remedios
 2. Segunda   "   "   "
 3. Derrubada de Sr Archias
 4. Derrubada que fiz em principio de 1857.

"California" de
Maulaz Jeanmonod & Giroud.
principiado em 1849.

Dado pela Camara de Viçoza ao Chaves e ... 1841
vendido por este á Carlos A. Faelmer e por este a
Aug. Béguin em 1851.

Dado pela Camara de Viçoza á Netto. Herdado pelo
filho d'este da S^a Netto e vendido por este á
Aug. Béguin, estabelecido em 1849.

Dado pela Camara á Joze Correia de Nascimento, hoje
de Aug. Béguin C^a.

Joze Dias de Azevedo e
Sympheroza Ribeira Dias } hoje de varios donos

Licença da Camara de Viçoza e varios donos.

N. S. dos Remedios 1851 e 52

Braço do Norte
Rio do Sul
Rio Primeiro
Ribeiro Matheus

700 braças
400 braças
500 braças
200 braças
1100 braças

The French translation of a bill introduced by deputy Wilhelm Joos (1821-1900) and dated July 13, 1864, calling on the Federal Council to produce a report on banning the slave trade practiced by Swiss colonists living in Brazil.

"The Federal Council is invited to examine and draft a report on the question of whether the lot of many Swiss sharecroppers who are in Brazil could not be improved by adopting penal measures against Swiss who buy or sell slaves after the Confederation Councils have declared this traffic unworthy of the Swiss name."

Federal Archives, Bern, Switzerland

Wilhelm Joos was a fierce opponent of slavery. His bill was based on the desire to improve the living conditions of Swiss sharecroppers in Brazil. The members of the Swiss parliament agreed to transmit his bill to the Federal Council to prompt that authority to draft a report. The Council, however, concluded that the initiative appeared to be unfair and could harm the financial interests of certain Swiss.

Proposition.

Traduction.

Le Conseil fédéral est invité à examiner et à faire rapport sur la question de savoir si le sort de beaucoup de colons partiaires suisses, qui se trouvent au Brésil ne pourrait pas être amélioré par l'adoption de dispositions pénales contre les Suisses qui achèteraient ou vendraient des esclaves, après que les Conseils de la Confédération auraient déclaré ce trafic indigne du nom de Suisse.

Berne, 13 Juillet 1864.

sig. Dr Guillaume Joos,
Membre du Conseil National.

Copie.

Colonie Leopoldina, le 22 Août 1888

Monsieur E. Schläpfer
Consul Suisse
Bahia.

Monsieur le Consul,

A cette date j'ai disposé Rs. 100,000 sur la maison Franc.co d'Asis Souza en payement de frais des documents que je vous ai remis pour Mr. le Consul Général Raffard, je vous prie de bien vouloir remettre cette somme le plutôt possible à Mr. Asis.

Tout va mal par ici, je ne sais comment nous nous en tirerons, nous restons avec des plantations, des dettes et personne pour travailler, s'il n'y a aucune indemnisation pour les ex-esclaves nous sommes tous ruinés, Mr. Bornand seul excepté. ~ Je ne vois pas de quelle manière on pourra liquider la succession Voegelin, ceux qui doivent à la succession sont sans rien comme tous les autres.

Agréez Mr. le Consul, l'assurance de ma parfaite considération

signé Fred. L. Jeanmonod
Vice Consul Suisse

CONSULAT DE SUISSE.

BAHIA
Brésil.

F. St. Itaparica

N° 2.

Bahia, le 22 Janvier 1895.

Monsieur le Consul Général,

J'ai l'honneur de répondre à votre office N° 3 du 5 crt. par lequel vous me demandez mon opinion sur l'utilité de continuer le Vice-Consulat de Caravellas & Colonie Leopoldina ou sur les inconvénients qu'il y aurait de le supprimer.

En vue du nombre considérablement diminué de ressortissants suisses demeurant dans le district en question, l'existence d'une représentation officielle ne me paraît guère de nécessité, d'autant plus que le Vice-Consul démissionnaire Monsieur L. Bornand s'était dès son entrée en fonctions et plusieurs fois depuis plaint du peu d'égards que les autorités brésiliens de son district montraient vis-à-vis de notre représentant. En outre, comme j'ai déjà eu l'honneur de vous le dire, Monsieur L. Bornand a cru devoir me remettre l'archive du Vice-Consulat lors de son départ de Caravellas, parceque l'opinion qu'il disait avoir de son frère Monsieur Ch. Bornand à cette époque ne lui paraissait pas assez favorable pour le proposer comme successeur et que en dehors du nommé il ne voyait personne à qui confier la gérence du Vice-Consulat.

Il est vrai que sous ce point de vue Monsieur L. Bornand a depuis changé d'opinion, mais les termes de la réponse qu'il a reçu de son frère, déclarant

Inventaire.

Des archives du Vice-Consulat de la Confédération Suisse à la **Colonie Leopoldina** .

N.°	Documents anciens	N.°	Documents nouveaux.
1.	Titres Fallet	29.	Correspondance L. Bornand 1891
2.	„ 9 possession d'esclaves (Fallet)	30.	„ „ „ 1892
3.	2 Circulaires du Conseil Fédéral	31.	„ „ „ 1893
4.	1 broch. J. Neutralité de la Suisse, Willy	32.	„ „ „ 1894
5.	2 réglements p.° fonctionaires consulaires 1869/8.		**Autres objets**
6.	2 conventions consulaires avec Brésil	33.	1 Copie de lettres manuscrit
7.	Succession Fallet, correspond.ce p.culier.	34.	1 „ „ „ p. presse à copier
8.	Comptes acquittés (Fallet)	35.	1 Livre protocole
9.	Correspondance 1851-67	36.	1 „ registre matricule
10.	„ Kessler, Bahia	37.	1 „ p. Caisse
11.	„ Louis Meyrat (1841-49)	38.	Sceau et timbre
12.	Plans et dessins (Fallet)	39.	1 timbre ancien
13.	Correspondance Jeanmonod	40.	1 broch. legislation civile des cantons p. Lardy
14.15.16.	„ diverses	41.	1 guide p. officiers d'état civil
17.18.	„ Jeanmonod	42.	1 „ question de l'alcoolisme
19.20.	„ „	43.	1 Délibérations p.° provésintés p. della p.eilles
21.	Dossier J. Girond	44.	2 Tarif des douanes Suisses
22.	„ Naras	45.	1 „ d'usage des „ „ 1893
23.	Documents relatifs à l'arrelam.to p. cimetières, Flack	46.	1 code fédéral des obligations
24.	Dossier J.-M. Vogelin	47.	1 „ pénal fédéral
25.	Ottaire Flack Consandier	48.	Constitution fédérale 1874.
26.	Correspondance 1877-85 ⎱ avec Jeanmonod		— Colonie Leopoldina, 14 Mai 18..
27.	„ 1886-89 ⎱ classée par		sig: L. Bornand
28.	„ 1890 — ⎱ L. Bornand.		ex- Vice-Consul de Suisse

Mocambos, *Quilombos* and Rural Black Communities in Brazil: Histories and Memories

Flávio dos Santos Gomes

In Brazil, slavery lasted more than 350 years (1516–1888), affecting indigenous and African workers in the early plantations in the northeast of the country during the early sixteenth century, as well as slave laborers in major cities and particularly in centers of coffee production in the southeast. In "Black American" countries, runaway slaves and their descendants formed communities in the colonial era, when slavery and trans-Atlantic trade in African slaves flourished. In Colombia and Ecuador, these settlements were called *palenques*, while in neighboring Venezuela they were known as *cumbes*. In the Caribbean they had a wider variety of names: maroons and *maronage* in the English and French Caribbean, respectively; in Cuba and Puerto Rico, the phenomenon of escaped slaves was known as *cimaronaje* and in the Guianas such fugitives were called bush negroes. In colonial and post-colonial Brazil, fugitive slave communities became known as *mocambos* and *quilombos*, which derived from *mukambu* and *kilombo*, terms commonly used in various parts of Central Africa to describe makeshift settlements, huts or camps.

Between the sixteenth and nineteenth centuries, *mocambos* and *quilombos* of various sizes proliferated across Brazil. They formed around plantations (Pernambuco and Bahia) and in the mining regions of Goiás, Mato Grosso and Minas Gerais, in the eighteenth century, as well as on the borders with the Guianas, Argentina and Uruguay. Colonial legislation only defined fugitive slave communities in 1740, when it defined *mocambos* and *quilombos* as "any remote settlement with more than five runaway Black slaves." However, almost two centuries previously town councils already had official records of such communities, even referring to their economic activities – some had farm buildings and pestles [for crushing grain] – designed to lay the foundations for lasting rural communities.

More fugitive slave communities formed in Brazil than any other country due to their ability to integrate into local economies, including through barter trade with other agricultural sectors to provide supplies in certain areas, such as the production of flour and other foodstuffs. Many of these Black communities survived for several generations, while others were repressed and forced to relocate. *Mocambos* and *quilombos* were swiftly suppressed, both to recover fugitive labor and to prevent the demographic and socioeconomic expansion of these communities. In Bahia, this suppression of *mocambos* began as early as in 1575, and reports existed of *mocambos* in Bahia's southern region of Recôncavo in the 1580s.

A predominantly Black, rural community of freed slaves, slaves, former slaves, laborers, tradesmen and also fugitives began to develop – particularly from the eighteenth century onward – based on the experiences of the *mocambos* and *quilombos*. These newly established and remote communities were notable for their non-isolation. They continued to exist at the time of slavery and in the post-emancipation period, undertaking migrations, forming alliances, and resisting acts of repression, supported by other sectors of the colonial and post-colonial society's economy. *Quilombos* in a single region could function in various ways, forming communities of rural workers who gradually established rural villages. These socioeconomic interactions allowed several small-sized rural Black settlements to develop unique local cultures and traditions that combined African, indigenous and European influences.

The widespread rural Black communities established themselves in various ways: on lands inherited from runaway slaves, *quilombo* settlers and their descendants; donated by the religious orders to former slaves; bought by freed slaves and then passed down the generations; distributed by the state in exchange for conscription in wars; and also following the many migrations of freed slaves and their families immediately after abolition. Communities of *quilombo*-descendants have been identified in various locations as traditional rural Black populations, rural Black communities and rural Black neighborhoods.

With its descendants of Brazilian-born slaves of African origin, in addition to the emancipated Black population after the abolition of slavery, Helvécia's Black community is an example of a group of rural *quilombo*-descendants. It was formed by small groups of itinerant fugitives, migrations of former Black slaves freed during the final decades of slavery and, above all, by the ownership and working of the land by rural Black slave-descendent families. This community exemplifies the experiences of *mocambos* and *quilombos* and various other rural Black communities, forming part of a broader historical process connecting experiences of slavery and emancipation for rural and semi-urban Black populations, occupying lands and producing ethnic and cultural identities that underwent constant transformations.

What defined the cultures of Brazil's various *quilombos* and *mocambos*? What little we know about daily life in these communities we owe to the records – from the sixteenth to the nineteenth centuries – left to us by those bent on eradicating them. Accounts of the economies, populations and defense strategies are often incomplete, missing or else exaggerated. It was essential to show *quilombos* as being hard to wipe out; these communities posed a challenge economically and in their ability to organize and put up resistance. We only have a scanty understanding of *quilombo* residents' actual lives, family customs, worldviews, kinships, appointment systems, and so on. However, some signs reveal their cultural and socioeconomic form of organization. *Quilombo* culture is often first associated with African culture, based on a deeply engrained romantic idea of *quilombos* as supposedly remote settlements as one might find in Africa. But the available evidence points to *quilombo* culture as a particularly American phenomenon, in the case of Brazil. Even though *quilombos* resulted from a collective escape of African slaves, they also brought together people from various origins. Living together in *quilombos*, members of these communities had to adapt practices and customs from various origins and shared ethnic perspectives, possibly including both African influences and cultural reinventions in the diaspora. This was the background of the Black population of Helvécia – recognized in 2005 as being *quilombo*-descendants. Located in the municipal district of Nova Viçosa, in the south of Bahia, this settlement developed out of the haciendas of Swiss and German colonists in the second half of the nineteenth century, as descendants of the *quilombos* on lands occupied by rural Black villagers.

Some information is available today, but there is a notable silence about how these communities formed, leading to a situation of invisibility, non-history, non-territory and non-memory. The lack of surveys and the non-recognition of territories and cultures led to racial exclusion, obscuring from view these rural Black communities and their traditions of resistance to slavery and their fight for emancipation. In Helvécia, memories and cultural representations point to historical complexity: a rural Black community of *quilombo*-descendants with land, kinship and memories. Research on Helvécia has produced records on the experiences of slavery and post-abolition records: generational histories that reconstruct local Black families' ethnic relations and their various material and symbolic expectations for work. There are also images on the origins of Europeans' presence, amid narratives that shed light on different stages in the community's history, both of the arrival of the Swiss colonists, the acquisition and ownership of slaves, and even earlier, from the time of Africans' disembarkation in ports in the south of Bahia.

In this way, the history of Helvécia is mixed with the formation processes of Black communities in the final decades of slavery and in the twentieth century. In the past twenty years, several scholars, social movements, federal, state and local authorities have actively recognized *quilombo*-descendants. Since Brazil's 1988 Constitution granted them land ownership rights and deeds, hundreds of rural Black communities, spread across Brazil, have been struggling for citizenship and land. "*Quilombo*-descendant" was used as an all-encompassing term in the Constitution itself, which officially recognized rights to land and citizenship. However, many communities have faced various difficulties on different scales, partly due to delays by the state and federal authorities in granting definitive land deeds or else as a result of mistakes in legal interpretations and even in the understanding of experts and social movements. The main problems include the expectations raised that these communities may have preserved specific pieces of history and are able to recover factual historical records about their existence during the period of slavery.

Researchers of the historical experiences of *quilombos* and *mocambos* in the seventeenth, eighteenth and nineteenth centuries, or who produce contemporary ethnographic studies have proposed broadening the definition of *quilombo* and "*quilombo*-descendant." In their struggle for recognition, community members and leaders have formed a movement to re-semanticize the meaning of *quilombos*. The definition of the term "descendant" and the policy developed for members of these communities could be conceived as having four theoretical underpinnings: memory, ethnicity, territory and citizenship.

Helvécia and various Black communities in Brazil today remain invisible, although some important post-abolition studies have unearthed some records. Some racist perspectives on certain social beliefs from the first half of the twentieth century designed a supposedly capitalist and civilizing mindset in which race and the slave-owning past stood in the way of modernity in Brazilian society. Images of cities and their cosmopolitanism invented obtuse rural worlds in which the past of slavery and the early post-emancipation decades needed to be forgotten. Beyond this persisting structural racism, the stories and images of Helvécia are essential for investigating the experiences and lives of Blacks in rural areas. There are the memories and hopes of Black families (descendants from African slaves) dreaming of the lands granted by landowners or seized for the construction and inhabitation of *mocambos*.

Helvécia = Switzerland?
Countering the Colonization of Attitudes,
Perspectives and Remembrance

Izabel Barros, Rohit Jain, Shalini Randeria

Will readers react to the title of this book, HELVÉCIA: A Swiss Colonial History in Brazil, *with astonishment or even incredulity? What does Switzerland, a European country without any colonies, have to do with far-flung Brazil? Will readers expect the images in this volume to provide traces of heroic emigrants or an alpine Swiss folk culture in faraway Latin America? Or will they unconsciously seek Europeanness in the names, and whiteness in the faces, of the people from Helvécia?*

The study of Swiss colonialism, especially in Brazil, has gained prominence in recent years. A striking example of this newfound interest was the Swiss celebration of the two hundredth anniversary of the founding of the city of Nova Friburgo in 2018. In the nineteenth century, the Portuguese crown and Swiss trading networks actively recruited hundreds of Swiss families from Fribourg to colonize the hinterland of the royal seat of Rio de Janeiro and contribute to the country's *branqueamento* ("whitening" policy).[1] The anniversary celebrated in Switzerland as a heroic epic of emigration was, from an Afro-Brazilian perspective – that is, from the perspective of indigenous communities and of formerly enslaved people (*quilombolas*) – a reminder of a brutal colonial regime that resulted in thousands of deaths over the course of several decades.

Today *Quilombo* Helvécia, located in the south of the state of Bahia, is overshadowed by Nova Friburgo in the state of Rio de Janeiro, which enjoys greater political and economic importance. However, Helvécia is not entirely unheard of in Switzerland. Some decades ago linguists studied the remnants there of what might have been a Creole influenced by Swiss German,[2] while historians attempted to quantify the fortunes that Swiss families had amassed in Helvécia and Switzerland.[3] In 2017 Denise Bertschi, an artist, tasked herself with revealing the seemingly invisible material traces that Helvécia's colonial past had left on its buildings, streetscapes, landscapes, and everyday objects.[4] This book, *Helvécia,* by Swiss-Brazilian photographer Dom Smaz and Brazilian journalist

Milena Machado, is the result of research conducted since 2015 which takes the reappraisal of Swiss colonialism in Brazil an important step further. For the first time, the consistent perspective is that of the Afro-Brazilian, resistance-based reality of *Quilombo* Helvécia. Those photographed either look directly into the eyes of the viewers or deliberately elude their gaze. This assertiveness, or casual disinterest, toward onlookers challenges us to exoticize Afro-Brazilians, forcing us instead to confront ways of life and attitudes marked by centuries of resistance that reject the white, Eurocentric gaze. What kind of interaction does such an image trigger? Do the people in the photos and those gazing at them belong to the same history? Do the photographs open up a horizon for us to reflect upon the postcolonial entanglements that bind us and invite us to (re)establish new, different relationships?

1. Free of Guilt? Colonialism without Colonies à la Suisse

The use of a postcolonial perspective for Switzerland may seem at first sight to be rather implausible or irrelevant. Indeed, the Swiss government has repeatedly emphasized that it has had nothing whatsoever to do with colonialism. It stated this officially at the World Conference against Racism in Durban in 2001. Foreign Minister Ignazio Cassis reiterated it after his tour of Algeria, Mali, Gambia, and Senegal in 2021.

Yet as the example of Helvécia shows, though Switzerland like many European societies did not have colonies of its own, it nevertheless participated in, and benefited greatly from, the colonial project. Not only did the Swiss travel to and settle in areas colonized overseas by their European neighbors, they also engaged in trade with European colonies, missionized there, explored the terrain, and exploited natural resources. As plantation owners, engineers, investors, and traders, or as missionaries and mercenaries, Swiss men and women were involved in local colonial exploitation and plunder, including the slave trade. In academia as in popular discourse, a distinction is still often made between the differences of British, Dutch, German, and French colonial rule. However, it is important to realize that colonialism was a pan-European, multinational project, one that cannot be defined in national terms. It was the commonly shared ideology of "race," and the claim that by virtue of their superiority "whites" are entitled to rule over others, that led to cooperation and solidarity among the white settlers of various nations within any colony. In short, the Swiss at home and abroad not only benefited from the imperial rule of other European powers. But many Swiss public and private actors actively contributed to the maintenance and expansion of the colonial world order. And, in the other direction, goods, people, assets, images, and narratives that flowed into Switzerland from the colonies created the structural conditions that enabled modern Switzerland to be built. Without the trade in cotton, sugar, coffee, gold, and enslaved people, industrialization in Switzerland could not have occurred the way it did; its machine and chemical industries, its railroads and its banking system could not have been established the way they were. Besides economic interdependence, it was human zoos, advertisements for colonial goods, schoolbooks, nursery rhymes, museum collections, adventure films, and carnival customs which shaped the Swiss imagination, influencing institutions and public discourse. In the process of modernization, the Swiss learned to perceive and identify themselves – like their European neighbors – as "white" and civilized, distinguished from non-white "Others" who were, and often still are, regarded as exotic, barbaric, primitive, or as "noble savages." These colonial relations, which have brought forth our world with its binary worldview, are often overlooked in the current perception and treatment of Swiss history. Neither acknowledging nor revising these centuries-old relationships thus perpetuates them.

The power of the images and localizations in this volume allows us to question this deliberate forgetting and leads us to reconsider the spatial boundaries of Switzerland. It allows our historical consciousness to extend beyond the limited territory of the nation-state to encompass the networks and interchanges that tied Swiss cities, institutions, and families to specific places and people in the global South. In *The Satanic Verses* Salman Rushdie, the British-Indian novelist, points out that the British were not familiar with their own history because so much of it had taken place overseas. This is also true of Switzerland, for Helvetia also occurred in Helvécia. And Helvécia is also Switzerland. Such a perspective of entangled histories[5] transcends the simplistic juxtaposition of metropolitan center and colony by locating Switzerland's past and present identity within a transnational, postcolonial framework.

Attention has been drawn of late to a "raceless racism" in Switzerland that renders itself invisible and, therefore, justifies the claim that Switzerland was, and is, not part of the colonial project.[6] Switzerland's highly idealized portrayal of its neutrality, benevolent internationalism and humanitarianism abroad have shaped this national narrative since the Holocaust and decolonization, thus virtually whitewashing the country's colonial, racialized entanglements. This continuous struggle to be "free of guilt" is probably much more laborious than an honest confrontation with the country's own past.

In recent years, scholars, activists, and artists in Switzerland have begun to address the heritage of colonialism and migration in Switzerland.[7] The Black Lives Matter movement catapulted these efforts into Swiss mainstream consciousness in 2020. The urgency of addressing this heritage is obvious. But the challenges it involves should not be underestimated: How can the stories obscured over the centuries be told in the absence of institutional, documental archives that contain them? How can race and resistance to colonialism be rendered visible without creating new violent forms of representation? What role can art – in this case, photography – play in creating new forms of representation and interaction that do not once again reduce people, their culture, and their histories to objects of vicarious consumption? And how can new, postcolonial relationships be established that not only acknowledge historical violence and present-day injustices but also open up paths toward a different, reparative future?

2. The Immortal *Quilombola* and the Slave Revolt of 1881/82, or: A Short History of Resistance in Helvécia

The Leopoldina colony, as Helvécia was called when it was founded, was the first colony established in Brazil by non-Portuguese European settlers in the nineteenth century. It was founded in southern Bahia in late 1818, one year before the Portuguese government officially opened the first colony, Nova Friburgo near the royal seat of Rio de Janeiro. The Leopoldina colony's remoteness from the capital of the empire and its rural setting necessitated particularly strong networks as well as an especially brutal spirit of conquest.[8]

It was Auguste-Frédéric de Meuron "de Bahia" (1789–1852) from Switzerland who, in the mid-1820s, acted as a liaison between the local authorities and Swiss merchants and investors. These in turn were followed by families from Switzerland and Germany, who became plantation owners, but also craftsmen, foremen, and accountants. We can certainly speak of an international commercial empire centered on the hub of Lisbon. By the late eighteenth century, Swiss merchants, mainly from Neuchâtel, were key players in the coffee, sugar, cocoa, and cotton trades; they were also exporters of manufactured goods from Europe such as "Indienne" textiles, which served as a currency for the purchase of enslaved people on the West African coast.[9] The most notorious exponent of this trade was David de Pury (1709–1786), an Anglo-Swiss banker for the royal court of Portugal, founder and shareholder of the firm Pury, Mellish & Devisme, which held a monopoly on the export of pau brasil wood, and one of the principal shareholders of the general commercial company of Perambuco and Paraíba. To this day, his statue proudly adorns Neuchâtel, where he was born, and his wealth lingers in prestigious buildings and assets in the city.

Barely six years after it was founded, the plantation was said to resemble a Garden of Eden. When co-investor Charles-Louis Borrel visited the colony in 1826, he was delighted. "The avenue of orange trees leading from the river to my pavilion was overgrown with fruit, the flowers were fragrant, the hummingbirds with their metallic luster sparkled in the sun like the most beautiful diamonds."[10] Despite this glorified view, Leopoldina was marked by violence and slavery from the beginning and grew into a massive colonial enterprise. By 1850, coffee production in the region accounted for as much as 90 percent of the total in Bahia, and the colony included two hundred whites and 2,000 enslaved people, according to sources. Coffee production brought with it a particular brutality in the management of the plantation and in the exploitation of enslaved people.

Starting in the 1860s, the Brazilian plantation economy became the target of criticism and local resistance to slavery, including in the northeast of the country. The long coast of São Mateus in the state of Espírito Santo (where Leopoldina was also located) was considered a particularly uncivilized area, where rebellious indigenous and enslaved populations repeatedly undermined efforts at colonization and either instigated revolts or fled the plantations.*

Very close to the Leopoldina colony is where Benedito Meia-Légua was born. He continues to be a legendary figure in the oral history of the region. As a fugitive slave, he always carried an image of Saint Benedict, the Black saint to whom he was devoted. Legend has it that Benedito Meia-Légua possessed supernatural powers, including the ability to be resurrected. Like other *quilombolas* in the region, Benedito's group was actively involved with sections of the local population as well as with peasants, who sympathized with his cause. The São Mateus region, where Benedito set up his base camp, saw an increasing number of uprisings: "Armed *quilombolas* attacked the farms, and more and more enslaved people fled their masters to join them. Fear of the tables being turned was so great that the inhabitants of São Mateus feared

* The term *aquilobamento* describes this tense liberation from colonial subjugation as well as the vision of autonomous management of land and cultural and political self-organization. Since the introduction of slavery, such liberated settlements, called quilombos in Brazil, characterized life in the New World (see the text by Flávio dos Santos Gomes in this publication, p. 179).

that this village would become a second São Domingos."[11] The residents of São Mateus were referring to the Haitian revolution of 1791–1804, which had led to the establishment of the first Black republic and the first modern constitution that enshrined participation in the political system irrespective of race. Uprisings in Brazil in 1881 and 1882 culminated in the violent murder of the owner of an estate by his enslaved people in April 1884. The landholding in question was one of the oldest, having resulted from a partnership between a lieutenant colonel in the Portuguese army, Augusto Beguim, and the Swiss vice-consul of Caravelas, Frédéric-Louis Jeanmonod. As even the Swiss colonizer Arnold Wildberger conceded, this uprising on the Monte Cristo plantation was caused by the "terrible treatment of the slaves by the Europeans, the owners of the colony."[12]

In a region where the confrontation between freedom fighters and slaveholders was particularly fierce, the resistance of the elite to the Golden Law of May 13, 1888, which decreed the immediate and unconditional abolition of slavery, was not exactly mild. The uprisings and newfound freedom of those enslaved terrified the owners of plantations and estates, who did everything in their power to mobilize the local authorities. Nevertheless, some 2,000 enslaved people from the Leopoldina colony, and the surrounding area, gained their freedom. The abolition of slavery ultimately resulted from small acts of rebellion that fueled political and legal struggles: carrying weapons, resisting arrest, claiming to be free, publicly admonishing known slaveholders. According to historian Flávio dos Santos Gomes, they constituted a "micro-politics forged with rare political skill by the freedmen and, before them, the enslaved."[13] In the end, all the colonizers gradually fled, and the former colony was refashioned as *Quilombo* by the insurgents and other liberated people from the region. Its colonial name, Leopoldina, also disappeared, and instead the name Helvécia came to be used commonly after the name of the most important plantation of the colony: "Helvetia." This plantation had originally belonged to Swiss colonizer Johann Martin Flach, then to his son João Flach, who had bought up another plantation called "Helvetia" and integrated them into one. Coffee cultivation and trade soon ceased, and Helvécia disappeared from the map of global trade, becoming instead a place of Afro-Brazilian lifestyle with its own subsistence economy.

Analyzing the effects of the Golden Law in Bahia, and especially in the colony of Leopoldina, Swiss colonizer Arnold Wildberger came to the following conclusion: "The inconvenience and damage that this law is causing to agriculture in the region of Salvador (*Recôncavo*) and in the southern part of the province are incalculable. This decree is a fatal blow to the Leopoldina; the emancipated are abandoning their rural properties; they seek no other freedom than the right to live in cities; disorder and misery follow. The large and prosperous coffee farms soon fell into disrepair, the wealthy owners returned, the less adventurous emigrated to the cities of Bahia or Rio de Janeiro, and the lush lands were abandoned because there were no hands to harvest the fruit."[14] Even today, the end of the Leopoldina colony is often portrayed as the story of a company bankrupted by the abolition of slavery, or as the abandoning of a hard-earned civilized place that was consumed once again by the wilderness. From the perspective of the community in Helvécia, the end of the Leopoldina colony was achieved instead through a long history of struggles which led to freedom and autonomy.

3. Excursus: Cosmologies of Resistance

Seen in this context, the images of everyday life in Helvécia that this volume brings together take on a new meaning: they document an Afro-Brazilian culture of resistance made up of many voices, one dating back to the nineteenth century, and thus even to the beginning of slavery. As the Brazilian historian Luiz Antônio Simas reminds us, the violence of European conquests was aimed first and foremost at the body: "The first attack of colonialism is directed against the body. The Christian catechism domesticates the body through sin. It is also the body that has been domesticated through the logic of labor. Through enslavement, the body became a tool; the body of the colonized woman was domesticated through rape, and the body was also domesticated through the logic of masculinity and formed into the body of the producer. The colonial project is reflected in the body."[15]

Just as colonial violence is inscribed in the bodies of the people in local communities, so, too, are moments of resistance and hope. These continue to be reflected in social relationships, food, and dress, and especially in Afro-Brazilian cosmologies, including *umbanda*, *candomblé*, and *encantaria*.* These spiritual ways of life carry traces of a diversity of African and indigenous traditions that shaped, and continue to shape, relationships with ancestors and spirits of nature into worldviews that are held by entire societies. In European historiography and academic literature, the millions of enslaved people brought to the New World are often portrayed as an undifferentiated mass, ignoring the fact that their languages, religions, customs, and political institutions were heterogeneous and varied. Transcultural intermingling during exile and resistance gave rise to new cults, rituals, deities, and ghosts, which in turn forged new identities and communities of trust in the New World.[16]

Christianity was undoubtedly one of the most powerful weapons used to colonize these spirits. However, it is precisely in the syncretic appropriation of Christian symbolism in *umbanda*, *candomblé*, or *encantaria* that the most effective form of resistance is also revealed: in indigenous and Afro-Brazilian cosmologies, it is the body that receives the ancestors, the *encantados* and the *orixás*. The polytheism of these cults easily integrate and absorb the Euro-Christian god; the latter becomes one among many. In fact, Christian symbolism is omnipresent in the rituals and processions; the statues of the Virgin Mary and crucifixes become sacred vessels in which the spirits of the ancestors, or their own deities, are received. In these cosmologies rooted in the *território*,* there is no separation between man and nature, nor between human beings, nor between the visible and the invisible. Here it is the drum that invokes the cosmological collective; it has its own rhythm, which is able to contradict the words being sung and to reverberate in people's bodies, in their movements, their facial expressions. It is the beat of the drum that summons the *encantados*, the *orixás*, and the ancestors to this day, and that is found in virtually all popular Afro-Brazilian forms of expression such as *samba*, *capoeira*, the *tambores de mina*, *de criola*, and *congada*.

These rhythms and physical expressions of the sacred continue to be closely linked to the resilience of Afro-Brazilian nations, conveying history, knowledge, and myths. It is, therefore, not surprising that expressions and rites linked to cults of African origin were banned by the authorities until 1940. And even today, when *samba* and *capoeira* are marketed as national cultural assets, the Afro-Brazilian cultural traditions that underlie them are frowned upon. Nevertheless, or precisely because of this, these forms of expression are thought to reflect secret knowledge that only reveals itself to those to whom it has been handed down. The existence of this knowledge in the bodies of the people, in their oral histories, in the rituals, and in the território preserves the stories of resistance in Helvécia and in other *quilombos*. It is living proof that the colonial project failed but also that it has not yet been fully defeated. The colonial missionary "development" of society was actually a de-envelopment of all things human and natural, of the human and the nonhuman, the visible and the invisible. It continues to hold sway unabated. However, the decolonial cultures of everyday life, like that of Helvécia, serve to remind us of the extent to which colonial violence shaped the cosmologies of modernity as well as postcolonial relationships into the present.

4. The Intersection of the Past and the Present

Let the daylight in, Tijuca
The time is now
We're going to fight
The alarm sounds
Here come the pros
They're from Borel
The samba's Nobel Prize

Carnaval!
Eternally as one
How good to be back
Reliving the emotion
I'd love to be with my father again
So many magical stories
The dream came true, and I don't want to wake up
Winged beings, castles high
A giant blow, fearless hero
In the snowy mountains an angel to protect
Best friend that a man can get

The world turns in time
Temple of invention
Everything fits in the pocket or in the palm of your hand
"The sound of the drum," precious gem
Whoever seeks will find
The password of love

A new era
"Relative age" of knowledge
Brilliant ideas
Explain life in every way
"Wise mind," the time flies with the traveler
The sun shines in a flash
Warming so many generations
I now see that yesterday
Is knowledge for tomorrow
Switzerland, inspiration in your history
With your flavors on the road
Show your feathers; the peacock has arrived.[17]

In 2015 Unidos da Tijuca, one of the most famous samba schools in Rio de Janeiro, staged "A Tale Marked in Time: The Swiss Look of Clóvis Bornay." This procession at a cost of 4.5 million reais (about US$ 1.5 million) was financed by private companies and the Swiss Confederation. It aimed to give the Brazilian public a sanitized representation of Switzerland that omitted any mention of the relationship between the Unidos da Tijuca samba school and Swiss colonialism. Auguste-Frédéric de Meuron (1789–1852), who had already brokered the founding of Leopoldina, built his second snuff factory near Rio de Janeiro in 1832. When de Meuron died in 1879, his nephew Frédéric Edouard Borrel, the namesake of Charles-Henri Borrel, who had co-founded Leopoldina, took over the company. He changed the name of the company to Borrel & Cie. The name Borrel then began to refer not only to the snuff factory, but also to the hill it was located on and ultimately to the favela that populated that hill starting in 1949. The tobacco products produced at the *fazenda* bore the name Borel; their symbol was a peacock. The headquarters of the Unidos da Tijuca samba school are in the Morro do Borel favela, and the symbol of the samba school is the same peacock that adorned the Borel cigarette packets that left Rio for Europe.

As this anecdote suggests, decolonization is far from complete as a process, for there are many continuities between the past and the present which remain deliberately unacknowledged. Switzerland's economic interests in Brazil are constantly growing, and the trade in raw materials and agricultural exports is flourishing. An unequal economic relationship continues to exist even if it is now often labeled as partnership and cultural exchange. Colonial images and resonances also live on, even if these have been given a new economic and cultural value. Issues of recognition of historical injustice and trauma inscribed in this shared history remain unaddressed. Emerging fascist tendencies in Euro-America and in postcolonial states such as Brazil, directed against indigenous minorities, migrants, and formerly enslaved people, demonstrate the need to come to terms with an unfinished, violent colonial past that continues to haunt us. At the same time, decolonial and anti-racist movements around the world continue to struggle to overcome the history of colonial violence. Is it possible to decolonize our world, or at least to build postcolonial relationships that acknowledge and, at best, can adequately address the ghosts of a long-buried past?

5. In Lieu of a Conclusion: An Appeal for a Reparative Present

New forms of history and memory must be created if this question is to be answered in the affirmative. Contrary to the invented traditions of nation-states confined to a defined territory and whose origins are stretched into glorious mythical pasts, history has always played out beyond present national borders and was always seen from a variety of perspectives, just as it has included both the violence of colonialism and forms of solidarity and resistance. But is it possible to wrest these entangled histories such as those of Helvécia and Switzerland from the grip of postcolonial amnesia, especially in the absence of written sources, or of only those produced by the colonizers, missionaries, or white abolitionists? Whose voices can be recovered and heard? Whose memory counts? How can these histories from a variety of different perspectives be negotiated in dialogue or integrated into a single narrative?

As Helvécia shows, the history of Switzerland also played out in Brazil – and vice versa. What was celebrated in Switzerland as a heroic epic of emigration and a civilizing project appears from the perspective of communities of former enslaved people as brutal colonial conquest. As historians Izabel Barros and André Nicacio Lima have pointed out,[18] using the history of Nova Friburgo as an example, what is needed to resolve this "clash of histories" is a historiography that both connects different geographical perspectives and incorporates non-academic, resistance-based forms of historiography. Not only is it necessary to simultaneously sift through archives in Brazil, Switzerland, Portugal, and elsewhere; it is also important to make visible transnational networks of voices and perspectives that conjointly report from the counter-archives of resistance-based knowledge.

Artistic (as well as ethnographic, activist, and spiritual) forms of action and expression use the body, the senses, and social relationships to uncover latent knowledge. And indeed, forgotten and repressed histories are embedded in emotional, moral, and aesthetic forms that may not be adequately rendered using academic modes of enquiry alone. In Europe, too, artistic strategies are becoming increasingly important in breaking postcolonial silences and creating new archives, memories, and relationships. At the same time, however, there is always the risk of drifting into appropriation, exoticism, and commodification, which have been inherent in modern European art since its inception, whether in the orientalism of a Gustave Flaubert, or the exoticism of Paul Gauguin, or the ironic appropriation of the "Other" in Dadaism.

Dom Smaz's sociological artistic depictions of everyday street scenes, *candomblé* rituals, and people from Helvécia represent an attempt to combine art in a different register with a postcolonial ethic. The photographer both participates in social life and observes it while following the rhythm of quotidian life in Helvécia. The images presented in this volume are as a result embedded in a composition that involves multiple historical and personal vantage points. This enables us to immerse ourselves in a world in which people rebel against the imposition of colonial authority to inhabit their own time and space – then as now.

This poetic, political journey could familiarize us with a world of anti-colonial resistance and portray past interconnections between our two worlds. It may stimulate new debates, research, and other projects. It may also engage a new audience. But is this enough? What must be done to preserve the relations between Switzerland and Helvécia that are conjured up as one looks at these pages? How could these relations be sustained beyond the moment of subjective aesthetic enjoyment or cultural consumption? And what does it take to avoid drifting into deep guilt or into exoticization of the "Others," or even into a desire for a common humanity, as if there were no existential differences based on one's location in different postcolonial geographies? Can equality and difference be accepted simultaneously?

In her essay on the European reception of the Haitian revolution, philosopher Susan Buck-Morss notes that "human universality emerges in the historical event at the point of rupture. It is in the discontinuities of history that people whose culture has been strained to the breaking point give expression to a humanity that goes beyond cultural limits."[19] In that sense, humanity exists only as a possibility. For the idea of universal humanity in the sense of the Eurocentric Enlightenment is an abstract illusion that always excludes certain "Others," thus displacing them from memory, from the narrative, from history, and from the world. This idea of a common humanity is realized only in very specific moments when people acknowledge and engage with postcolonial relations and, working together, establish them anew; when we enter the flow of intertwined histories and listen to voices full of rage, grief, and laughter calling for forgiveness, justice, reparation, and liberty. It is only in the existential experience of the "Other" that the idea of a shared humanity as a possibility surfaces on the horizon. The experiences of voices united in resistance to the colonial project, whether in *Quilombo* Helvécia or at the Black Lives Matter demonstration on the Bundesplatz in Bern, call for more than historical justice. These experiences embody the complexity, power, and beauty of humanity.

A postcolonial project of shared humanity therefore necessitates not only a different historiography and representation, but transnational processes of reparative justice as well. Neither empty political gestures nor intellectual or artistic engagement can suffice. It is known, for instance, that David de Pury bequeathed part of the fortune he accumulated in Brazil to the city of Neuchâtel. Moreover, he and his colonial compatriots funded the construction of villas and parks, and gave to Swiss society through philanthropy. Max Frey, who went on to establish the Frey chocolate factory in the Canton of Aargau, was undoubtedly present in Helvécia when he earned his wings in the Swiss commercial firm Cramer-Frey in Bahia, where he accumulated wealth for further business in Switzerland. Many a merchant, plantation owner, and naturalist amassed vast fortunes or large collections of cultural artifacts in colonial Brazil. In this sense, the history and prosperity of Helvécia is mutually imbricated with that of Switzerland.

Fragments of these stories that tie Switzerland to Helvécia appear and disappear. Once they have taken shape as images, faces, stories, sources, and witnesses, they can no longer be suppressed. They are also an antidote to imperial nostalgia. Dissipating colonial amnesia, they also signal the end of Swiss innocence. Helvécia and its people, their cosmologies and continuities are proof that the colonial project ultimately did not achieve its goals and that history has not come to an end. In Switzerland, what is called for is a different historiography and a policy of reparations that recognizes the legacy and continuities of colonialism.

1	Izabel Barros and André Nicacio Lima, "Geschichte dekolonisieren. Ein kritischer Beitrag zu einer globalen Schweizer Geschichte," in *Handbuch Neue Schweiz*, ed. Institut Neue Schweiz (Zurich, 2021).

2	Dante Lucchesi and Alan Baxter, *A comunidade de fala de Helvécia-BA*, Projeto Vertentes do Portugês Popular do Estado da Bahia (Salvador: Universidade Federal da Bahia, 2022), http://www.vertentes.ufba.br/a-comunidade-de-fala-de-helvecia-ba.

3	Béatrice Ziegler, "Schweizerische Kaufleute in Brasilien im 19. Jahrhundert," in *Jahrbuch für Geschichte Lateinamerikas* (Hamburg, 1988).

4	Susan Buck-Morss, *Hegel, Haiti and Universal History* (Pittsburgh: University of Pittsburgh Press, 2009).

5	Sebastian Conrad, Shalini Randeria and Regina Römhild, eds., *Jenseits des Eurozentrismus. Postkoloniale Perspektiven in den Geschichts- und Kulturwissenschaften* (Frankfurt am Main / New York, 2013).

6	Pinto dos Santos, O. Jovita Dankwa et al., eds., *Un/Doing Race. Rassifizierung in der Schweiz* (Zurich, 2022).

7	Among others, Patricia Purtschert, Barbara Lüthi, and Francesca Falk, eds., *Postkoloniale Schweiz. Formen und Folgen eines Kolonialismus ohne Kolonien* (Bielefeld, 2012); Patricia Purtschert and Harald Fischer-Tiné, eds., *Swiss Colonial Encounters and Postcolonial Assemblages* (Basingstoke, 2015); Institut Neue Schweiz, ed., *Handbuch Neue Schweiz* (Zurich, 2021).

8	Lucelinda Schramm Corrêa, "O resgate de um esquecimento. A colônia de Leopoldina," *GEOgraphia 13* (2005); Lucelinda Schramm Corrêa, *A torturante ausência de uma presença. A imigração alemã na Bahia do século XIX* (São Paulo, 2003).

9	Schweizerisches Landesmuseum, *Indiennes. Ein Stoff erobert die Welt!* (Zurich, 2021).

10	Christian Doninelli and Milena M. Neves, "Als Schweizer Sklaven hielten," *Neue Zürcher Zeitung Magazin*, March 2, 2018.

11	Yuko Miki, "Política antiescravista na fronteira. São Mateus, Espírito Santo (1884)," in João José Reis and Flávio dos Santos Gomes, *Revoltas escravas no Brasil* (São Paulo, 2021), 587.

12	Arnold Wildberger, *Os presidendes da provinvia da Bahia, efectivos e interinos (1824–1889)* (Salvador, 1949), 716.

13	Iacy Maia Mata and Ricardo Tadeu Caires Silva, "Resistência e rebeldia. Escravidão e pós-abolição no extremo sul da Bahua (1880–1889)," in João José Reis and Flávio dos Santos Gomes, *Revoltas escravas no Brasil* (São Paulo, 2021), 658–59.

14	Ibid., 650.

15	Luiz Antônio Simas, "Encontro entre Walter Benjamin e o Caboclo da Pedra Preta: O espaço escolar a contrapelo," in: Faculdade Getúlio Vargas, *Didática e prática de ensino de História II e Sociologia da educação*, May 12, 2017, https://www.youtube.com/watch?v=V5lRcTgd14Y.

16	Susan Buck-Morss, *Hegel, Haiti and Universal History* (Pittsburgh: University of Pittsburgh Press, 2009), 124 ff.

17	Translated by Quentin Pope: Samba Enredo 2015 – Um Conto Marcado no Tempo – O Olhar Suíço de Clóvis Bornay G.R.E.S. Unidos da Tijuca (RJ), Composição: Caio lves / Carlinhos / Cosminho / Fadico / Gustavinho Oliveira / José Luis / Josemar Manfredini / Rafael Tinguinha, in *Letras e musica Brasil*, https://www.letras.mus.br/unidos-da-tijuca-rj/samba-enredo-2015-um-conto-marcado-no-tempo-o-olhar-suico-de-clovis-bornay/.

18	Izabel Barros and André Nicacio Lima, "Geschichte dekolonisieren. Ein kritischer Beitrag zu einer globalen Schweizer Geschichte," in *Handbuch Neue Schweiz*, ed. Institut Neue Schweiz (Zurich, 2021).

19	Susan Buck-Morss, *Hegel, Haiti and Universal History* (Pittsburgh: University of Pittsburgh Press, 2009), 133.

This text is exactly what it describes and demands: a short history of the interconnectedness of Switzerland and Helvécia which itself emerged from the linkage of various transnational strands of knowledge and biographical information.

The input of Shalini Randeria, Rohit Jain, Izabel Barros, Dom Smaz and Milena Machado Neves, and the dialogue with the publishers, represents a demand to forge transnational alliances that will enable new postcolonial narratives and forms of solidarity.

In retrospect, this constellation is at best as coincidental as it is inevitable. Rohit and Shalini met a good fifteen years ago. At the time, Shalini was a professor of social anthropology at the University of Zurich. Having grown up in India, she studied there as well as in England and Germany. She has done more than anyone else to establish the postcolonial discourse in Europe in recent decades. At the same time, she always remained in touch with the concerns of grassroots movements and non-governmental organizations in South Asia. Full of enthusiasm, her young doctoral student Rohit learned to think of research and politics as a unit and developed a self-confident postcolonial stance. Growing up in Switzerland as the son of Indian parents, he was looking for a way to feel at home and found the means to do so in ethnography and inventing anti-racist happenings. Since then, he and many comrades-in-arms have helped to shape new postcolonial spaces in Switzerland in order to strengthen a diaspora of the many. In this critical-carnivalesque struggle, the paths of Rohit and Izabel crossed. Having lived in Switzerland since 2005, she has, in the face of much structural resistance, established herself as a decolonial, feminist historian and an activist for human and environmental rights. In doing so, she draws connections between transnational struggles involving Brazil, West Africa and Switzerland and reflects on them from an indigenous and Afro-Brazilian perspective.

As a professor and migrant of color, as a second-generation Swiss-Indian and a social anthropologist, and as a historian and activist socialized in Brazil, we apply our different experiences, intersectional privileges and stakes to the history of Switzerland and Helvécia. At the same time, we are affectively, politically and intellectually caught up in the transnational and postcolonial entanglements.

Being invited to write about Switzerland's relationship to its colonial history using Helvécia as an example required linking different points of view. The exchange with Dom and Milena was a further productive and necessary node in this transnational network. They, too, were in search of connections: historical, political, visual. Like all of us.

This interplay has resulted in an associative text, indeed a fragmentary journey, that connects generations, continents and life experiences. It is an experiment in learning from each other about how Europe's identities, histories and image archives can be rethought. In the nineteenth century, Europe was defined as white, homogeneous and modern. In this text, we subscribe to the far older tradition that Europe has always been – and continues to be – a cosmopolitan land at the crossroads of Asia, Africa and the Americas: home to a global diaspora.

I. B., R. J., S. R.

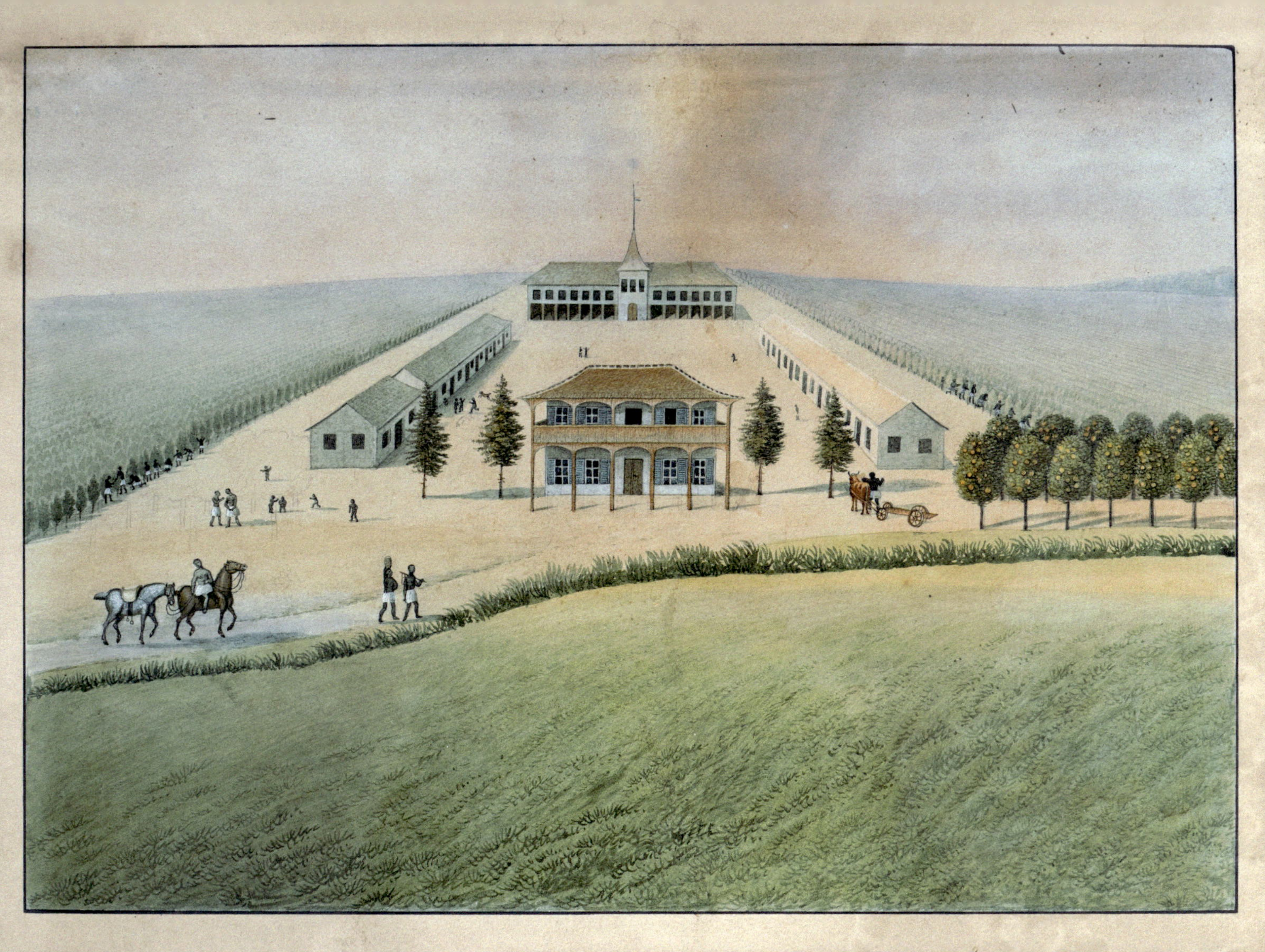

"The lane of orange trees leading from the river to my house was covered with fruit, the flowers filled the air with a sweet fragrance, the hummingbirds with their metallic glints shone in the sun like the most beautiful diamonds."
Charles-Louis Borrel visiting his Brazilian farm in 1826.

The Castel de Pombal (Dovecot Château) Plantation of Charles-Louis Borrel, the father of Eugène Borrel, one of the cofounders of the Leopoldina colony.

Jean-Frédéric Bosset de Luze (Geneva 1754-1838), between 1826 and 1838 (watercolor drawing on paper, 33 x 48 cm). Private collection, Geneva, Switzerland

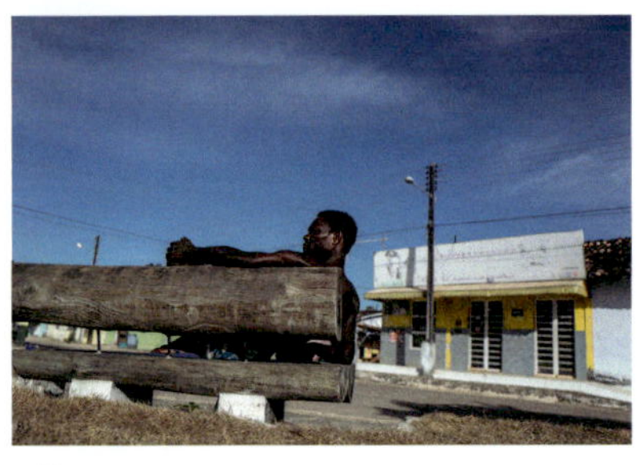

→ 7

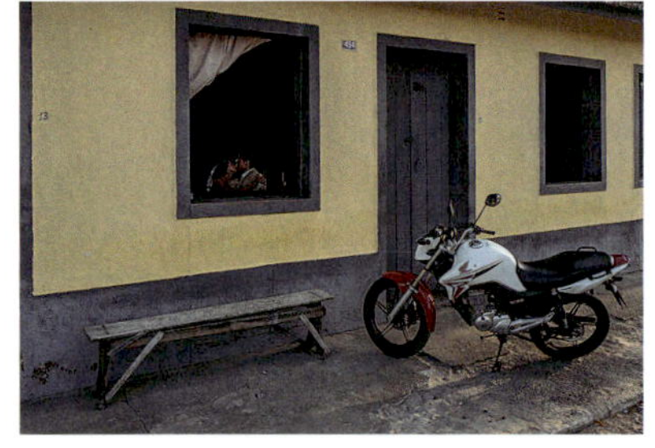

→ 18

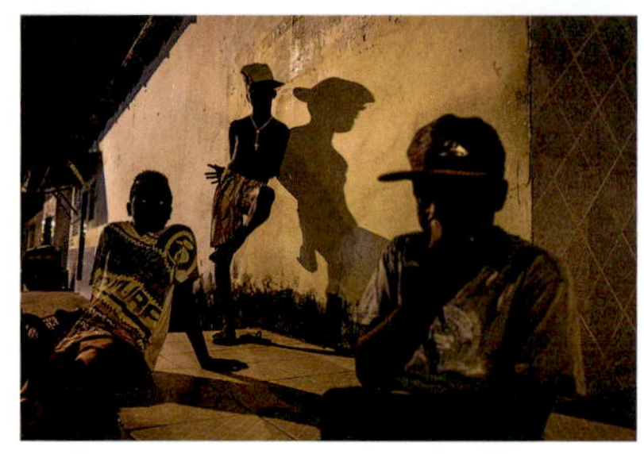

→ 30

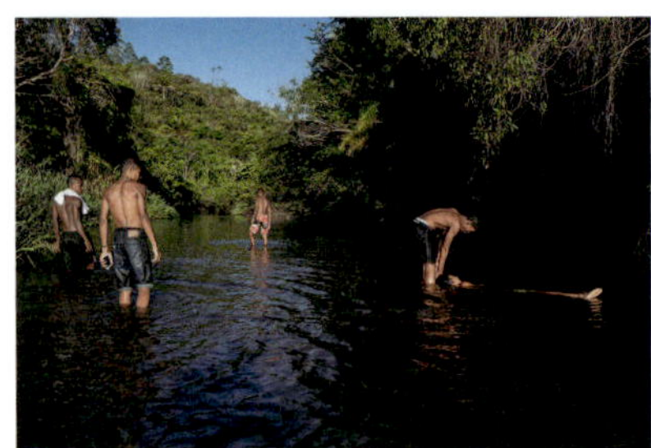

→ 8

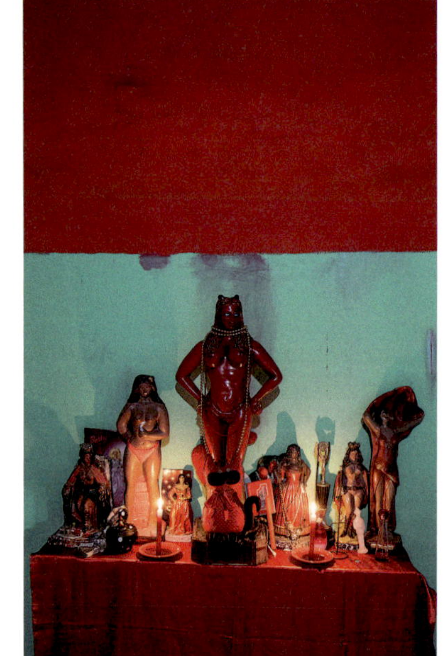

→ 23

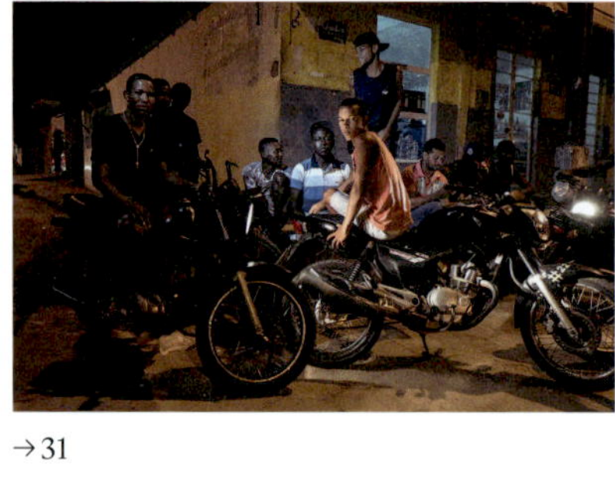

→ 31

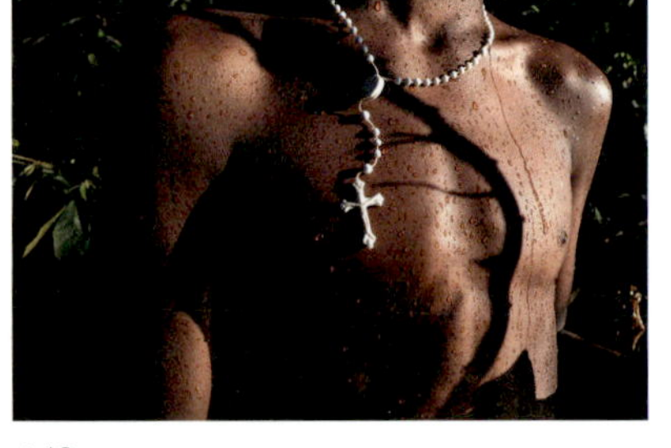

→ 10

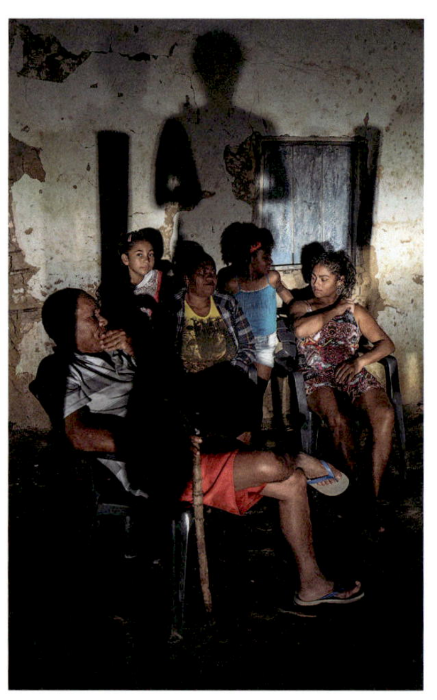

→ 39

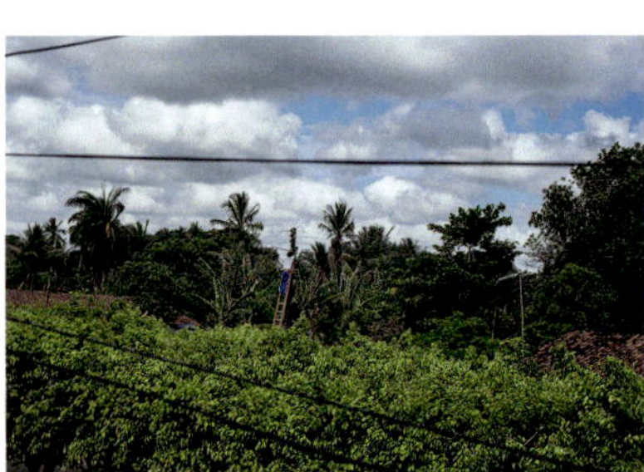

→ 13

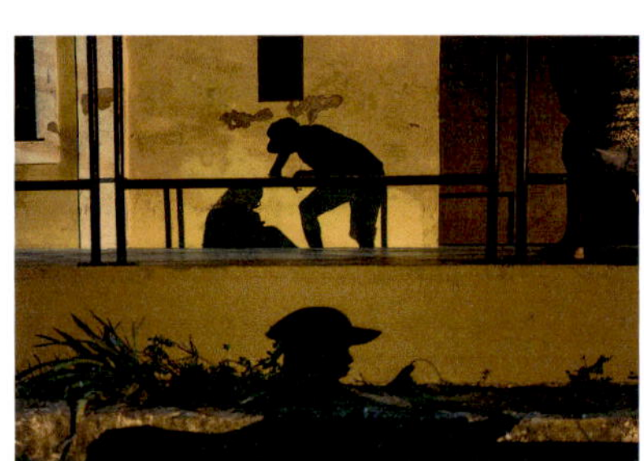

→ 25

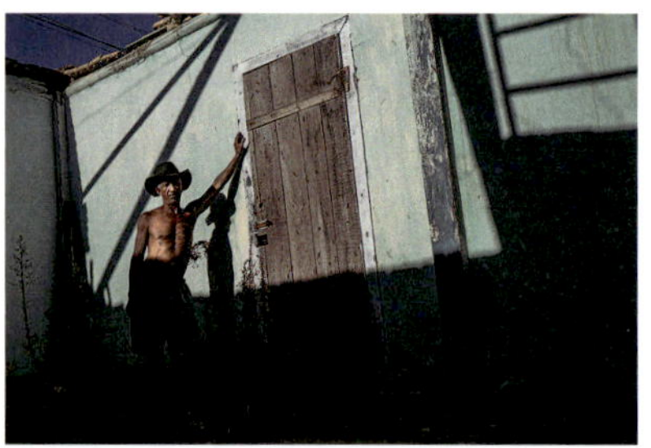

→ 40

→ 14

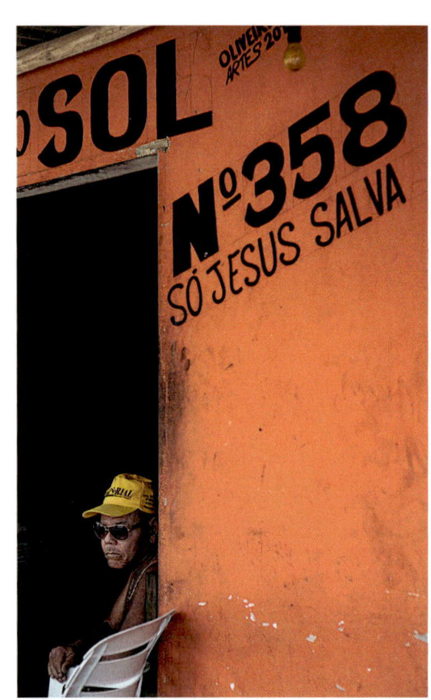

→ 29

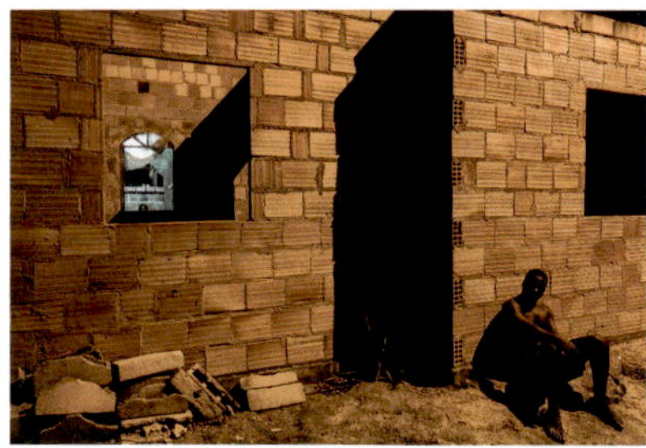

→ 42

→ 15

2015 – Persival, nicknamed "Pé," talking to himself in the village streets.

2015 – The house of Rosemar Cerqueira Rafael, a descendant of the Sulz family, has been restored to its original colors.

2015 – Atila (center) and his pals on the village square.

From our very first visit to the village, Atila guided us around the former colony. I saw him as an allegory of Saci-Pererê, a figure that haunts the popular imagination and is linked to Brazilian folklore. He is a one-legged Black boy who lives in the forest and moves about smoking a pipe and playing tricks on people. Many legends try to explain why the little fellow is missing a leg. One says that Saci was a slave and apparently lost a leg while practicing *capoeira*.

2015 – Young villagers walking in the Peruípe River, which is drying up; the prized coffee the former colony produced was shipped abroad from this river.

2016 – An altar in honor of Pomba-Gira, a spirit from the *Candomblé* and *Umbanda* religions representing the power of the sensual female body. Popular belief imbues her with gifts associated with questions of sexuality and sexual relations.

An *Umbanda* altar is a point of force, a kind of sacred table by which divine rays reach the faithful who are gathered in front of it. The chief function of this type of altar is to create a magnetism, a connection between the heavens and the earth. Through this table the vertical rays of the divinities come down upon the altar and are then spread horizontally, occupying the entire space dedicated to the practice of the religion.

2016 – "Why are you shining the light on me? Is it because I'm the darkest one, is that it?" Damacio Jesuino Merilho (center)

2015 – "Atila, are you religious?" "Nah, it's just for the look."

2016 – My shadow cast on a family in the village seated in front of their house.

2016 – "My mother asked me to take part in this celebration. I was 14. Now I'm *capitão*, but it's too much anymore; I'm going to give up my spot as captain to somebody else." Eldertrudo Milo, 83 years old

The Feast of São Sebastião is Helvécia's largest cultural event. This traditional celebration was brought by the Europeans and reenacts, as it were, the medieval struggle between the Moors and the Crusaders. It lasts two days and is the most important event in the village.

2016 – Young people spend their evenings connected to the public Wi-Fi network on the village square.

2015 – Repairing a telephone line.

2018 – Ponto do Sol bar, House no 358, SÓ JESUS SALVA.

2015 – José Maia, an inhabitant of Helvécia, sold all the tiles of his roof for a low price to a stranger passing through who was very interested in them. Those period tiles had been produced by enslaved individuals.

2015 – Pupils from the Arte Capoeira Bahia School in front of the former train station.

2016 – The Swiss Johann Martin Flach was the owner of a brick factory in Rio de Janeiro when the government of Brazil granted him the lands that became the Helvetia plantation.

At the time, *senzalas* were made of wood or clay. For years they remained the houses of the poor, before gradually disappearing and being replaced by brick houses.

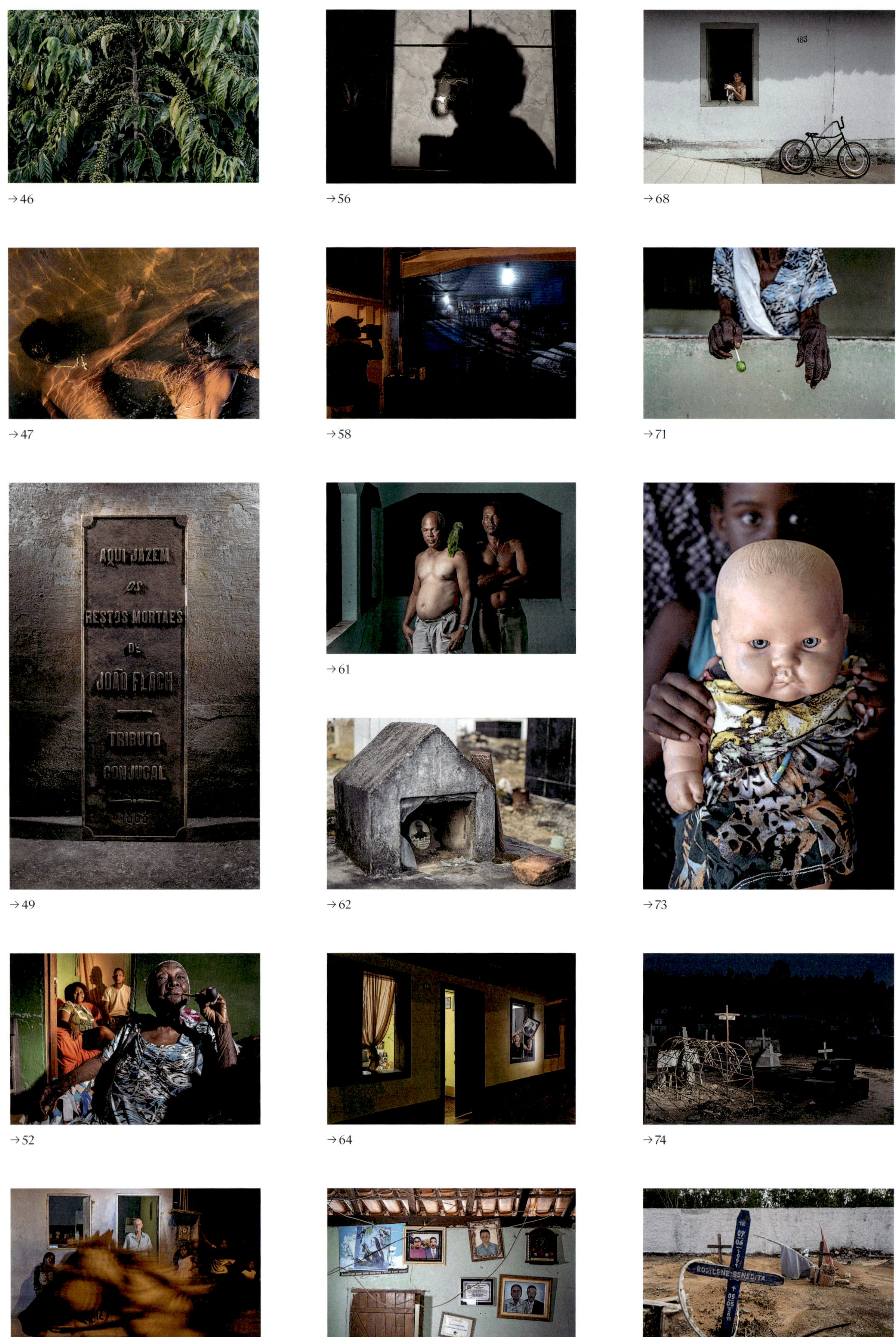
→ 46

→ 56

→ 68

→ 47

→ 58

→ 71

→ 49

→ 61

→ 62

→ 73

→ 52

→ 64

→ 74

→ 55

→ 66

→ 77

2021 – Coffee tree.

In Helvécia, coffee growing came to an end in the past but a landowner restarted a plantation just a few years ago.

2018 – My shadow.

2015 – Iracema Sulz Metzker, a descendant of the Swiss Sulzes and the German Metzkers.

2015 – Atila and one of his friends looking for a small tortoise in the Peruípe. It was from this river that the coffee grown in the former colony was shipped out of the country.

2016 – The shopkeeper Adalto Início readying his bar before the celebration. Each year, for five years now, he goes to Helvécia for the Feast of São Sebastião.

2021 – Dona Cocota's hands. At 110, she is the matriarch of the village.

Dona Cocota's legal name is Maria da Conceição. She was a midwife and says she helped birth 318 babies in her lifetime.

2018 – The commemorative monument to João Flach was found in what had been the colony's cemetery. After the death of his father Johann Martin Flach, one of the first Swiss to settle in the colony, João returned from Switzerland, where he had been studying agronomy, took over the family plantation, and expanded it considerably. He drowned in the Peruípe River in 1868 and left an estate worth around one million Swiss francs (in 1987 francs), a huge sum in his day.

2015 – The Krull de Souza brothers, Domingos (left) and Ednilson, are likely descendants of one of the richest families of the Leopoldina colony. The first members of the Krull family to arrive in the region (the brothers Ernesto and Francisco) were nephews of the Hamburg consul in Bahia, Peter Peycke, one of the founding members of the colony and from whom they inherited their lands. In the 1850s, over one hundred enslaved men and women worked for them in their plantations.

2017 – White dolls continue to show up everywhere in the games played by young girls in the village.

2016 – Commemorative stone dedicated to Bela Sofia Krull (1887–1976), paternal grandmother of the brothers Domingos and Ednilson Krull.

2015 – Dona Cocota (Maria da Conceição) was 105 years old in this photo, the oldest person in the former colony.

2015 – "I had to ask the museum to look after this portrait of my great-grandfather. My son Normam had always been scared to death by it. He thought his ancestor was staring at him at night!"
Rosemar Cerqueira Rafael

Rosemar Cerqueira Rafael's great-grandfather was Henrique Sulz.

2017 – Legend has it that after being buried, the former *mãe de santo* (literally the "mother of the saint," the priestess performing an *Umbanda* religious service) Zuza would appear each night to different members of her family, always requesting the same thing, that her body be buried even deeper so that she could rest in peace. After being disturbed for weeks, the family dug up the corpse and reburied it, then installed a kind of metal cage so that she wouldn't return. The apparitions stopped after that.

2017 – Carlos Henrique Cerqueira is a grandson of Henrique Sulz, the first Sulz to arrive in the colony. Carlos's mother, Emilia Sulz, was the village's first teacher.

Of all the Swiss families to have settled in the colony, only the Sulzes have descendants who are still living there today. The name Sulz, originally Schulz, is the result of an incorrect transcription of the name upon arriving in Brazil.

2018 – Old portraits of Dona Cocota and her husband hanging on her wall.

2016 – The "combatants" of the Feast of São Sebastião are faithful to their team even beyond the grave.

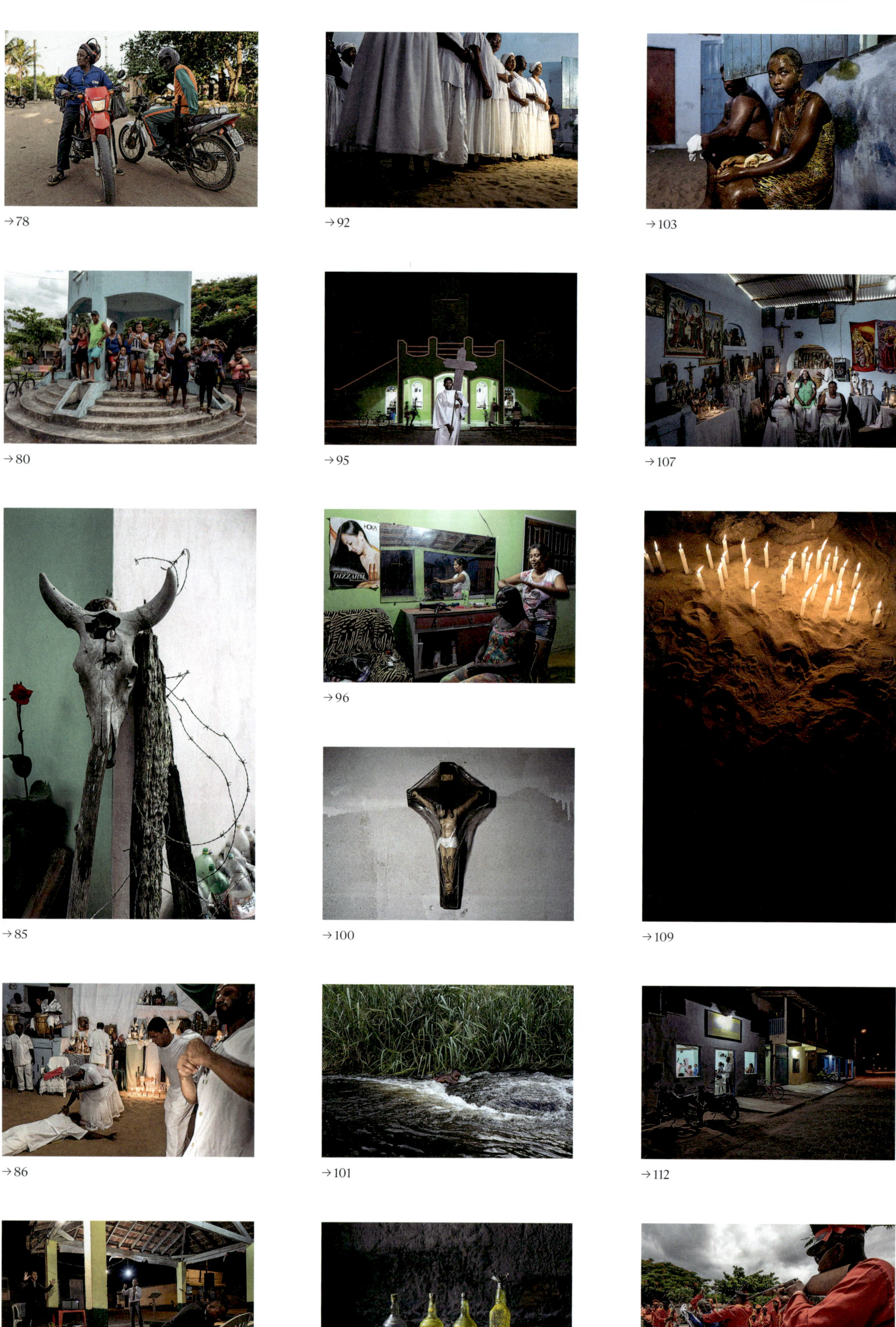

→ 78

→ 92

→ 103

→ 80

→ 95

→ 107

→ 85

→ 96

→ 100

→ 109

→ 86

→ 101

→ 112

→ 89

→ 102

→ 116

2015 – Back from work.

2016 – Viewers who have come to watch the traditional celebration of the Feast of São Sebastião.

2016 – A cow skull, which is a sentry in the *Umbanda* religion.

2016 – Believers in a trance in Mãe Maria's *terreiro*.

2015 – Adilio Brito de Souza, an evangelical minister (center), and Fabio Teixeira de Jesus (left) celebrating a service on the village square.

2016 – Worship by the faithful at a service celebrated by Mãe Maria.

2015 – Elvis Elisiario de Jesus, deacon of the Catholic Church of Helvécia, holding an iron cross from the nineteenth century that was recovered from the historic cemetery, one of the rare vestiges of the colonial era.

In July 2019, Elvis Elisiario de Jesus would become the first ordained priest from the community.

2015 – Straightening hair at Katia Pinheiro's hair salon.

2018 – Crucifix still in its original plastic wrapper.

2015 – A young villager plunged in the waters of the Peruípe River.

2016 – Small bottles filled with *dendê* oil used in *Umbanda* rituals.

2016 – Young woman, her body anointed with *dendê* oil, during an *Umbanda* initiation ceremony.

2016 – The *terreiro* of Mãe Maria, *mãe de santo*.

2016 – Candles for the spirits of Mãe Maria's *terreiro*.

2015 – Evening service in one of the evangelical churches.

2016 – The Feast of São Sebastião depicts the war between the Moors and the Crusaders as a kind of clash.

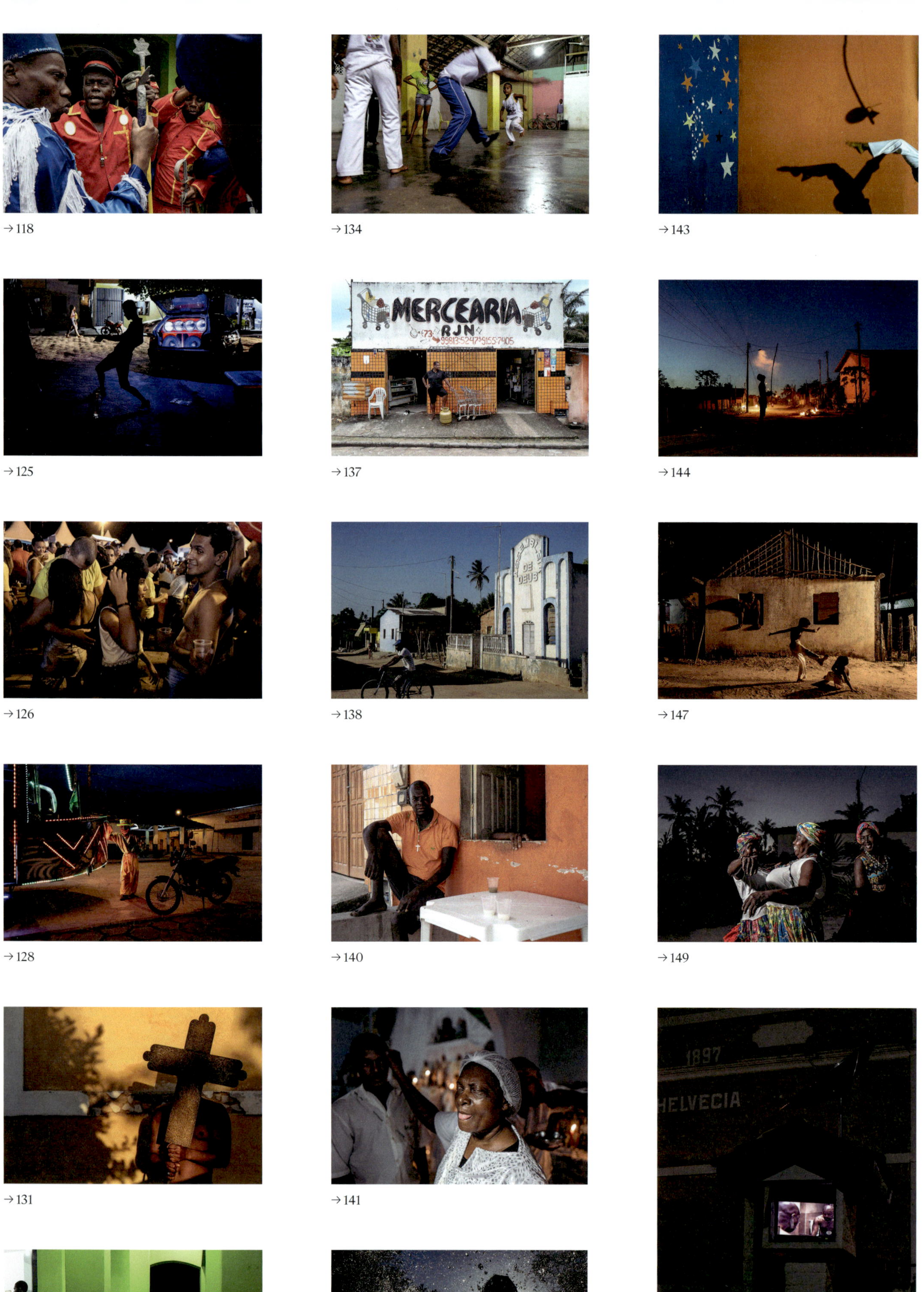

2016 – The team in red represents the Moors, in blue the Crusaders.

2016 – The Feast of São Sebastião draws young people from outside of Helvécia. Vinicius is dancing to the *baile funk* music blasting from the speakers in the trunk of his car.

2016 – Young people at the Feast of São Sebastião.

2021 – For a few coins, clowns give children a ride through the village streets in a disco-bus.

This form of entertainment, which is regularly seen in the streets of Helvécia, is a great success in cities and towns in Brazil's interior.

2017 – Danilon Luiz, Helvécia's community leader, holding a nineteenth-century iron cross, recovered from the historic cemetery.

Luiz is part of the association that worked to bring about in 2005 Helvécia's being recognized as a *quilombola* community.

2015 – Elvis Elisiario de Jesus, deacon of the Catholic Church of Helvécia, standing next to a young seminarian, late for Mass, at the entrance to the village's Catholic church.

2015 – Reginaldo Cecilio Antonio, Helvécia's *capoeira* instructor, is a passionate teacher of the discipline to a new generation.

2022 – *Mercearia* (grocery).

2015 – "Assemblia de DEUS," an old evangelical church that has since been razed.

2018 – An inhabitant lost in thought on the terrace of the Ponto do Sol bar.

2016 – "Each son has a saint, each saint has their food. So I prepare and I give it to them to eat."
Mãe Maria

The *mãe de santo* is inhabited by an *Umbanda* deity that seeks to communicate with their followers while the latter eat in order to feed this spirit.

2015 – Glints and gleams playing on the river.

2015 – A move in *capoeira*.

2015 – A player of the berimbau, traditional instrument in *capoeira*.

2015 – "My ancestors were African. Their blood flows in me. Through *capoeira*, I defend their culture. It's my heritage."
Reginaldo Cecilio Antonio

Reginaldo at the window of a pau a pique house, a building technique that dates from the time when slavery was legal.

2015 – Faustina Zacharias Carvalho, Maria Piedade Tersilha, and Maria D'ajuda Tersilha dancing *bate-barriga*.

2016 – Movie night in front of the village television set.

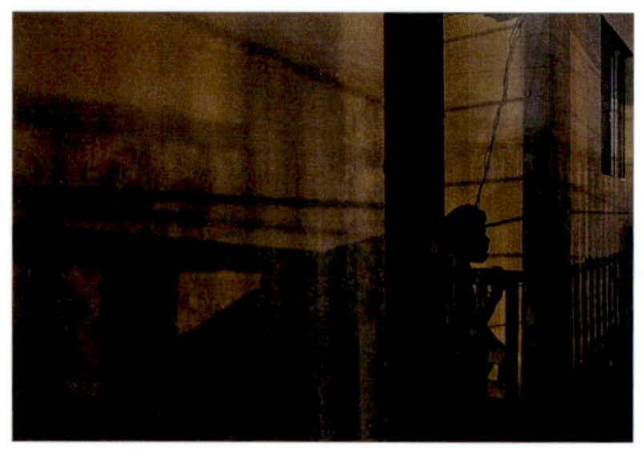

→ 152

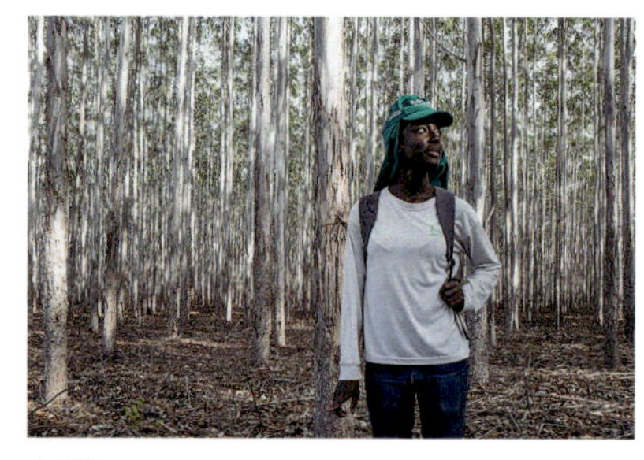

→ 161

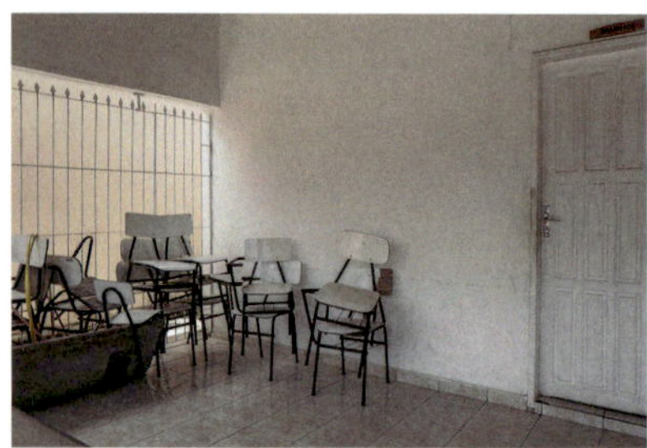

→ 154

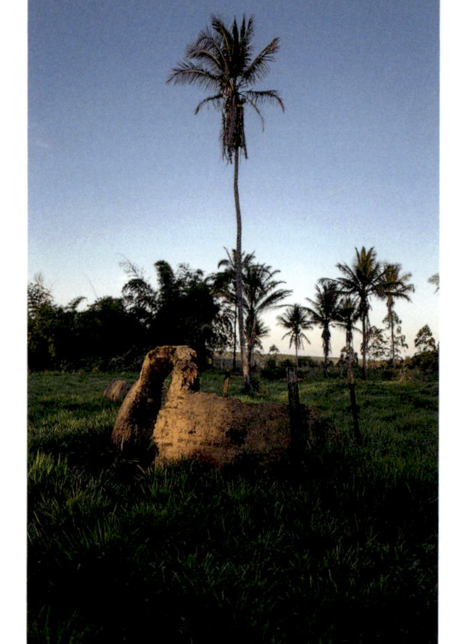

→ 163

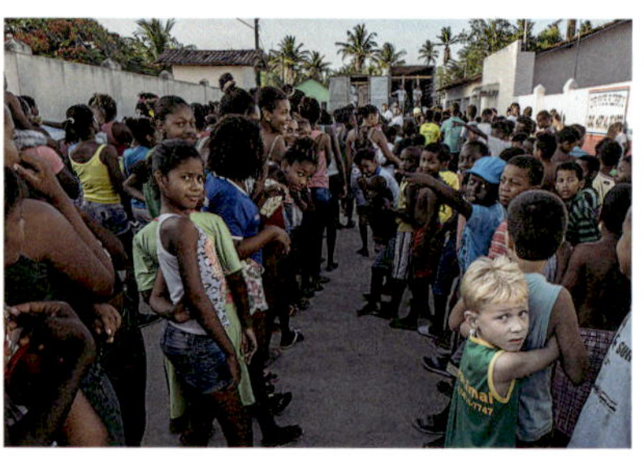

→ 155

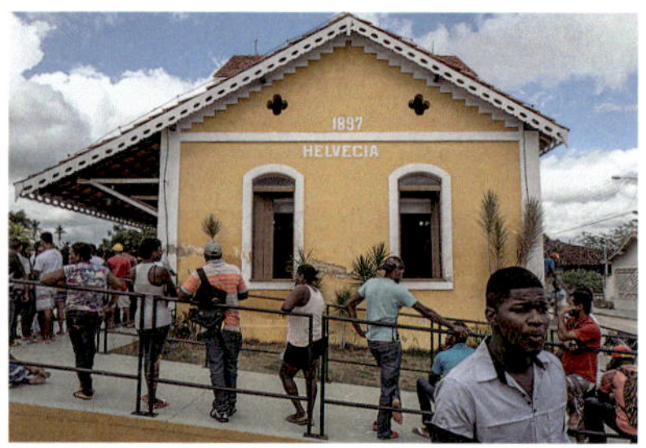

→ 157

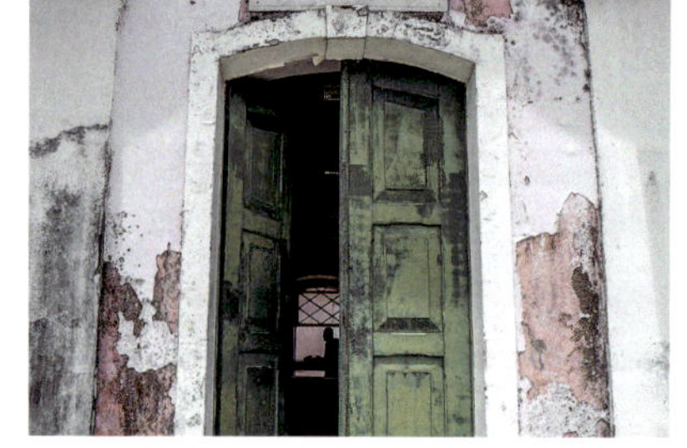

→ 164

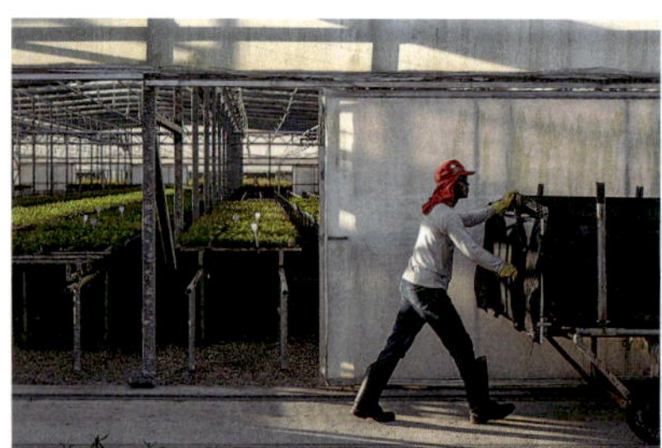

→ 158

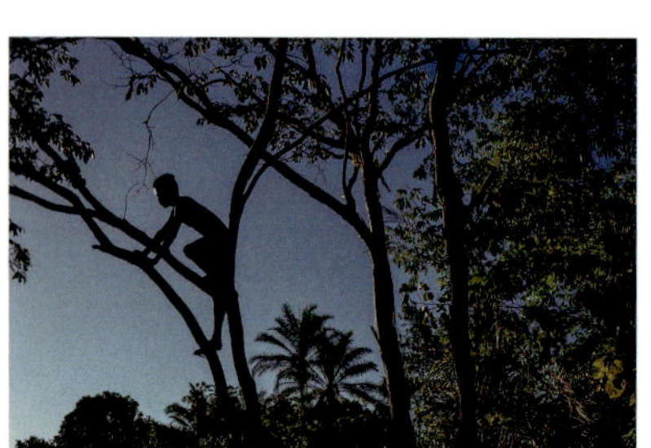

→ 160

2016 – My shadow.

2016 – In the village school.

Many of the young people do not know the connection between their village of Helvécia and Switzerland.

2015 – Lines of children waiting for the distribution of Christmas gifts by an evangelical group. Handing out miniature trucks and white dolls takes place to the refrain of "JESUS loves you, JESUS loves you!" which the members of the group repeat over and over.

2016 – A long line of villagers formed one Saturday morning in front of the former train station. The Brazilian company Fibria came to the village looking to hire.

2015 – An employee of Fibria sporting a red cap with a white cross indicating that he was familiar with safety measures to be taken in case of an emergency.

2015 – Atila in a tree, looking like Saci-Pererê, protector of the forest.

2015 – Miriam Santos is one of the many villagers who work for Fibria, the Brazilian company that is one of the leading producers of cellulose.

Currently, Helvécia is lost in a vast monoculture of genetically modified eucalyptus trees that is so extensive it even covers the former colony's historic cemetery.

2016 – An old oven used for making carvão (charcoal). Some people illegally cut down the eucalyptus to make charcoal, which they then sell.

This parallel economy is commonplace in the region. The oven was demolished by the police about three months prior to shooting the photograph.

2016 – Entrance to the Public Archives of the State of Bahia in Salvador.

Photographs and co-publication

Dom Smaz is a Swiss-Brazilian photographer who is based in Lausanne, although he often works in Brazil. He is a five-time winner of the Swiss Press Award and for some ten years now has regularly contributed to both the national and international press, including *Le Temps, Neue Zürcher Zeitung, Tages Anzeiger, Sunday Times Magazine, The Guardian,* and *Die Zeit*. His photographs often deal with the themes of colonial heritage, social differences and marginalization. In 2018, he took part in the show Mobile Worlds, mounted by the Museum für Kunst und Gewerbe (MK&G), Hamburg, in partnership with the Johann Jacobs Museum, Zurich. In 2019, part of Mr. Smaz's *Helvécia* project, which is the basis for the present publication, was featured at the Festival Internacional de Fotografia of Bogotá, Colombia. Mr. Smaz graduated from Vevey's School of Photography in 2012. He is a member of the French photography agency Hans Lucas.

Historical research and co-publication

Milena Machado Neves is a journalist and freelance curator who has developed numerous cultural projects in Brazil. She has worked closely with Dom Smaz in documenting their joint project on Helvécia, drawing on her professional experience, but also her deep knowledge of this region in Northeastern Brazil where she hails from. She currently lives and works in Lausanne, where she is a regular contributor to Radio Télévision Suisse (RTS).

Historical research and text

Christian Doninelli is a Swiss journalist and science writer with a Licence in geography and history from the University of Neuchâtel. In 2012, coming back from Nova Friburgo, he discovered Helvécia by chance and published a TV report for *La Télé* and several features and news articles on this former colony in *Swissinfo*. With Milena Machado Neves, he has also copublished pieces on the same subject in *La Liberté* and *Neue Zürcher Zeitung*.

Historical analysis

Flávio dos Santos Gomes is a Brazilian historian and professor at the Federal University of Rio de Janeiro (UFRJ). A specialist of the history of slavery in Brazil, he contributed a text on the Black farming community of the country's rural regions and *quilombo*, the special status granted certain towns and villages, the history of its development and its challenges.

Essay

Shalini Randeria is a social anthropologist and sociologist. She is among the leading intellectual voices in the study and analysis of postcolonialism, global inequalities, and democratization. Currently, she is rector of the Central European University in Vienna. Earlier she was rector of the Institute of the Humanities (IWM) in Vienna and professor of social anthropology and sociology at the Graduate Institute of International and Development Studies (IHEID) in Geneva. Her publications on entangled modernities and the critique of Eurocentrism have introduced postcolonialism into the German-speaking world and contributed to its development internationally. Besides her academic publications, Ms. Randeria is a regular contributor to major publications like *Die Zeit, Süddeutsche Zeitung,* and *Neue Zürcher Zeitung,* and to renowned cultural venues like Zürcher Theaterspektakel, the Haus der Kulturen der Welt, and the Maxim Gorki Theater in Berlin. Her podcast *Democracy in Question,* launched in 2021, is in its fifth season.

Rohit Jain holds a PhD in social anthropology and is an art researcher who has specialized in migration, postcolonialism, and the politics of representation. He has taken part in a range of art research projects at Zurich University of the Arts (ZHdK) on the gold trade in Switzerland, and urban citizenship at Zurich's Shedhalle. Mr. Jain is a cofounder of several political-cultural initiatives, including the Institut Neue Schweiz INES, the Berner Rassismusstammtisch, and Schwarzenbach-Komplex, a long-term politico-artistic project on antiracist memory. He teaches at the University of Zurich's Department of Social Anthropology and Cultural Studies, and recently co-published the *Handbuch Neue Schweiz* (diaphanes, 2021).

Izabel Barros is a historian, decolonial feminist, and antiracist activist in Brazil and Switzerland. She is an FNS PhD candidate in history as part of the project "Moral and Economic Entrepreneurship in Asia, Africa, Latin America, and Europe. A Collaborative History of Global Switzerland, c. 1830-1900" (IEP-UNIL). From 2020 to mid-2022 she was a program officer for feminist peace policy at cfd, the Feminist Peace Organization. From 2013 to 2020, she served as a researcher in Switzerland and program officer for Brazil at the Cooperaxion Foundation. In Maranhão, she collaborated with local civil society organizations, *quilombos* and indigenous communities engaged in the defense of their territory and self-determination. She is active in the Taoca, Livingroom and Berner Rassismusstammtisch collectives. She has also overseen numerous cultural and artistic initiatives, including *Wie die Geranie nach Bern verschleppt wurde* (2020), *Black Box Bern* (2020-2021), *We Talk. Schweiz ungefiltert* (2021), and *Das Wandbild muss weg!* (since 2021).

Christian Doninelli

- Arlettaz, Gérald, "Émigration et colonisation suisses en Amérique 1815-1918," *Études et Sources*, no. 5, 1979.
- do Carmo, Alane Fraga, *Colonização e escravidão na Bahia: A Colônia Leopoldina (1850 –1888)*, thesis of the federal university of Bahia, 2010.
- Lucchesi, Dante et Alan Baxter, "A comunidade de fala de Helvécia na Bahia," *Jornal Grande Bahia*, March 2017.
- n.n., *Diverses lettres adressées à Frédéric de Gingins concernant la botanique, avec une lettre de M. Langhans sur le Brésil*, 1820, Château de La Sarraz D 57, Archives cantonales vaudoises.
- Neeser, Hermann, "A colônia Leopoldina (1858)," *Centro de Estudos Bahianos*, no. 5, 1951.
- Oberacker, Carlos H. Junior, "A Colônia Leopoldina: Frankenal na Bahia meridional, uma colônia européia de plantadores no Brasil," *Revista do Instituto Histórico e Geográfico Brasileiro*, vol. 148, no. 354, 1987.
- Pache, David, *Letters to his sister Mélosine*, Archives cantonales vaudoises, ACV P Jaïn 79.
- Pereira de Jesus Moreira, Ramom, "De imigrantes a senhores de gente: a formação da colônia Leopoldina, trabalho livre e trabalho escravo no sul da província da Bahia (1818-1888)," communication au 31° Simposio Nacional de História, Rio de Janeiro, 2021.
- Quelle, Otto, "Das Deutschtum im Staate Bahia. Ein methodischer Versuch," *Ibero-amerikanisches Archiv*, vol. 7, no. 1, 1933-1934, pp. 38–54.
- Raffard, Henri, *La Colonie suisse de Nova Friburgo et la Société philanthropique suisse de Rio de Janeiro*, Rio de Janeiro, 1877.
- Schramm Correa, Lucelinda, "O resgate de um esquecimento – a colonia de Leopoldina", *GEOgraphia*, vol. 7, no. 13, 2005.
- von Spix, Johann Baptist, and Carl Friedrich Philipp von Martius, *Reise in Brasilien auf Befehl Sr. Majestät Joseph I, König von Baiern in den Iahren 1817 bis 1820 gemacht und beschrieben*, Munich, 1823-1831.
- Dr Stauffer, "Voyage au Brésil de M. Charles-Louis Borrel 1826-1828, *Nouvelles Étrennes neuchâteloises*, 1922, pp. 65–89.
- Tadeu Caires Silva, Ricardo, "Criminalidade, resistência escrava e abolicionismo na Colônia Leopoldina, Bahia (1880-1888)," *Revista de História Regional*, vol. 21, no. 1, 2016.
- Tölsner, Dr Carl August, *Die Colonie Leopoldina in Brasilien, Schilderung des Anbaus und der Gewinnung der wichtigsten dort erzeugten Culturproducte, namentlich des Kaffees, sowie einiger andern während eines langjährigen Aufenthaltes daselbst gemachten Beobachtungen und Erfahrungen*, Göttingen, 1858.
- von Tschudi, Johann Jakob, *Reisen durch Südamerika 1818–1889*, Leipzig, 1866.
- Miki, Yuko, *Frontiers of Citizenship. A Black and Indigenous History of Postcolonial Brazil*, Cambridge, 2018.

Newspapers

- *Berlinische Nachrichten von Staats- und gelehrten Sachen*, 1/3, January 5, 1819.
- *Feuille fédérale suisse*, April 15, 1896.
- *Frankfurter gemeinnützige Chronik*, 1842, pp. 4–5.
- *Gazette de Lausanne et journal suisse*, June 16, 1820, Archives en ligne du Temps.
- *Journal des voyages, découvertes et navigations modernes*, 1, 1818–1819.
- *La Renommée*, June 25, 1819.
- *Lesefrüchte, belehrenden und unterhaltenden Inhalts*, 3, 1829.
- *Lesefrüchte, belehrenden und unterhaltenden Inhalts*, 3/4, 1829.
- *Morgenblatt für gebildete Stände*, November 16, 1820.
- *Neue Zürcher Zeitung*, July 23, 1884.
- *Oppositions Blatt oder Weimarische Zeitung*, December 6, 1819.
- *Bremer Zeitung für Politik, Handel und Literatur*, 321, November 17, 1821.
- *Zürcherische Freitagszeitung*, November 19, 1819.
- *Zürcherische Freitagszeitung*, June 16, 1820.

Flávio dos Santos Gomes

- Acevedo Marin, Rosa Elizabeth; Castro, Edna M. Ramos. *Negros do Trombetas. Guardiões de matas e rios*. Belém, UFPA, 1993.
- Anjos, Rafael Sanzio Araújo dos, *Territórios das Comunidades remanescentes de Antigos Quilombos no Brasil - Primeira Configuração Espacial*. Brasília, Mapas Editora & Consultoria, 2000.
- Carvalho, José Jorge de, ed., *O Quilombo do Rio das Rãs: histórias, tradições e lutas*. Salvador, CEAO/EDUFBA, 1996.
- Gomes, Flávio dos Santos; Reis, João José, *Liberdade por um fio. História dos quilombos no Brasil*. São Paulo, Cia. das Letras, 1996.
- Gusmão, Neusa M. Mendes de, *Terra de Pretos. Terra de Mulheres: terra, mulher e raça num bairro negro*. Brasilia, MEC/Fundação Cultural Palmares, 1996.
- Leite, Ilka Boaventura, ed., Negros no Sul do Brasil: invisibilidade e territorialidade. Santa Catarina, *Letras Contemporâneas*, 1996.
- Mattos, Hebe. "Remanescentes das comunidades dos quilombos:" Memórias do cativeiro e políticas de reparação no Brasil. *Revista USP*, São Paulo, no. 68, 2006, pp. 104–111.
- Moura, Clóvis, ed., *Os Quilombos na Dinâmica Social do Brasil*. Maceió, EDFAL, 2001.
- Price, Richard, ed., *Maroon Societies. Rebel Slave Communities in the Americas*, 2nd ed., Baltimore, The Johns Hopkins University Press, 1979.
- Schwartz, Stuart B. "Mocambos, Quilombos e Palmares: A resistência escrava no Brasil Colonial." *Estudos Econômicos*, São Paulo, vol. 17, special issue, 1987, pp. 17–61.

Izabel Barros, Rohit Jain, Shalini Randeria

- Barros, Izabel, and André Nicacio Lima, "Geschichte dekolonisieren. Ein kritischer Beitrag zu einer globalen Schweizer Geschichte," in *Handbuch Neue Schweiz*, ed. Institut Neue Schweiz, Zurich, 2021.
- Barth, Hans, "1864: die Schweizer Beteiligung am Verbrechen der Sklaverei," 2015, https://archiv.louverture.ch/KAMPA/AGASSIZ/barth_BR_joos.pdf.
- Baxter, Alan, *The Context of Language Acquisition Among Slaves of the Colônia Leopoldina*, Research Seminar of the Institute of Latin American Studies, La Trobe University, Victoria, 1999.
- Baxter, Alan, and Dante Lucchesi, "Un paso más hacia la definición del pasado criollo del dialecto afro-brasileño de Helvécia (Bahia)," in *Lenguas criollas de base lexical española y portuguesa*, ed. Klaus Zimmermann, Madrid, 1999.
- Buck-Morss, Susan, *Hegel, Haiti and Universal History*, Pittsburgh, 2009.
- Coindet, Jean-Jacques François, *Fábrica Meuron no Andaraí*, nineteenth century, oil on canvas, 85.4 × 130.2 cm, Rio de Janeiro.
- Casa Fiat de Cultura, *Olhar Viajante*, Coleção Brasiliana / Fundação Estudar da Pinacoteca do Estado de São Paulo, Belo Horizonte, 2008, http://www.casafiat.com.br/wp-content/uploads/2017/05/catalogo_olhar_viajante.pdf.
- Conrad, Sebastian, et al., eds., *Jenseits des Eurozentrismus. Postkoloniale Perspektiven in den Geschichts- und Kulturwissenschaften*, Frankfurt am Main / New York, 2013.
- Corrêa, Lucelinda Schramm, "O resgate de um esquecimento. A colônia de Leopoldina," *GEOgraphia 13*, 2005.
- Corrêa, Lucelinda Schramm, *A torturante ausência de uma presença. A imigração alemã na Bahia do século XIX*, São Paulo, 2003.
- dos Santos Pinto, O. Jovita Dankwa, et al., eds., *Un/Doing Race. Rassifizierung in der Schweiz*, Zurich, 2022.
- David, Thomas, et al., *Schwarze Geschäfte. Die Beteiligung von Schweizern an Sklaverei und Sklavenhandel im 18. und 19. Jahrhundert*, Zurich, 2005.
- Doninelli, Christian, and Milena M. Neves, "Als Schweizer Sklaven hielten," *Neue Zürcher Zeitung Magazin*, March 2, 2018.

- Ferreira, Carlota, "Remanescentes de um falar crioulo brasileiro," in Carlota Ferreira et al., *Diversidade do português do Brasil*, Salvador, 1984.
- Institut Neue Schweiz, *Handbuch Neue Schweiz*, ed. Mirjam Fischer et al., Zurich, 2021.
- Lima, Renata Azevedo, "Conflitos de terra e Quilombos na colonização do Rio de Janeiro (1808-1831)," Niterói, 2013, https://www.historia.uff.br/stricto/td/1704.pdf.
- Lucchesi, Dante, and Alan Baxter, *A comunidade de fla de Helvécia-BA*, Projeto Vertentes do Português Popular do Estado da Bahia, Universidade Federal da Bahia, Salvador, 2022, http://www.vertentes.ufba.br/a-comunidade-de-fala-de-helvecia-ba.
- Maia Mata, Iacy, et al., "Resistência e rebeldia. Escravidão e pós-abolição no extremo sul da Bahia (1880-1889)," in João José Reis and Flávio dos Santos Gomes, *Revoltas escravas no Brasil*, São Paulo, 2021.
- Miki, Yuko, "Fugir para a escravidão. As geografias insurgentes dos quilombolas brasileiros, 1880-1881," in Petrônio Domingues and Flávio dos Santos Gomes, *Políticas da raça. Experiências e legados da abolição e da pós-emancipação no Brasil*, São Paulo, 2014, pp. 35–68.
- Miki, Yuko, "Política antiescravista na fronteira. São Mateus, Espírito Santo (1884), in João José Reis and Flávio dos Santos Gomes, *Revoltas escravas no Brasil*, São Paulo, 2021.
- Wildberger, Arnold, *Os presidendes da provinvia da Bahia, efectivos e interinos (1824-1889)*, Salvador, 1949.
- Purtschert, Patricia, and Harald Fischer-Tiné, eds., *Swiss Colonial Encounters and Postcolonial Assemblages*, Basingstoke, 2015.
- Purtschert, Patricia, et al., eds., *Postkoloniale Schweiz. Formen und Folgen eines Kolonialismus ohne Kolonien*, Bielefeld, 2012.
- Schweizerisches Landesmuseum, *Indiennes. Ein Stoff erobert die Welt!*, Zurich, 2021.
- Ziegler, Béatrice, "Schweizerische Kaufleute in Brasilien im 19. Jahrhundert," in *Jahrbuch für Geschichte Lateinamerikas*, Hamburg, 1988.
- Zimmermann, Klaus, "O português não-padrão falado no Brasil. A tese da variedade pós-crioula," in *Lenguas criollas de base lexical española y portuguesa*, ed. Klaus Zimmermann, Madrid, 1999.

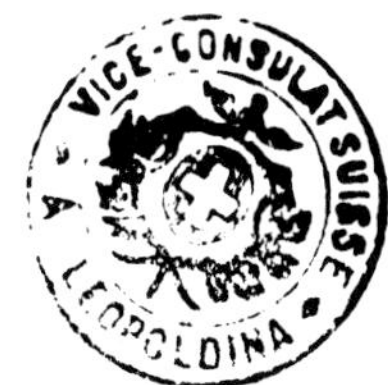

The official seal of the Swiss vice-consul for the Leopoldina colony, dating from October 9, 1891.
Federal Archives, Bern, Switzerland, 2019

Acknowledgments

We would like to express our sincere gratitude to all the people who have supported our work and made this publication possible, in whatever way they were involved.

We would first like to thank all the inhabitants of Helvécia and the surrounding region. They have opened their homes to us, told us their stories, and graciously accepted being photographed: Wingles Vieira, Wlisses Francisco Gerlin, Atila, Gilsineth Santos Silva, Maria Aparecida dos Santos, Domingos and Ednilson Krull de Souza, Faustina Zacharias Carvalho, Maria da Conceição (known as Dona Cocota), Mãe Maria, Elvis Eliziario de Jesus, Iracema Sulz Metzker, Fabio Teixeira de Jesus and Eldertrudo Milo, Damacio Jesuino Merilho, Carlos Henrique Cerqueira, Rosemar Cerqueira Rafael, Katia Pinheiro, Maria Piedade Tersilha, aria d'Ajuda Tersilha, Reginaldo Cecilio Antonio, and Persival (known as Pé), along with Danilon Luiz Francisco, whom we would like to thank as well for his commitment to and support of our work on site.

We would also like to thank Rafael Cerqueira, Bruno Duque, Valdir Nunes dos Santos, Jean Alburquerque, Armando Antonio de Amorim, Rodrigo Zagonel, Thiago Sarmento Correia, Joseane Oliveira, Antonio Rego Júnior, Antonio Artur Teixeira, and Robson Leite, for sharing their contacts and paving the way for us to get in touch with certain people and documents that were important to our work.

Many thanks go out to Milena's parents, Gilda Costa Machado Neves and Dorivaldo Almeida Neves, for the welcome assistance they provided in terms of research, logistics and contacts, as well as the interest they have shown in this story. And great thanks to Dom's family, Ana Freire, Santiago Lema, Pascal Schmidt, Caroline Malik Schmidt, and Maude Schmidt. Along with their moral support, they encouraged and aided us in our initial translations and generously provided financial assistance to enable us to hire a number of professionals to transform this documentary into a book project.

Our thanks to Thomas Kern of swissinfo.ch, Gilles Steinmann of the *Neue Zürcher Zeitung*, Catherine Rüttimann of the Swiss-French newspaper *Le Temps*, and Carol Körting of Leica magazine for having believed in this story from the outset and publishing it.

Our thanks as well to Roger M. Buergel and Sophia Prinz of the Johann Jacobs Museum for having hired us so that we could continue our research on the subject. This allowed us to participate in the "Mobile Worlds" exhibition mounted by Hamburg's Museum für Kunst und Gewerbe (MK&G).

Thanks to the employees of the Public Archives of the State of Bahia in Brazil, and to all those who are fighting to ensure that this vital institution remains open. Its existence enabled us to research and retrace the history of Helvécia. Our thanks go likewise to the Federal Archives of Switzerland, the Archives of the State of Neuchâtel, and the Archives of the Canton of Vaud, for having welcomed us and allowed us to pursue our research in their records.

Thanks to the Pinacoteca of São Paulo and the collector Jules Petroz, for sharing with us their paintings of the colony.

Many thanks to Christian Doninelli for having agreed to work with us, then going on to spend so many years tirelessly researching the subject simply out of pure passion.

Thanks to Tamara Leuenberger and Thomas Schmid for their instruction and translation.

Thanks likewise to Adrien Moreillon for his exacting graphic-design work, as well as his unstinting commitment to this publication for over two years.

Thanks to Klaus Kehrer, who offered us a warm welcome in Arles and believed in the potential of our project.

Many thanks to Lars Müller and his team, whose commitment was indispensable for this book to become a relevant publication. Thanks to him, we developed the content of the present work, offering high-quality contributions that draw on serious scholarship and research. We are sincerely grateful for his seemingly hopeless struggle to make this shared dream a reality.

Thanks to Luiza Goulart, who generously and for no charge provided her invaluable help in the publication of several texts until we were able to hire her to work with us on the present book.

Many thanks to Chantal Courtois, a curator at MEG, the Musée d'ethnographie de Genève, who spent over two years talking about our project at her institution until it took shape as an exhibition. We shall be forever grateful to her for her thoughtfulness and care. We have included in the present work several captions she wrote, as well as her chronology, which was further developed and refined by Martin Vercampt, whom we would like to thank as well.

Thanks go out to all the people who, for over six years, lent us an ear and never turned us away, in particular Julien Nosten, Raphaël Hugentobler, Vincent Balet, Pedro Gustavo da Costa Borges, Kevin Melkior, Rachel Guillemin, Yann Gross, Raniere Kepler de Santana, Mariana Vilhena, Fernanda Castro, Ludmila Neves Bercaire, Ana Salac, Letícia Rabelo Beckers, Christian Brokatzky, and Eloisa Abussamra.

Thanks to Albertine Bourget of ESH Médias, along with Julie Body, Régine Buxtorf, and Caroline Zingg of *L'Illustré* magazine, for previously publishing this story and having mentioned our book project.

And finally, thanks to all those who generously took part in our crowdfunding initiative. Whatever your level of participation, we are extremely touched by your gesture.

With love and gratitude.

Milena and Dom

Imprint

Dom Smaz
Helvécia – A Swiss Colonial History in Brazil

- Editorial Board: Dom Smaz, Milena Machado Neves, Lars Müller, Adrien Moreillon
- Photography: Dom Smaz
- Texts: Dom Smaz, Milena Machado Neves, Christian Doninelli, Flávio dos Santos Gomes, Shalini Randeria, Rohit Jain, Izabel Barros
- Historical Research: Christian Doninelli, Milena Machado Neves, Dom Smaz
- Interviews and Photography Assistance: Milena Machado Neves
- Text Editing: Luiza Goulart (Essay Flávio dos Santos Gomes, Captions), Martin Vercampt (Chronology), Chantal Courtois (Captions)
- Translations: John O'Toole (French–English), Mike Pilewski (German–English), Quentin Pope (Portuguese–English)
- Proofreading: Kristie Kachler
- Project Coordination: Miriam Eickhoff, Marius Wenger, Fanny Rakeseder
- Design: Adrien Moreillon
- Lithography: Seraphin, Bad Münstereifel, Germany
- Printing and Binding: DZA Druckerei zu Altenburg, Germany
- Paper: Arctic Volume White 1.1 vol., 130 g/m²

© 2022 Lars Müller Publishers, Dom Smaz and the authors

No part of this book may be used or reproduced in any form or manner whatsoever without prior written permission, except in the case of brief quotations embodied in critical articles and reviews.

Lars Müller Publishers is supported by the Swiss Federal Office of Culture with a structural contribution for the years 2021–2024.

Lars Müller Publishers
Zurich, Switzerland
www.lars-mueller-publishers.com

ISBN 978-3-03778-701-4, English
ISBN 978-3-03778-702-1, French
ISBN 978-3-03778-720-5, German

Distributed in North America
by ARTBOOK | D.A.P.
www.artbook.com

Printed in Germany

With the kind support of:

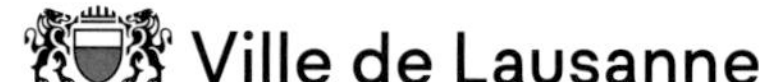

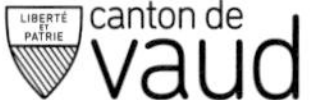

Volkart Foundation

Erna and Curt Burger Foundation

Maya Behn-Eschenburg Foundation

Blaser Trading AG

And the people who contributed to the crowdfunding campaign substantially: Ana Freire, Santiago Lema, Pascal Schmidt, Caroline Malik Schmidt, Félix Schmidt and Daniel Robert Prinzing.

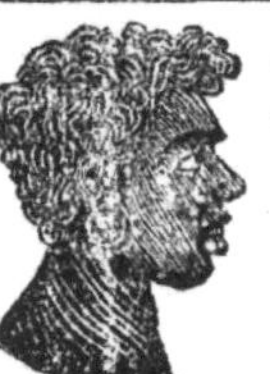

Advertisement for À la Case de l'Oncle Tom (At Uncle Tom's Cabin), a shop located on the Rue des Alpes in Geneva, offering "Caravellas" coffee, the beans produced in the Leopoldina colony. Excerpt from the *Journal de Genève*, March 3, 1870.

The Castel de Pombal (Dovecot Château) Plantation →
Jean-Frédéric Bosset de Luze (Geneva 1754-1838), between 1820 and 1838 (watercolor drawing, 25.5 x 57 cm). Collection of the Pinacoteca of the State of São Paulo, Brazil

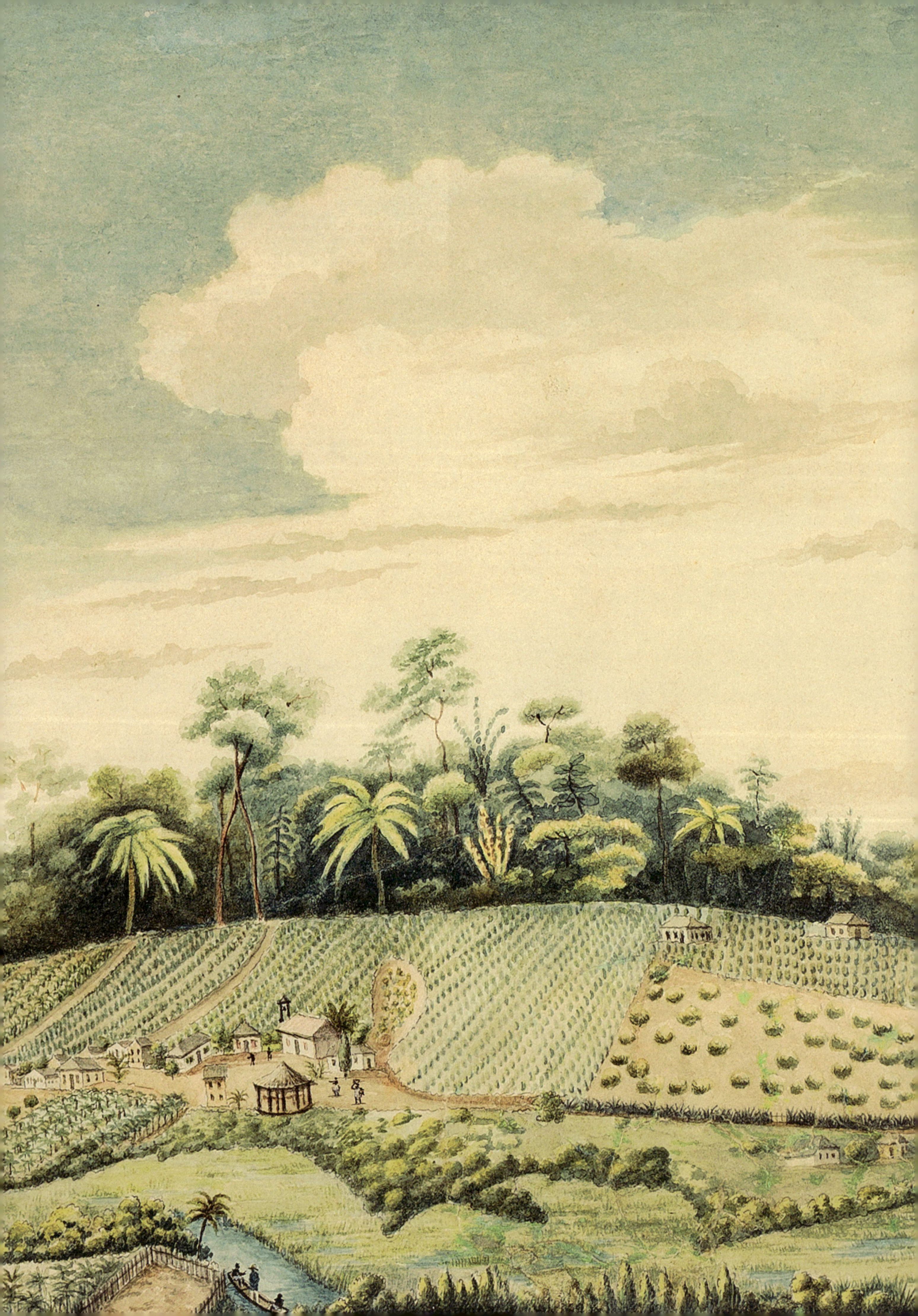